THE POETIC JUSTICE

To: Carela Mendez

The Poetic Justice

A Memoir

JOHN CHARLES THOMAS

John Charles Thomas
July 2023

HAK Summer Associates
D.C.

UNIVERSITY OF VIRGINIA PRESS
Charlottesville and London

University of Virginia Press
© 2022 by John Charles Thomas
All rights reserved
Printed in the United States of America on acid-free paper

First published 2022

9 8 7 6 5 4 3 2 1

Library of Congress Cataloging-in-Publication Data

Names: Thomas, John Charles, author.
Title: The poetic justice : a memoir / John Charles Thomas.
Description: Charlottesville : University of Virginia Press, 2022.
Identifiers: LCCN 2022008346 (print) | LCCN 2022008347 (ebook) |
    ISBN 9780813947839 (hardcover) | ISBN 9780813947846 (ebook)
Subjects: LCSH: Thomas, John Charles, 1950– | Judges—Virginia—
    Biography. | African American judges—Virginia—Biography. | Virginia.
    Supreme Court.
Classification: LCC KF373.T515 A3 2022 (print) | LCC KF373.T515 (ebook)
    | DDC 347.73/14092 [B]—dc23/eng/20220430
LC record available at https://lccn.loc.gov/2022008346
LC ebook record available at https://lccn.loc.gov/2022008347

[handwritten, mirror-reversed inscription: July 2023 / HHS Summer Research / D.C., with signature]

Cover photo by John Charles Thomas Jr.

❖ CONTENTS ❖

Illustration gallery follows page 110

❖ FOREWORD ❖

Some books must be written because they have timeless significance. *The Poetic Justice* is such a book. Written in its author's inimitable voice, it speaks of being Black in America, of indomitable will, and of signal accomplishment.

John Charles Thomas grew up in Norfolk, Virginia, in the 1950s and '60s. He knew the searing prejudice of segregation in his city and the corrosive pain of grinding poverty, alcoholism, and violence in his home. Adversity could easily have broken John Charles. But he wouldn't let it.

Because of his academic prowess, John was sent to one of Norfolk's white high schools during the early days of integration in the city.

Then he was among the early Black undergraduates at the University of Virginia. On Mr. Jefferson's grounds, he was one of three Blacks in a class of fourteen hundred males. He was not a silent member of that body.

After law school at UVA, John was the first Black lawyer hired by the august Richmond firm then called Hunton, Williams, Gay & Gibson. Following seven years spent climbing the firm's intensely demanding and competitive ladder, he was the first Black elected to its partnership, thus becoming the first Black lawyer to rise through the ranks and make partner in any major law firm rooted in the South.

Shortly thereafter, John Charles Thomas was appointed by Governor Charles S. Robb to the Supreme Court of Virginia. Again, he led the way—as the court's first Black justice and its youngest member ever.

This is an extraordinary constellation of accomplishments. And it is just the beginning of his story.

John Charles is gifted. Poetry—writing it and reciting it—is but one indicator of his prodigious talent. While in study hall in high school one day, he suddenly remembered an assignment for his advanced English class, due in about half an hour. A poem would meet the need. With stunning speed, John conceived of a beautiful poem, wrote it down, and shortly thereafter added it to the pile of papers on the teacher's desk. Later in the class, the teacher approached John, holding his poem as if she could barely bring herself to touch it, and threw it on his desk, contemptuously declaring, "I reject this! I do not believe a colored child could write this." This egregious act of racial cruelty visited by a teacher upon her student shattered John's confidence in his poetry for quite some time. He continued writing poems, but put them in a drawer, not sharing them with others.

On a February evening in 2013, in New York City's Carnegie Hall, John recited a compelling selection of his poems, accompanied by music. His program was titled "The Allure of the Muse." The performance was a triumph.

For more than forty years I have heard John speak to countless groups, large and small, often at my request. Long ago he honed his capacity to stand before crowds and speak eloquently, powerfully, spontaneously, with few if any notes. His poetry often graces his remarks. John in full oratorical cry is an elemental force. Majestic at the podium, he commands all before him.

John Charles and I have known each other for close to half a century. I saw him as a young lawyer gallantly swimming upstream in a white sea. He and I have seen our families form and flourish. I saw him battle the brain tumor that forced him from the Supreme Court and brought him back into the nurture of his and my old law firm. More recently, though neither of us went to school at William & Mary, we both came to love the Alma Mater of the Nation, John as a member of its board of visitors for eleven years and I as its president. The judge was a strong force on the board, always focused on the good of the university. He was the sort of board member presidents cherish.

We talked often about the need for him to write this book. John did, finally, sit down and write it. The result, in my judgment, will be read for generations to come. It tells of stunning achievement in the teeth of fierce odds. It deals graphically and frankly with race at a time when our country still struggles to overcome its original sin. It is inspiring.

It is also a good read. Many important books, though substantively significant, get cluttered, trodding turgidly along page after page. *The Poetic Justice* moves at a brisk pace, urged along by vivid detail and powerful facts. By any measure, John Charles Thomas's memoir is engrossing. You will not want to put it down.

W. Taylor Reveley III

❖ PREFACE ❖

As I write these words, I am in my seventy-first year. From the time I first was in the news as a member of the Virginia Commission for Children and Youth when I was nineteen, I have heard several recurring questions: "How could you do these things at such a young age?" "How could you have known enough or had experience enough to take on these assignments?" "How could a child like you—who was raised without many if not most of the things that society considers normal—turn out to be a positive individual? And, given what you have lived through, why aren't you bitter?"

I never thought about such things as I was growing up. I did not have time to reflect on the philosophical questions posed by the ups and downs of my life. All I could do was get over the hurdle that was in front of me and try to be ready for the next obstacle that was sure to come.

As a child, it seemed that I hardly ever had enough of anything. I usually wore hand-me-downs from family members or secondhand clothes from the Goodwill. Steak was never on my menu; the best I could hope for was a small piece of hamburger.

When I lived at my grandma's house, I was assigned one chore after the other: pulling crabgrass, raking the pebbles along the side of the house, and picking figs from the tree in the yard; delivering packages to her friends; being responsible for the newspaper route that my uncles and aunts had started. I had to do as I was told and get on with it.

With this book, I now have the chance to think about the forces that shaped me and how my life experiences put me in position to become the first Black and the youngest Supreme Court justice in the history of Virginia.

THE POETIC JUSTICE

The First and the Youngest

O n the afternoon of April 25, 1983, I stood before the six justices of the Supreme Court of Virginia. I was very aware of the empty seventh seat on the right side of the bench as I faced the court with my wife, Pearl, holding the family Bible. I raised my right hand and took the oath prescribed for a new justice of the Supreme Court. At that moment, I was thirty-two years, seven months, and seven days old. It had been 376 years since the first permanent English settlement in America at Jamestown. It was 364 years after the arrival of the first enslaved Africans at Jamestown. After all those centuries, all those generations, all the struggles for freedom, the marches, the demonstrations, there I stood: the first African American and the youngest person in history to take a seat on the Supreme Court of Virginia—the oldest court in the new English-speaking world.

My transition from lawyer to Supreme Court justice had been so swift that I didn't have time to get my own robe for the ceremony. I was sworn in wearing a robe borrowed from Chief Justice Harry Carrico, which led to a now iconic photo of him on the bench with me adjusting the robe. And, yes, the Justice Carrico whose robe I wore was the same Justice Carrico who had written the decision in *Loving v. Commonwealth,* 206 Va. 924 (1966) that upheld Virginia's miscegenation laws until the decision was reversed by the Supreme Court of the United States in *Loving v. Virginia,* 388 U.S. 1 (1967).

The courtroom was packed for the ceremony. For the first time in history, cameras were allowed in the courtroom, and overflow rooms with televisions had been set up around the courthouse. A host of family members and friends were there. My pastor, Rev. Dwight C. Jones of the First Baptist Church of South Richmond, gave the invocation. Governor Charles Robb, who had appointed me to the court, remarked that all Virginians could walk a little taller that day with the integration of the commonwealth's highest court. My former law partner and law firm mentor, Tim Ellis, talked about my career as a young lawyer. Dennis Montgomery spoke on behalf of my friends and fellow law school classmates. My former law partner Joseph Spivey III read a resolution from the Richmond Bar Association. My friend and fraternity brother Charles D. Chambliss Jr. read a resolution from the Old Dominion Bar Association. Another former law partner, D. Alan Rudlin, who was the key figure in suggesting my name to Governor Robb, read the commission that put me on the bench. Bobby B. Stafford, president of the Old Dominion Bar Association, made the motion to the court regarding my qualification to serve on the bench. Then Chief Justice Carrico administered the oath of office.

Following the proclamations, the resolutions, the speeches, and the prayers, my robing committee—consisting of John J. Brown Jr., Michael Clark, Kester Crosse, Joel Cunningham, Douglas Davis, and W. Taylor Reveley—came forward, helped me into my borrowed robe, and escorted me to the right side of the bench, where I climbed a short flight of stairs and took my place in the empty seventh seat at the end of the bench, where the junior justice always sits. With those few steps I had ascended to the highest court in Virginia. I had broken what many had thought was a near impossible barrier, and I had become a visible example of the efforts to create a more inclusive commonwealth of Virginia.

When I took my seat on the bench, my brother-in-law Bill broke the decorum in the courtroom and let out a loud cheer. As if on cue, the rest of the audience erupted into shouts and cheers and leapt to their feet in sustained applause. Chief Justice Carrico, who had announced that this was a court session and thus there should be no outbursts, sat there with a look on his face that seemed to say "Oh, well, what can one do?" and allowed the applause to continue.

From the bench, I could see several of the great civil rights leaders in Virginia, including the pioneering lawyers Oliver Hill and Sam Tucker.

I could see friends from my childhood, from high school, from college, from law school, and on. Senior members of Virginia's government were there. My mother was there and several of her brothers and sisters. Uncle Tom and Uncle Charles, both retired U.S. Army lieutenant colonels, were in their dress uniforms. Pearl's mother, father, and siblings also were there, as were my brother and sisters. A real family gathering. There was a lot of excitement in that room. I knew that by joining the court I was fulfilling the dreams of many people who had struggled for years to fully integrate the commonwealth.

There was a low but discernible buzz. People were smiling and joyful, pointing this way and that, taking in the scene. Yet, amidst all that emotion, surrounded by all those people, I felt alone. It was not the physical loneliness of someone locked away in solitary confinement; rather, it was more the loneliness of a runner at the start of a marathon, as he contemplates what lies ahead and understands that despite the cheering crowds, he has to run this very long race by himself.

I knew that only I would feel the twists and turns, the ups and downs, the pounding of the pavement, the weariness, the effort. I knew that after the handshakes, smiles, and hugs were over I would be there by myself with all those briefs, appendices, and cases to read. I knew I had to hire a law clerk, get my office set up and operating. I knew that soon I would be writing questions in the briefs and making notes in the margins to prepare for oral argument. But I also knew that for a few more hours that day, I had to meet those who had attended the ceremony and share in their joy at this pivotal moment in Virginia history.

Though the effort to integrate the commonwealth's courts had been decades if not centuries long, the immediate events that put me on the bench had taken place in only about thirty days. It started when the General Assembly could not agree on a new justice to fill a vacancy on the court.

In Virginia, judges and justices are elected by the General Assembly. In early 1983, the House of Delegates supported one candidate for the Supreme Court and the Senate supported another. When the House sent the name of its candidate to the Senate, the Senate voted it down. When the Senate sent the name of its candidate to the House, the House voted it down. After several such votes, the General Assembly went out of session, leaving a vacancy on the court. Under these circumstances, the governor has the power to make what is called a recess appointment. He can fill the vacancy, and the next session of the General Assembly can accept or reject his appointee.

In 1983, I had no thoughts of becoming a judge, to say nothing of becoming a Supreme Court justice. I was a newly minted partner in my law firm, Hunton & Williams. I had made partner on April 1, 1982, thus becoming—according to the news accounts of the day—the first African American lawyer to move up the ranks from associate to partner in a formerly all-white southern law firm. I was busy trying cases in the state and federal trial courts then arguing appeals at the Supreme Court of Virginia, the Fourth Circuit, and elsewhere. In October 1982, I had married Pearl Walden, and we were just starting our life together. So, in early 1983, becoming a justice was the furthest thing from my mind.

But when the General Assembly went out of session and left a vacancy on the Supreme Court, pressure on Governor Robb to appoint a person of color sprang up instantly. Names were floated in the press. Civil rights groups suggested candidates. My name was not mentioned. Pearl and I were in the car when a story about the vacancy came on the radio, and I said, "It might be me." She replied, "They're not thinking of you because you are not on their radar."

But unbeknownst to me or Pearl, my friend and law partner Alan Rudlin—who had made partner at our law firm the same time that I did—had written to Governor Robb urging him to put me on the Supreme Court. The two had been moot court partners at the University of Virginia Law School. In those days, first-year law students were divided alphabetically to create what were called small sections, which are the classmates you tend to get to know best. Robb and Rudlin had been in the same small section. They were third year when I was first year, thus we were at the law school at the same time.

Rudlin did not tell me that he was urging Robb to appoint me. In fact, about the time he sent the letter, Pearl and I had left Richmond and driven to Cincinnati to visit her sister's family for Easter, which in 1983 was on April 3.

I later learned that when Governor Robb got Rudlin's letter, he called Hunton & Williams asking to speak to his old moot court partner. Robb placed the call himself, and his very familiar voice startled the secretary who answered the phone; she was not used to talking directly to the governor. Robb asked Rudlin to come to the Capitol. He wanted Rudlin's candid assessment of me because Robb didn't want any surprises to crop up if he appointed me to the court. Rudlin apparently reassured the governor, who then asked him to set up a second meeting with several senior lawyers from Hunton & Williams. Robb also asked Rudlin to bring to the next meeting copies of my briefs at the Supreme Court of Virginia. While all this was going on, I was still in Ohio, completely unaware.

At the second meeting, the governor told the group that they needed to pick someone to communicate with the bar organizations, to deal with the media, and to research the number and ages of persons of color on high courts across the country. My law partner Joe Spivey attended this second meeting. He called me in Ohio and said, "John, if I had not seen this with my own eyes and heard this with my own ears I might not believe it, but I was just in a meeting with the governor of Virginia and I believe he means to appoint you to the Supreme Court of Virginia. So, I just want to tell you to get ready." I hung up the phone, told Pearl what I had heard, and we started packing in a hurry to return to Richmond.

When we got home, Pearl and I started to look at the financial impact of me leaving the law firm. The numbers were sobering. Not only would the move cause my income to drop by more than $36,000, I would abruptly realize two years of partnership income by withdrawing from the firm. Basically, I would take a serious pay cut and then owe so much in taxes that I would have to borrow money to pay the bill.

There I was, a kid who had grown up in the kind of poverty that caused the church to send food baskets at Thanksgiving, whose clothes had come from the Goodwill or were hand-me-downs, who had hardly had money for anything—being asked to give up a job that I had worked seven hard years to achieve and that paid more than I had ever made, in order to take a seat on a court that had been all-white for centuries. It was a lot to think about, and I did not immediately say yes.

Near the end of that first week in April, Lieutenant Governor Dick Davis called late one night and said, "John, make up your mind! If you do not take this chance to sit on the Supreme Court of Virginia, there will not be a Black person on the court this millennium. The governor is ready to act, so make up your mind!" Pearl and I prayed over what

I should do. I remember thinking that Black people had been pushing for a change like this for decades, and now the burden was on me to see it through. I understood that the weight of history was on my shoulders. I could hear my mother repeating to me the words from the story of Esther: "You do not know but that you were placed in the Kingdom for such a time as this." I returned the lieutenant governor's call and said, "Okay, let's do it."

Governor Robb asked to see me at the Capitol on the evening of Sunday, April 10. Alan Rudlin went with me. We first met with several of the governor's aides. Tim Sullivan, an advisor to Robb who would later become president of the College of William & Mary, asked me questions that would help the group draft a press release. Then I was taken to the governor's small private office on the third floor of the Capitol.

The governor and I shook hands. We knew each other, but not all that well. We had been on a program at UVA when I was an undergraduate and he was in law school. He had also seen me at staff events with Pearl, who was a special assistant to the governor for cabinet support.

I was waiting for him to ask me to serve on the Supreme Court or to tell me why he had decided to appoint me. But all he said was, "When you come here tomorrow morning, do not come to the west side of the building because all the reporters will be camped out over there. Instead, come to the east side, where the Capitol police will be waiting to bring you up to my office." I said, "Okay." And that was it. I never got to say, "It is my honor to accept this historic appointment" or the like. All we talked about was logistics.

When Rudlin and I left the Capitol, we exited through the doors on the west side near the statue of George Washington on horseback. It was dark and stormy. As soon as we stepped outside there was a clap of thunder. I thought to myself that God in Heaven was applauding this change in Virginia.

The next morning, Pearl went to her office at the Capitol. I went to my office on Main Street. When I got there, I asked Rudlin and another law partner, Doug Davis, to walk with me to the Capitol, which we approached from the east side as I had been told. When we arrived, a Capitol policeman was there to take me upstairs.

In the governor's office, Pearl was waiting with a large group of staffers and state officials. Governor Robb said, "Let's go to the press conference." When we got downstairs, I saw Chief Justice Carrico and several of the justices of the Supreme Court of Virginia sitting together near the front of the room. The governor introduced me, took a few questions, and turned the podium over to me. A reporter asked, "What kind of person are you? How would you describe yourself?" I responded, "I'm the kind of person that if you needed to go through that brick wall, you would want me with you."

Later in the day, I said goodbye to my law firm, where my friends and colleagues were in shock about the speed of my transition from lawyer to justice. Some were tearful, some were excited. No one knew what my rapid departure would mean for the firm, but they all understood that a big change had occurred.

Over the next four days, I packed up my law office and moved books, papers, and knickknacks to my chambers at the courthouse. When I got to the Supreme Court building there was no one to help me move in, so I found a hand truck, unloaded my car by myself, and brought my things upstairs. I saw that the desk in my chambers was broken, so I found another one, tipped it on its side, put it on the hand truck, and hauled it to my chambers. My investiture was ten days away. The next court session would begin shortly thereafter, so I had to start reading the briefs and appendices that were sitting in big wooden boxes on a side table in my chambers.

I sat there alone, hoping that I would have enough time to get ready. I was determined to be prepared the first time I went on the bench for oral argument. I had never practiced criminal law, so I paid special attention to the criminal cases on the docket. Indeed, there were several areas of law that I felt the need to focus on, like juvenile and domestic relations and divorce and child custody. Basically, I had been a civil litigator handling commercial matters. I had a lot to learn and a short time in which to learn it. I felt that loneliness again, that feeling that nobody could help me, that I was in a do-or-die, sink-or-swim situation. I had had that feeling more than once in my life, because being lonely is a large part of being the first. It is a feeling that can either overwhelm you or motivate you. It motivated me to get ready.

Injury, Poetry, and Childhood

I was born on Monday night, September 18, 1950, upstairs in my grandparents' house at the corner of Washington Avenue and Proescher Street in the old Huntersville section of a very segregated Norfolk, Virginia. My mother, who was a registered nurse, decided that she would have me at home rather than at a hospital. My birth was more difficult than she had anticipated. In a prolonged labor and delivery—as she pushed—my head was deformed along the right side. My aunts who were present that day later talked about how badly misshapen my head was. They told me that my mother held my head in her hands and pushed it back into a more normal-looking shape. It would take almost forty years to understand what really happened to me on the day that I was born.

I was my parents' first child. My father, John Thomas, was born in Staunton, Virginia, in July 1920. I met my paternal grandparents, King Edward Thomas and Estelle Thompson Thomas, when I was quite young, but I never knew them well and have little memory of them. My mother was born in Norfolk in February 1925. She was the eighth of fifteen children born to my grandfather William Harvey Sears and my grandmother Eunice Virginia Mears Sears; their children were born from 1912 to 1941, with no twins. When my mother was born she was named Virginia Bell Floretta Sears, but as she got older she did not like that name because her initials, V.B.F.S., led her classmates to dub her Virginia Big Fat Sears. To avoid this she simply changed her name to

Floretta Virginia Sears. As far as I know she never sought court approval for this change; she just did it.

The story is that my mother and father met in New York City, where she was a nurse working at Brooklyn Jewish Hospital and he was a merchant seaman on shore leave. My mother was at a deli and ordered something; the waiter, who was not looking in her direction when she spoke, reportedly mistook her contralto voice for that of a man's and responded by saying, "Sir, I'll get to you in a minute." My father—on hearing the waiter call my mother "sir"—reportedly said, "Hey, that's no sir, that's a lady talking to you. Pay attention." My mother was apparently beguiled by this stranger coming to her aid and got to know him.

I do not know how the story evolved from New York City to Norfolk, but somehow she decided that she wanted to marry this man and plans were made for a wedding. Prior to the wedding my mother apparently changed her mind. But when she told her mother that she did not want to go through with it, her mother slapped her and said, "You can't back out now. We have made plans, and we have told everybody." They got married February 14, 1948, four days before my mother's twenty-third birthday.

When I was born, my father wanted me to be John Thomas Jr. My mother wanted me to have a middle name, as she and all her siblings did. She won; I was named John Charles Thomas, with the Charles coming from my mother's brother, my uncle Charles Walter Sears, with whom she was very close among her siblings.

For the first six years of my life, I lived upstairs in the house where I had been born. When I was an infant, my grandparents had a store downstairs in the front of the house. They sold sodas, postage stamps, money orders, razors, and other incidentals. To keep me occupied, they put me in a small cradle on the store counter beside the cash register. The family told me that almost all the customers would talk to me or tickle me or otherwise try to get my attention, and I would giggle or laugh or make some noise in response. I have often wondered whether my perch on the counter of the store where everybody talked to me helped me develop my language skills.

As a young child I was always asking questions, so much so that my Grandmother Sears would say to me, "Don't ask so many questions.

Go make yourself small." Although she tried to stop me from pestering her with questions, she was happy for me to sit and read. She could see that I was learning all the time and that I had a serious nature, so she knew that I would sit quietly reading a book all day long. Once when I was still quite young, she told me, "You are the oldest little boy I have ever seen." I understood that she meant that I acted much older than my age, and I was fine with that.

When I wasn't asking my grandma questions and being told to be quiet, I was sitting on the side porch with my granddaddy, William Harvey Sears, listening to his stories. He was born in 1890 in Waverly, Virginia, so he was about sixty years old when I was born. I am told that he had once been a big, strong, six-foot-tall man who raced cars, ran a boxing arena, built houses, and ran a business. But I only knew him as an old man who had had a stroke and whose right arm was bent permanently at the elbow. He would sit on the side porch and pull a handle attached to a strong spring to try to straighten that arm, but it never straightened out. My granddaddy would sit there and read the newspapers and chat with his old buddies who would walk up, lean on the railing, and tell him things like who had been injured on the job, who had gotten a raise, or who might be a good man to join the Prince Hall Masons.

Over the course of my many conversations with my granddaddy, he noticed that I had a strong memory. I will never know precisely what caught his attention. He was a Master Mason who loved oratory and poetry, so when he discovered that I had a strong memory he decided to teach me poetry. I wasn't reading then—I was only four years old—so he had to teach me poetry by rote memory. He would go line by line through a poem and make me repeat what he was saying.

The first poem he taught me was "Thanatopsis" by William Cullen Bryant. The title means "a view of death." It is a long poem with a lot of big words. He would read a line, then make me repeat it. He would add another line and tell me to repeat the two lines, and so forth. We went on like this for maybe a month or so until I could repeat most of the poem. I am not sure why my granddaddy chose this poem to teach me. But all his children including my mother seemed to know all or part of it because he had either taught it to them or recited it in their presence. Its length and complexity made it a favorite of his and his buddies. It

sounded so lofty; its themes of death and nature were rich with mean-
ing. To recite it seemed to them to require great oratorical skills. And
the poem is lyrical, which means that if you can figure out its rhyme
scheme and recite it in the proper meter, it is almost hypnotic. The
idea of a mere child reciting this colossal poem must have been akin
to a four-year-old hitting a home run at Yankee Stadium or throwing
a touchdown pass from one end of the field to the other. And that was
basically how my granddaddy's friends reacted when he called on me
to recite the poem for them.

When a group of his buddies gathered at the railing, Granddaddy
would call me over and say, "Charles, recite that poem." I always had
to begin by stating the name of the poem and the name of the author.
Then he would say, "Stand up straight; put your hands to your side;
hold your head up. Now say that poem." "Yes, Granddaddy." Then I
would launch into the poem. His face would light up and so would
the faces of his old buddies. If I stumbled over a word, he would supply it. If my voice lost volume, he would admonish me to "speak up."
As I continued, the old men would cheer, "Go! Go!" You would have
thought I was a sports hero shooting the winning basket at the last
second. When I got to the end of the poem, those old guys would be
beside themselves with joy. Hearing me recite serious poetry seemed
to make these old Black men so happy that I continued doing it. And
because I had to stand and recite at such a young age, I have never had
stage fright. It has never bothered me to talk an audience.

When a little kid can recite a big old poem, the word gets out. Before
too long I was called on to recite Bible verses and say prayers at church
on youth Sundays. At school I was called on to make announcements
over the public address system and to speak at school programs or act
in school plays. Next came the taunts of "teacher's pet" from my classmates. The taunts bothered me as they would most young kids, but I
kept learning and reciting poetry because I knew it made my granddaddy so happy. He could not have known that he had started me on
a path that would stay with me all my life and that would come to my
rescue when I was sent to the white high school in 1965.

Grandma was a stern disciplinarian who was not reluctant to spank
her grandchildren. One day I was playing with other kids on the sidewalk, just running up and down. As was often the case in Norfolk's

black neighborhoods, the sidewalk was in disrepair. Some portions were broken and crumbling; other portions jutted up, exposing raised edges that were tripping hazards. As I ran, I tripped over a protruding edge of concrete and went flying face-first toward the ground. I put my hands out to break my fall, but I had fallen into Miss Owens's "garden." This so-called garden was about two feet by two feet, bordered by sidewalk and front walkway and covered with chicken wire. The only thing you could see growing in it was weeds. I never thought that this little patch of dirt looked much like a garden. No matter, by the time I got up and dusted myself off, Miss Owens had called my grandma to report that I had messed up her garden.

When I got home Grandma said to me, "Come here, boy. Why did you mess up Miss Owens's garden?" I said, "Grandma, that's not what happened. I was playing and I tripped on the broken sidewalk, and I just put my hands out so I wouldn't hit my face on the ground." Grandma responded, "Well, you shouldn't have been running. Now hold out your hand." So, I got spanked for trying not to hit my face on the ground. But that's not all. When my mother got home from work, Grandma said to her, "Flo, Charles messed up Miss Owens's garden today. What are you going to do about it?" Grandma didn't tell my mother that I had already been spanked for falling into the garden. So, my mother told me to go get the belt. And then I got a second whipping for the same thing. I was just a little boy; I had not heard of double jeopardy, but I sure knew that it wasn't fair to get two whippings for the same thing.

I soon realized that if you stayed around my grandma too long you would wind up with some chore to do: pulling weeds in the yard, taking packages to neighbors, picking figs from the wasp-laden fig tree where if you found a ripe fig you were sure to be stung trying to pick it. Grandma simply did not like for children to be what she called "idle." The way she looked at it, if you were not doing some chore, you would get in trouble.

Grandma used to wash clothes for some of the real old ladies in the neighborhood, and she'd then send one of her grandchildren to deliver the laundered, folded clothes. One Saturday when I was around eleven or twelve years old, she gave me a bundle to deliver to a lady who lived several neighborhoods away. Just before I left to make the delivery

Grandma said to me, "Now don't take any money from her, you hear?" "Yes, Grandma," I said. Then off I went, all the way up Washington Avenue across Tidewater Drive, up St. Julian Avenue, past the Black cemetery, through the housing projects, to Virginia Beach Boulevard over near Norfolk State College. Basically, it was an "over the river and through the woods" kind of journey, a very long walk for a little boy.

When I finally got to the lady's house and rang the doorbell, she opened the door, took the bundle of laundry, patted me on the head, told me that I was such a sweet little boy to come so far to deliver her clothes, dropped a nickel in my shirt pocket, and closed the door. When I got back to Grandma's house, I told her what had happened. She said, "I told you not to take any money from her. Take it back." "But, Grandma, I didn't ask for this. She just dropped it in my pocket and closed the door." Grandma said, "I don't care. I told you not to take any money from her. Now take it back." "Yes, ma'am." And off I went, retracing my long journey. When I got to the lady's house, I rang the doorbell, handed her the nickel, and said, "My grandma said I have to give this back to you." I guess the lesson was to do precisely what your grandma tells you to do. But as I look back over the years, it strikes me that it never occurred to me to just keep the nickel and not tell my grandma what had happened.

In addition to the discipline I received at the hand of my grandma, I was raised by a committee of aunts and uncles and with a whole slew of cousins. When I was very young my mother, my brother Clarence (who was born in 1954), and I lived upstairs in Grandma's house in the rooms where I had been born. I lived there from 1950 until the fall of 1956.

During that time, my father was convicted of rape and sent to the State Penitentiary on Spring Street in Richmond. My mother always maintained that he did not rape that woman, because in her mind he was "too good-looking a man to have to rape anybody." I know that such a comment sounds woefully wrongheaded, but I heard her say this with my own ears. I guess that despite my father's many character flaws, my mother always felt pleased that this handsome man had married the girl who had once been called Virginia Big Fat Sears.

I remember visiting my father in prison. There was a grassy area where the families gathered before they were allowed inside to see the inmates. And apparently the families of white and Black inmates mingled there together before entering the prison. My mother took this small amount of desegregation as a sign of progress in Virginia. She would talk about how wonderful it was to see the little white children and little Black children all playing together outside the penitentiary.

Aunt Evelyn and her children, Bucky, Eunice, and Pat, lived downstairs in the back of the old house. Bucky and I were both born in 1950, he in January and me in September. Uncle Henry's son, Waddell, who was born in 1949, also lived there, and we all played together. We climbed trees, shot marbles in the dirt, and played cowboys and Indians on Granddaddy's piles of lumber in the backyard. We used his sawhorses as our pretend horses. We would make the sawhorses rock back and forth while we were in hot pursuit of imaginary bad guys.

Bucky, Waddell, and I also played at Barraud Park, off Tidewater Drive near the Lafayette River. It was the public park for Negroes. We played at the park when we weren't playing in the streets. We had never been inside any of the white parks, so we did not know the kinds of playthings they had there. The most we ever did was drive past City Park on Granby Street and marvel at how big it was compared to Barraud Park.

Barraud Park, small though it was, had merry-go-rounds and swings and places to play football, baseball, and tennis. It even had a concession stand and a picnic area. It also had cages with baboons and monkeys. Basically, this was the Black zoo. Many of the children would climb up on the fences and shake them while yelling at the monkeys. They were delighted when the monkeys would climb the fences in their cages and howl back, or when the baboons would yelp. Sometimes the children would throw rocks and dirt at the animals to get a reaction. The animals would bare their teeth and snarl in response.

The Lafayette River ran behind the park. Across the river was a white neighborhood. We could see the white children playing in their backyards and they could see us. We would yell at each other across the river and throw rocks at each other. But, the river was wide, so it was not possible for a little kid to throw anything all the way across. We could hardly hear what we were yelling at each other, but we did it anyway until we got tired and walked off. Nobody told us to throw rocks and to taunt each other. It seemed a spontaneous thing. It didn't happen every day, but when they saw us and we saw them, the white children would yell at us and we would yell at them. I guess it was about the racial divide that we have lived with so long in our country.

When we didn't feel like going to Barraud Park, we would play in the streets and on the sidewalk outside Grandma's house. We would take a piece of coal and draw the boxes for hopscotch on the front sidewalk. We played hide-and-seek between parked cars, behind bushes, and behind the woodpile in the backyard. On rainy days we sat on the side porch drawing pictures on the big blank pieces of newsprint that came wrapped around the *Norfolk Journal and Guide*. Sometimes we would read books and make up stories. There were no sidewalks on the Proescher Street side of Grandma's house, only pebble-strewn dirt, so that's where we would sweep out a big area in the dirt, draw a rough circle, and shoot marbles.

The old house was big and creepy. Granddaddy bought the land for the house on February 16, 1911, for five hundred dollars, paying twenty dollars down and agreeing to pay five dollars per month. He bought the land from George L. Proescher and his wife. I guess this explains the location of the property at the intersection of Washington Avenue and Proescher Street.

Granddaddy built the house not long after he married Grandma in 1911. He was always proud to say that he had built that old house himself. There were only two bathrooms in the whole house, one upstairs and one downstairs. The place was always dimly lit; Grandma did not want to waste money on electricity, so throughout the house she used 15- and 20-watt bulbs. There were no closets, so clothes were hung on nails driven into the backs of doors or thrown over the backs of chairs. The dim lights and the clothes hanging all over cast shadows on the walls that made the house eerie. Every floorboard seemed to creak. To walk about at night was to bump into things, to hear creaking and groaning noises, to see shadows on the walls that could be any monster you could imagine.

The rooms we lived in upstairs did not have much heat. We had a small coal stove. But often we couldn't even afford a few lumps of coal. There was a lumberyard on St. Julian Avenue up near Calvary Cemetery. I remember going there with my mother in the dark of night, in the cold, carrying empty paper bags that she and I would fill with tree bark that had been stripped from the lumber and was lying on the ground under the woodpiles. There was no fence around the property, so we would just walk along the road until no car was visible, then quickly duck under the timber that was propped up on supports a few feet off the ground. I would then crawl beneath the woodpiles to fill the bags with wood chips. The bark made great fires because it burned easily and quickly, so if you wanted to heat your place with wood chips you needed a lot of them.

In our neighborhood such hardscrabble living was the norm. Hardly anyone had the luxury of an oil stove connected to a tank in the yard. Almost everyone I knew lived a hand-to-mouth, day-by-day, catch-as-catch-can existence.

The Sears family attended First Baptist Church on Bute Street in Norfolk. My cousins and I would walk from Grandma's house several miles to get to church, but we never thought about the distance. It was just the way we got around. We seemed to walk everywhere, and as we walked we talked. We told jokes, asked riddles, gave each other quizzes, recited Bible verses, and basically made a game of everything.

Rev. Dr. E. Paul Simms was our pastor. There was a white First Baptist Church in Norfolk, too, and its minister was Reverend Mimms. The similarity between the names of the pastors of the two First Baptist churches always caught my attention: Simms and Mimms, Black and white, divided by race even while both were preaching Christianity.

Reverend Simms was also a professor at Norfolk State University. He was a light-skinned Black man from Boston who had worked at Harvard Law School as a messenger when he was young. He told me that only a very few Black students were studying at Harvard when he was there. He had observed a Black law student who tried to speak in class, but every time he tried to talk some of his white classmates would scrape their feet on the floor and make loud noises to drown him out. According to Reverend Simms these disruptions did not last long, because when the professor saw what was going on, he turned to the class and said, "Gentlemen, this is 'fair Harvard,'" then he walked out of the classroom. Reverend Simms said the disruptions stopped after that. I think this story shows that a teacher can change the conduct of his students by confronting their prejudices. And I have always liked the idea of "fair" Harvard, and I have hoped for fairness everywhere.

On Sundays, we all went to Sunday school in the morning then to the main church service at 11:00 a.m. We sang in the choir, played roles in the Christmas pageant, and were generally involved in the life of the church. But what we really liked were the church's summer outings to Seaview Beach. This was an all-Black beach that had an amusement park with bumping cars. Black people from all around Tidewater would come to Seaview Beach, bringing fried chicken, potato salad, homemade rolls, and all the other picnic favorites. We had the best time running into each other in the bumping cars.

We also loved being at our church at Christmastime. Down in the basement the children would sing Christmas carols and bob for apples. A lot of our friends and almost all our cousins would be there. We always had a church Christmas pageant where we got to wrap ourselves in sheets and play shepherds watching their flocks at night. The highlight of the evening was leaving church with bags of candy canes, walnuts, apples, and that lovely Christmas spirit.

Every summer we looked forward to Daddy Grace's parade on the Fourth of July. Sweet Daddy Grace of the United House of Prayer for All People would ride through the narrow streets of Huntersville, sitting on a throne on the back of a flatbed truck and throwing Hershey's kisses to the children who would run ahead of the float hoping to snag some candy. Daddy Grace's bodyguards tried to shoo the children away, but it was an impossible task because the children so wanted the candy. And because the parade was in the heat of July, the candy wrapped in aluminum foil was virtually liquid by the time you could get a piece and unwrap it. But we did not care. It was free chocolate candy; too bad that it got all over our face and clothes.

Daddy Grace's parade had marching bands, marching units made up of old war veterans, and women with parasols and long dresses just strutting along. There were jazz ensembles and blues bands all sauntering down the street in the July heat making music. People on upstairs porches along the parade route leaned precariously over fragile railings that looked like they might give way at any moment. Others sat in folding chairs in the street or on the sidewalk, trying to find shade under the few trees that lined the street and eating watermelon and drinking ice water trying to stay cool. Units in the parade tied wet handkerchiefs around their necks to keep cool.

The parade distracted us from how we lived day to day. It brought music, excitement, and flair to the somber streets we lived on. For just a little while, despite the heat, we could cheer and dance and laugh and be transported. We loved that parade and we wanted it to last all day, but it didn't. What was lasting was the poverty and segregation we lived in.

❖ 3 ❖

Education, Racism, and Meeting JFK

I attended Mount Olive Kindergarten in Lindenwood, a more well-to-do Black neighborhood in Norfolk literally across the tracks from Huntersville. I remember being happy to go to Mount Olive. I was about five years old at the time. But something happened there one day that upset me. I cannot remember what it was, but I was not going to take it. I pretended to have to go to the restroom, which was down the hall. When I got outside the classroom, I got my coat, walked out of the building, and took my time going back home to Grandma's house. I knew the way home. I walked for a while beside the train tracks that ran near the church. When the tracks got to the point where they would go over Tidewater Drive, I crossed the tracks and several streets until I was near the house. I knew what time I usually arrived home, so I looked at clocks in the corner stores that I passed and kept walking around the neighborhood until the time was right for me to get home. I arrived at Grandma's house at the usual time.

When I went back to my kindergarten the next day, no one said a word to me about where I had gone the previous day. Apparently nobody had noticed that I had left. When I have told this story to family and friends, they have always wanted to know what made me get up and walk out. My best explanation is that I was not going to just sit there at that school being mistreated and do nothing about it. What I did that day might have been an early example of the idea that when something is wrong, you need to do something about it.

I did well in kindergarten. When I finished, my mother took me to a pharmacy at the corner of Church Street and Princess Anne Road for a piece of pie. It was the kind of place with a counter and a few permanently affixed stools where customers could sit. There was one little table with two chairs by the window. I was five years old. I had never been anywhere to eat outside the house. I had never had a piece of store-bought pie. I asked for the big slice of lemon meringue that was covered by a glass top. Boy, was it good. I gulped it down.

My mother had always told me to leave a little bit of food on the plate so that people would not think I was starving. I always thought that was silly advice because when I was little, I always felt like I was starving. So, I ate all the pie. The idea of leaving a piece of that store-bought pie just wasn't going to fly. And when I finished, I licked the plate. Right there in the little corner pharmacy I picked up the plate and licked it because the slice of pie was so good that I wanted every last bit. My mother was mortified. I got a spanking on the spot for embarrassing her in public. So, my graduation treat ended in a whipping.

We were still living at Grandma's house when the time came for me to go to the first grade. The elementary school in our neighborhood was John T. West. My mother and all her brothers and sisters had gone there. It was a small, old, outdated building that sat beside the train tracks. My mother did not want me to go there, so she used the address of a friend who lived in Lindenwood and enrolled me in Lindenwood Elementary School, a newer school beside the Lafayette River. There were tree-lined streets in Lindenwood and big houses with porches lived in by Black people who had steady jobs. I was happy to be going to the pretty new school, but it just wasn't in my neighborhood. And even though Mount Olive Kindergarten was in Lindenwood, it was located directly beside the train tracks that separated Lindenwood from Huntersville. So, having gone there did not really acquaint me with Lindenwood; it had been more like being on the boundary line of the two neighborhoods.

On the first day of school, the teacher gave the class a quiz, something to do with numbers and our ABCs, basic things that a first-grader might know. One part of the quiz asked us to color in a stoplight. I knew that stoplights were red at the top, yellow in the middle, and green at the bottom. I was about to color in my paper that way when I looked up and saw that another child had the colors in a different order. When

I saw this, I remember thinking that the stoplights in Lindenwood must be different from the ones in Huntersville. So, I colored in my paper the same way she had done. The teacher collected the papers, looked quickly at them, then said, "Well, boys and girls, it looks like we did very well on the test. Only two of you got it wrong." Because I wasn't from Lindenwood, I did not know that the girl I had copied from was learning disabled. The other children did, and they soon realized that I was the other student who had gotten the colors of the stoplight wrong.

I never again copied from another student's paper. I had learned the hard way that you can't know what the people around you know or don't know, so you may as well rely on your own learning. In retrospect, that is a profound lesson to have learned on the first day of first grade.

I didn't stay long at Lindenwood. My father had been released from prison, and he wanted to move from Grandma's house. My mother found a place in the Liberty Park housing project. All the housing projects in Norfolk had "Park" at the end of their name—Diggs Park, Bowling Park, Youngs Park, Roberts Park—as if by calling them parks you could transform them into fun places to live. Liberty Park was the oldest of the projects, built in the 1940s. One of my teachers years ago told me that Liberty Park had been built as temporary World War II housing "for the colored." The oldest parts of Liberty Park certainly looked temporary, and no white people lived there.

My mother came to get me from Lindenwood in late October on the very day that all the children were dressed in their Halloween costumes and were about to start trick-or-treating from one classroom to another. My mother arrived just as we were lining up to walk down the halls. I did not want to leave; I wanted pocketfuls of candy. My mother wouldn't wait and I wouldn't leave voluntarily, so she lifted me by my arms and dragged me to the car for the trip to Liberty Park. I was not happy.

Our unit at Liberty Park was deep in the old part of the projects near a swampy area. The units were side by side with a common wall that was not much more than plasterboard. You could hear through the walls, and worse than that, if you did not have a trusted next-door neighbor you were sure to be robbed, because all a thief had to do was break into the empty unit, punch a hole in the wall, and come through and take what he wanted from your unit. It happened all the time. Our unit had a front room, a kitchen, two bedrooms, and a bathroom, all in about fifteen hundred square feet. We were cramped for space and piled on top of each other.

Though housing projects have come to symbolize crime-infested, dead-end hopelessness, in the 1950s living in the projects was often a step up from the old Black neighborhoods like Huntersville. People who moved to the housing projects did not think that they were going to live there for the rest of their lives. In fact, the projects were looked upon as a place to live while you put together enough money to buy your own home. So, the housing projects back then were upwardly mobile places. In our little cul-de-sac at the back of Liberty Park, we had a sense of community, even pride. People cut the grass, washed their cars, had picnics, played outdoors. In all the time I lived in Liberty Park I never saw a gun or heard gunfire. Of course, there were thugs and hoodlums—they seemed to exist everywhere—but in those days they weren't armed with guns. They tended to beat you with their fists and with sticks and, sometimes, cut you with switchblades.

While we lived in Liberty Park, my mother was a night-duty nurse at nearby Norfolk Community Hospital, the all-Black hospital up the street from Norfolk State College. Other times she worked at King's Daughters and Norfolk General, but always as a night-duty nurse. My father was usually employed as a cook. That had been his job in the merchant marine before he went to prison. While we lived in Liberty Park, he was a cook at the Shoney's Big Boy restaurant.

There was never enough money for anything. We seemed to be the poorest kids in a neighborhood of poor kids. Every now and then my father would come home with one Shoney's hamburger, which we would divide among the whole family. At most you would get a bite. Everything had to be divvied up or diluted. In all my childhood, I never had a whole bottle of Coca-Cola or Nehi grape soda, and I hardly ever got to taste a soda at full strength. Our mother would take a soda, mix it with water, then put ice in it and pass it out. I never liked it that way, but that's the way things were. I think that the first time I had an undiluted bottle of soda was at the barbershop when I was a few years older. Some things in life ought not to be diluted.

Though my mother was a registered nurse who had graduated from the St. Philip School of Nursing at the Medical College of Virginia in Richmond, she never really liked being a nurse. She always wanted to be a performer. She wanted to sing and recite poems and passages from famous plays. She styled herself a "dramatic monologist," and she tried to earn extra money by putting on one-woman recitals at Black churches all over Tidewater. She would recite poetry and impersonate famous Black women while reciting things that they had said. She would end her program with a recitation of "Thanatopsis," and she had among her props a couch on which she would lie down while delivering the last lines of the poem. But given that we lived in a cramped two-bedroom unit, there was no good place for her to keep her props. Everything was just crammed into our apartment. There was hardly a place to sit. It was like living in a storage unit. But since my mother said she was no housekeeper, and since she was happy doing her recitals, the clutter did not seem to bother her. This enraged my father, who railed about all the "junk" in the house.

My parents had a horrible relationship. I never saw moments of tenderness between them. All I remember is tension. It is a wonder that four children were born of the marriage. I grew up amidst constant fighting, cussing, and fussing. Once during a fight she cut him with a knife. When they stopped fighting, she used her nursing skills to sew up his wound.

A particularly violent fight ensued after my father dragged all her props from our apartment and threw them into the swamp behind the building. When she came home and saw that her props were gone, she went down to the muddy swamp and dragged all that stuff back inside. He started beating her with his fists. I was six years old. I was afraid he would kill her, so I went into the kitchen, got the biggest knife I could find, got between them, and said, "If you hit my momma again, I'll kill you." He must have been able to tell from the sound of my voice that I meant what I said, so he stopped beating her and left the house. They would fight other times, but from that day on he was wary of me because he never could be sure what I might do to keep him from beating my mother.

Not long after I arrived at my new first-grade classroom at Liberty Park Elementary School, the teacher put all the children in a circle and handed us a book so that we could read a passage or two before passing it to the next child in the circle. When the book came to me, I read aloud the whole page and was about to turn the page to keep reading. The teacher walked over, took the book from me, took me out of the reading circle, and left me at a table by myself. She didn't say anything or give me an assignment, but apparently she saw no need for me to stay in the reading circle. So, while the other children continued reading, I looked around the classroom, found the biggest word that I could find on a map or a book or a calendar, wrote the word on my paper, then tried to find as many words as possible within that big word. That's what I would do when the other children were in the reading circle.

I liked reading books, so I got a job in the library at Liberty Park, rearranging the chairs, sweeping the floor, and putting books back on the shelves. For that, I could take home extra books, and I did.

Though I was doing well at Liberty Park, for the second time in my life I cheated in school. This time, the teacher had told the class to find out at home what "GOP" stood for. I forgot to do it. In class, the teacher said, "Yesterday I gave you boys and girls a little assignment. Now I'm going to find out whether you did what I told you to do." I figured, "Okay, I'll just listen to the answers my classmates give and then repeat the one that seems right to me." Well, it did not work out like that. The teacher went from student to student and made them whisper the answer in her ear. I was done in. My friend Melvin was sitting in front of me. I got his attention and said, "What does it mean?" He said, "Grand Ol' Party." Good, I had something to say. But I was hoping that the teacher would get to Melvin before she got to me, so that I could be sure that he had the right answer. No dice. She came from the back of my row and got to me first. I said what he had told me. She said "good boy," then went on to Melvin. That was the last time I cheated in school.

When I was in third or fourth grade at Liberty Park, no more than ten years old, I decided I was in love with one of the teachers. She was not my teacher. I thought she was pretty, and I think she had said something kind to me about a school program that I had been in. I decided I wanted to marry her. One day at recess I went to her classroom and said, "Will you marry me?" She looked up in surprise and said, "Thomas, go wipe that booger out of your nose." I was crushed. Even then I knew there was no recovering from being told by the woman you thought you loved to go wipe a booger from your nose. I said, "Yes, ma'am," and quickly left her classroom. I hope she doesn't remember me.

In November 1960, when I was in fifth grade, John F. Kennedy campaigned in Norfolk shortly before the presidential election. My mother—a lifelong political activist who earned small sums of money in get-out-the-vote drives—wanted to go hear Kennedy, and I did too. Even though I was just ten years old, I was captivated by this man with the funny-sounding voice who had Black people believing that he would be good on civil rights. He came to Norfolk to speak at Granby High School, the big white high school in the fancy white neighborhood. As often happened in the segregated South of the '60s, most of the Black people and most of the white people waited in two separate groups. The whites were waiting on Granby Street, in front of the school; the Blacks were waiting behind the school near the service entrance.

But, as luck would have it, Kennedy's motorcade arrived at the back of the school, where a narrow service road led to the football field, the site of the rally. A line of cars was already parked along the service road, making it even narrower than usual. So, when the motorcade turned onto that road, the motorcycles had to get in front and back of Kennedy's car and they all had to slow down. There I was with my momma standing between some parked cars. Kennedy was sitting in the back seat of a Lincoln convertible with the top down; it looked much like the car in which he would be assassinated. He was toward the right side of the car. As the car inched past me, I said, "Hello, Mr. Kennedy. I hope you become president of the United States," and I stuck out my hand. He shook it and said, "Thank you, young man, I hope I do too." I was so happy when he was elected. I couldn't wait for people to stop saying "President-elect Kennedy" and to hear him called President Kennedy, for I had touched this president with my own hand. Once he was elected, the excitement about what he would do to help the Black community grew. He put a Black person in his cabinet; he appointed other Blacks to high positions in the government; and he seemed to care about the Black community in a way that no other president had. I have always thought well of JFK. He was the first U.S. president that I had seen personally. He was one of the first national public figures that I had met. He inspired me to want to become involved in civic affairs, if not in politics.

Not long after the Kennedy encounter, my mother told me that we couldn't afford Liberty Park anymore and that we had to move back near my grandparents to a house that they owned behind their house. In other words, we were too poor for low-cost public housing in the projects.

The house to which we moved shared a yard with the house where I had been born, but it faced Proescher Street. It was old and dilapidated. There was no privacy. The rooms, all off one long hallway, had no doors, and as you walked from the front of the house to the back you could see into each room. It didn't have hot water or a full bath. There was one sink in the kitchen and an indoor commode. My momma put a huge vat with a faucet on top of the gas stove covering three of the burners. We would fill the vat with cold water and heat it over the gas jets. We used the hot water to wash dishes, to wash clothes in an old washtub with a scrub board, and to bathe in a galvanized metal tub on the kitchen floor. And everybody had to bathe in that one tub of water; by the end it was covered with scum. To this day I cannot stand to take a bath because of the thought of having to sit in dirty water.

When we moved to the house on Proescher Street, my mother's brother, Uncle Sammy, was living upstairs. Samuel Oliver Sears Sr. was his full name. He had been an auxiliary policeman in New York City in the 1940s and had received a citation from Mayor LaGuardia for saving a woman's life who had jumped from the Brooklyn Bridge. He had gone in after her and pulled her from the water. His exploits made it into the Movietone newsreels. But I don't remember Uncle Sammy as the hero he once was. When I knew him, he and his buddy "Good Britches"—who we had to call Mr. Good Britches because as children we always had to give our elders a title of respect—would pull a two-wheeled hand-made wooden cart through the streets of Huntersville picking up scrap metal and other junk and taking it to the junkyard on Church Street for money. Then they would buy cheap wine and sit on the curb or on the stoop to our house and get drunk. Uncle Sammy always looked disheveled and smelled like old booze.

Grandma would scold Uncle Sammy, but she would let him inside her house and feed him. I always wondered why she treated Uncle Sammy the way she did. The rest of us couldn't come into her living room unless we were dressed in our Sunday clothes and were on our best behavior. She was so stern with her grandchildren that it seemed odd that she would let Uncle Sammy inside all smelly and dirty. Later I found out why.

The story goes that he came home from New York for a visit and went down to Virginia Beach to some nightspot. As he was leaving, some white guys jumped him and beat him on the head with a bottle, crushing his skull. He stayed in Norfolk to recover, and his days as an auxiliary policeman were over. He told me that after the attack he always had headaches and that he drank to kill the pain. So, it turned out that Grandma treated Uncle Sammy the way she did because she had seen her son hailed as a hero only to be brutally attacked by white men; she felt the injustice of it all. Uncle Sammy died from exposure on the front steps of the house on Proescher Street one night in November. The family buried him in a tuxedo. From what I heard at the time from my aunts and uncles, they knew what Uncle Sammy had been and they knew how far he had fallen, but with that tuxedo they wanted to say to the world that their brother was better than the racist circumstances that had altered the course of his life.

It seemed that we were just as poor in Huntersville as we had been in Liberty Park, even though my mother didn't have to pay rent to her parents. We had a diet of day-old bread, oatmeal, and old military rations from my uncles who were in the army. Several times the power was turned off for nonpayment. During those times we would run an extension cord along a clothesline from Grandma's house to ours, through an open window. That way we had just enough electricity for the refrigerator and a lamp at night.

The house had almost no heat. There was a kerosene stove in the front of the house, but the heat from that stove just couldn't reach the back of the house, so we would turn on the oven and leave the oven door open. Then my brother and I would sleep together on the top of the bunk beds to feel the heat near the ceiling coming from the oven in the next room.

Because my father continued his drunken, violent ways, my mother finally got a restraining order against him. Despite the order, he continued to attack her. After one attack my mother called the police to arrest him for violating the order. When she told him that she had called the police, my father, half naked and drunk, came into our room, got into the bottom of the closet, and tried to cover himself with clothes. When the policeman arrived—a white man—I showed him where my father was hiding. I knew that if my father was not taken away, there would be more of the same violence. I have often wondered how that white policeman felt coming into our dirty, rundown house and having a little Black kid gladly turn his father over to the police.

Though we had moved back to Huntersville, I continued to attend Liberty Park Elementary School, which was miles away. I would catch a ride to school in the mornings, usually with Aunt Evelyn, who was a guidance counselor at Jacox Junior High, located about halfway between where I lived and Liberty Park. After school, I would usually walk from Liberty Park to Huntersville. I was not yet a teenager, but I did not think anything of walking such distances. I had no choice. Bus fare was too much, and the idea that someone would pick me up after school to give me a ride home was laughable. In my situation, I had to fend for myself.

Most of the children at Liberty Park were poor, some more so than others. One boy in my second-grade class came from a very large family and was desperately poor. His clothes and shoes were worn out. Once when the teacher called the roll at the start of the school day, this boy was missing. The teacher sent us looking for him. We looked in the restroom, on the playground, in the cafeteria, in the library. We could not find him. There was an old upright piano in the classroom that sat beside a wall with some space between the side of the piano and the back wall of the classroom. The teacher kept a broom in that corner. One of the children found the little boy in that narrow space. He was asleep on his feet, wedged between the piano and the wall.

The teacher pulled the kid out of the corner. "What were you doing beside the piano? Didn't you hear me calling for you? Don't you know that when you come into this room you are supposed to take your seat?" "Yes, ma'am," he said. "I'm sorry. I was sleepy." The teacher chastised him, telling him that he needed to sleep at home so he could learn while in school. We all thought that the kid sleeping with the broom was funny. But the teacher had not considered that he lived in a two-bedroom unit in the projects where eight people had to find a place to sleep. He had gone to sleep in the corner because he was desperate to find a place to sleep. When I was older, I recoiled at what that teacher had done because I could see that the last thing this kid needed was to be laughed at by his classmates.

Later, that same poor, tired little kid got in trouble again. At the time I just felt sorry for him, but when I was grown, I looked back with anger at the way that little boy had been treated. Even though he was terribly poor, he was going to school, he was trying to complete his assignments, and he wasn't one of the bullies or troublemakers. I remember him as a quiet, timid kid doing the best he could to cope with the life he had been born into.

The second incident involved a homework assignment. We had been told to go home and write down something like the names of our brothers and sisters. When we turned in our assignments, the teacher took this kid's sheet of paper and held it up for the class to see. "Boys and girls, look at this. This is disgusting. He turned in this dirty sheet of paper to me. Don't ever turn in your homework looking like this." "Yes, ma'am," we all said as one. The poor kid had taken a sheet of paper and had tried to erase what was on it so that he could write out his assignment. But he was just a second-grader, and he did not erase well nor did he write well, so the paper looked smudged and grimy.

As it turned out, that was the only sheet of paper this little boy had. He had done the best he could and ended up being humiliated in front of his class. Even then I felt sorry for him. I have tears in my eyes as I write this. I wonder why that teacher treated him that way. Why crush someone's spirit who was trying as hard as he could? Why not just give him a clean sheet of paper? I have often wondered what happened to him. I so hope that he found a way out of his tough circumstances.

4

Family Life, Integration, and Broken Glass

D espite the poverty that my family lived in, one of the things that we all loved while growing up in Huntersville was Christmas-time. We had the best time at our grandparents' house. Often our uncles, aunts, and cousins who lived far away would come back to Norfolk to the old house for Christmas. Because my mother struggled so much to make ends meet, the rest of the family used Christmas to give me and my siblings practical things like pants, shirts, underwear, notebooks, pencils, and school paper. They were trying to be helpful. For years they gave me underpants and handkerchiefs. Even after I had become a lawyer, they stuck to their old habits until I finally told them, "Look, y'all, thank you for your help, but I can buy my own underwear from now on."

During my childhood, one of the people we wanted to see most of all at Christmas was Uncle Dukie, who was in the army. His full name was Rufus Percy Sears. He was the youngest of the Sears men, and he was a prankster.

One Christmas he came home long before sunrise. He parked his car far from the house and walked the rest of the way, making sure that no one saw him. He slipped into the living room and hid himself under a pile of coats on a chair in the corner. When everybody woke up and came downstairs, we all wanted to know where Uncle Dukie was and why he was taking so long to arrive. We could not wait to see him. As the morning wore on, we started worrying that he may have had a flat tire or something. By then, there was a big crowd in the living room near the Christmas tree. Wrapping paper was everywhere; toys were all over the floor; Christmas music was playing; we were all talking and laughing. Amidst all that commotion, Uncle Dukie threw off the coats, stood up, and said, "Merry Christmas! Y'all should have known that I was not going to miss this." Well, the room just erupted in glee. Uncle Dukie had made a dramatic appearance. What could be better on Christmas Day!

Uncle Dukie was always up to something; he got the nickname Dukie because as a child he was all too happy to put up his dukes and fight. He had dark-brown skin and was slim and fit in his Army Dress Blue uniform. One of the family stories recounts that Uncle Dukie was in Norfolk when President Dwight Eisenhower made a visit to the city and had a motorcade down Granby Street. On that day Uncle Dukie was in his Dress Blues and driving his brand-new Oldsmobile, trying to get through the city to Grandma's house. He came upon a roadblock that had been set for the Eisenhower motorcade, but when the policemen saw this Black soldier in Dress Blues driving a new car, they assumed he was in the presidential entourage and waved him onto Granby Street, down which he drove until he came to a turn that would lead him home. I was too young to know the truth of that story, but it sure sounds like the Uncle Dukie I remember.

Like most of the Sears men, Uncle Dukie loved poetry. His favorite poem was "Be Strong" by Maltbie D. Babcock. He was keen on telling me and my cousins: "Be strong! We are not here to play, to dream, to drift; We have hard work to do and loads to lift; Shun not the struggle, face it, 'tis God's gift."

Uncle Dukie died in 1959. Because of the Korean War he had left college, joined the army, and served in Korea. Then he came back to the States and went to the University of Michigan, where he finished in the summer of 1959. That was the same year that Aunt Lula—the youngest of the fifteen Sears children—finished Booker T. Washington High School. We were living next door to Grandma's house. One evening I heard my momma break into a horrible sob. "What's the matter, Momma?" I asked. "Uncle Dukie's dead," she said through gut-wrenching sobs.

We soon learned that the day after Uncle Dukie graduated from Michigan he went with some of his classmates to a beach party on the shores of Lake Michigan. He swam out into the water and drowned. Someone from the army called Grandma's house, and Aunt Lula, the high school senior and the youngest sibling, answered the phone and was told, in an official, direct, blunt way, "Ma'am, we're sorry to advise you that Lieutenant Rufus Percy Sears is dead." Well, Aunt Lula about had a heart attack. She had just come from class night at Booker T., where she was one of the star performers, only to get word that the brother closest in age to her was dead.

I had never seen such sorrow in my life. I was eight years old. I had been to funerals before and knew of people dying. But the grief that swept through the Sears family on the news of Uncle Dukie's death was so palpable I have never seen its equal. The next day, as the family gathered at Grandma's house, they leaned against doorposts and cried, slumped over chairs and cried, put their heads down on the dining room table and cried. I wondered how many tears a person could cry.

In the immediate aftermath of Uncle Dukie's death, the family decided to send most of the young cousins to our Aunt Toppie's house in Hampton. Though we were all sad about Uncle Dukie, at least we would be together to cheer each other up.

While we were in Hampton, they took us to see the movie *Tom Thumb.* The movie theater in Hampton was not like the ones we were used to in Norfolk, where the Black community was large enough that we had our own all-Black movie theaters, largely on Church Street with one other on Brambleton Avenue near Norfolk State. When we went to the movies in Norfolk, we didn't see white people except for the cashier or the person selling popcorn. But in Hampton, I saw for the first time a movie theater attended by both whites and Blacks, with white people sitting on the ground floor and Black people sitting up in the balcony.

When we got to the theater in Hampton, I didn't know about the upstairs-downstairs seating rule, so I walked toward the main doors on the ground floor. I was intercepted by a great big white man dressed in a uniform with a long coat that went below his knees and with rows of brass buttons. (The uniform reminded me of the one worn by the palace guards in *The Wizard of Oz.*) He said, "Stop, you can't go in there." I said, "Yes, I can. I have a ticket." He said, "Colored people have to sit upstairs in the balcony. Now go upstairs." I turned and looked at my cousins and the adult who was with us, and we all headed to the balcony.

To tell you the truth, I liked sitting in the balcony. It was more fun. You were up high. The view of the screen was great, and the area felt like a private space. And so, though I was being discriminated against, I didn't much care because I was in a movie theater, and I had a clear view of the screen. I thought to myself that if white people could see the view from the balcony, they would wish they could sit up there too.

Later, at Uncle Dukie's funeral, all the cousins were dressed in white. I didn't really understand why, since I knew that at funerals you usually wore black. But that is what the family wanted to do because he had died so young. After the funeral my uncles Tom and Charles, Uncle Dukie's older brothers, decided to return to the cemetery to shape up his grave. They got shovels from the tool shed and put them in the trunk of the car. I said, "Can I go too?" They said yes.

On the ride to the cemetery Uncle Tom, the elder of the two, was advising Uncle Charles on how to position himself to advance in rank in the army. Both were officers, but Uncle Tom outranked his younger brother. They talked about leadership and taking charge and letting those in command know that one was willing to accept added responsibilities. The ride was short. Soon we were there tidying up the gravesite. I helped reposition the flowers, while my uncles piled dirt on the grave and tamped it into a more uniform shape, all the while trying not to weep aloud. They had tears in their eyes as they did this last act for their younger brother.

When I was on the verge of going to law school, the family said that I was doing what Uncle Dukie had wanted to do, that I was fulfilling his destiny to be a lawyer. As I progressed in the law, the family would say from time to time, "Just like Dukie." I did not mind having the fulfillment of his dreams placed on my shoulders. I even got a license plate that read "Dukie."

Back at Liberty Park, my cousin Bucky, Aunt Evelyn's son, and I were on the school's safety patrol. He was the captain. I was the sergeant. We got to wear white safety patrol belts that came across our chests and around our waists. We would tell the other students to line up or to be quiet or other things that the teachers wanted us to say, and we would patrol the halls while the other kids were in class.

After school, Bucky attended an afternoon program at Liberty Park nursery school, but my mother couldn't afford it. All I could do was stand at the fence and watch the other children play. I would watch for a while, then walk home to read books or do chores. I always walked away feeling that I was missing out on all the fun.

In elementary school, my closest academic competitor was a very smart guy from a prominent Black family. But often he did not try. He would give the wrong answer just to make people laugh, even when he knew the right answer. He always had money and was generous with it, yet he would steal things to prove how bold he was. He would snatch a bag of chips from the corner store and run away laughing, with other children egging him on. I remember him because everybody thought that he was destined to do great things in his life. But that is not how it turned out. As he got older, he got into more serious trouble. One day at the Supreme Court as I sat in my chambers looking at the names of the cases on our criminal docket, I saw my childhood friend's name. He had been convicted and was appealing his sentence to the Supreme Court of Virginia. It was sad to contemplate how much our lives had diverged, the kid who seemed to have everything and the poor kid who had hardly anything. It showed that where you come from does not determine where you end up.

While I was at Liberty Park, the city of Norfolk was experimenting with integration. This was the early '60s. It was the time of the freedom rides that challenged segregation in interstate commerce. It was the time of sit-ins at lunch counters, usually in college towns throughout the South. It was the time when Black people were fighting to integrate southern colleges and universities like the University of Georgia and Ole Miss. One of Norfolk's small steps toward integration was to invite schoolchildren from across the city to come downtown to a screening of Shakespeare's *Macbeth* at one of the big old white movie theaters on Granby Street. Though elementary-school children did not study *Macbeth*, we were invited anyway. The point was to show that the theaters were being integrated. So, my classmates at Liberty Park and I came to school that day dressed in our Sunday-best clothes. The boys had on their little suits and white shirts and ties. The girls wore dresses, hats, fancy socks, and patent leather shoes. As was typical for a field trip, they paired us up. My partner that day was a girl named Linda. She had on a kind of sailor's hat with a brim that was rounded upward and a blue ribbon that wrapped around the hat and hung off the back. We were all excited about the field trip, even though we did not know the first thing about *Macbeth*.

When our bus got downtown, we saw throngs of white children dressed for the most part in sneakers, blue jeans, and sweatshirts all milling around outside the theater. We got off our bus, quickly paired up with our partners for the day, and formed a line. We were like little soldiers, all in a row. The other children were not threatening us, but they were plainly not under the kind of supervision that we were. They were running and jumping and roughhousing. We filed quietly into the theater. We were seated on the main floor in the center, directly in front of the screen. From my experience at the white movie theater in Hampton, I guessed that they thought that they had put the colored children in the best seats.

We marveled at this place that we had only driven past and had always wondered what it was like inside. We were impressed with the recessed lighting and the plush seats and carpeting. None of us had ever been inside of a movie theater that looked like this. But there we were, Black children from schools across Norfolk, sitting in that one section, front and center.

When the screen came to life, it was bigger than any we had ever seen. We were amazed. But as soon as the lights went out, things started flying toward us: ice cream, ice, paper cups, soda, water, and popcorn were thrown front and center, where we were sitting ducks. We were bombarded. We didn't know what to do; our teachers didn't either. We were in the bullseye.

My field trip partner was sitting to my left. In the darkened room as the missiles flew, one struck with unerring accuracy. A scoop of ice cream, apparently flung from a cone, landed on the upturned brim at the front of Linda's sailor hat. It was the most perfect shot; the ice cream was balanced on the brim of her hat. It stayed there and started melting. As we sat there in the dark—in fear, under attack—the ice cream on Linda's hat dripped down past her eyes onto her best dress. We were all scared, not knowing what else would happen. She started crying. I held her little hand. Children were crying all around us.

There were exits directly in front of us on either side of the screen.

In the midst of the bombardment, our teachers passed the word for us to get up and move toward the exits. They had gotten our buses to come into the alley behind the theater to evacuate us. And that's what it was, an evacuation. We got up, not caring about the movie that we didn't understand in the first place, and made our way to the exits. We were happy to get out of there.

This was the first time that I realized that sometimes not even our teachers knew what to do, that sometimes even Black adults were as helpless as we were. I have often wondered whether the white teachers had tried to stop their students from making us targets. The whole episode taught me that I had to be on alert when I was in an integrated setting.

Maybe the white children throwing things at us that day in the movie theater were a version of the Black and white children trying to throw rocks at each other across the river behind Barraud Park. Maybe when your whole society teaches that one group is superior to another, hostility between those two groups is almost inevitable.

Near the end of my time at Liberty Park, I came upon another example of discrimination. This time it was not based on race but rather on my status as the child of a convicted felon. The sixth grade was the highest grade in elementary school; you graduated to junior high school after that. At Liberty Park the sixth-grade boy and girl with the highest grades were named king and queen of May Day. I had the highest grades among the sixth-grade boys, but because my father was an ex-convict some of the teachers thought that I would not be a good example as king. Someone at the school told my family about this, and my mother protested.

Ultimately, I was named king of May Day. But I have never forgotten that sometimes your own people will dismiss you, not because of anything you did but because of things done by your family members. The episode taught me that I could do my very best and still lose out because I came from the wrong family or the wrong part of town. I felt that was unfair, but there was nothing I could do. It is hard to know how many parties I was not invited to or the number of opportunities that were never presented to me.

My mother was always trying to find a job other than being a nurse. She thought she belonged in the public arena, standing before crowds performing or advocating for one thing or another. So, in addition to being a "dramatic monologist," she was also a political activist who wrote petitions to the city council demanding things like more resources for the Black schools. She worked for political campaigns as a local organizer in the Black community, earning small amounts of money here and there.

Out of her community activism she finally landed a job on a local radio station, WHIH in Portsmouth. The "Flo Thomas Show" was a talk show about public affairs. Her followers were called "the Girlfriends of Flo Thomas." This was the kind of job that she had been hoping for most of her adult life. She was in front of the public. She was free to cover a range of topics. She could express her opinion and persuade others to her viewpoint, and because she was on the radio she was invited to speak at programs and events in the area. She was having fun.

Around that same time, my father was able to open his own barbershop. It had three chairs and was directly across the street from one of the city's housing projects. A steady stream of boys and men came in each Saturday to get their haircuts for church on Sunday. But the barbershop was next door to a bar. Pretty soon my father was taking money out of the cash register and taking breaks at the bar. It was a losing proposition. Eventually, he lost the barbershop and kept drinking.

Often on weekends my mother would send me to find my daddy. Every time that I went looking for him, he was in a bar. I would walk inside and tell whoever was in charge that my mom had sent me to get my daddy. Sometimes he would leave with me and return home. Other times he would curse and say that he would come home when he damn well felt like it. I always thought that it was better not having him at home since that usually meant a drunken fight.

One day we were surprised when my mother drove up to our rundown house on Proescher Street in a new car. It wasn't a fancy car; it was the entry-level Chevrolet with blackwall tires and plastic seat covers. But it was the first new car we had ever had. My father wanted to know how she managed to get a new car. She said that it came with her job at the radio station. He didn't believe it. He said that she must have been screwing around to get a new car.

The car was parked near the side porch where my granddaddy sat. While I was sitting there talking to my grandfather, my father came outside drunk, picked up a brick, and smashed every window in the new car. Bam! Bam! Bam! The breaking glass sounded like firecrackers. My grandfather, who was very much an old man by then, could not do anything to stop my father, and he didn't try. He just sat there and watched. Then he turned to me and said, "Charles, you're going to be a preacher." I said, "No, Granddaddy." He said, "Yes, you are, because you have a lot to tell." I have always wondered why he said that to me during my daddy's drunken rampage. He had never said anything like that before. He had never talked about what I might be in the future. I had never seen my granddaddy go to church, and he had never talked to me about the Bible or about religion. But suddenly at that moment he told me that I was going to be a preacher. I guess he thought that his eleven-year-old grandson had already seen enough in his short life to have learned lessons that were worth repeating. Not long thereafter my mother lost the job at the radio station and had to go back to being a night-duty nurse.

In another conversation, my granddaddy told me that when he was thirty-nine years old he worked as a master shipwright at the Norfolk shipyard; he was a carpenter on the ships. He said that the shipyard hired a nineteen-year-old white guy to be his boss, and that the young white guy would order him around with commands like "Darkie, bring me that wrench." I said, "What did you do?" He said, "There was nothing I could do. I had to have my job because I had mouths to feed. But I never liked it." And I did not like it either. As I grew older I never forgot how my granddaddy had been belittled by a young white guy.

5

Survival, Resilience, and Bible School

I had a paper route to help make money. I carried the *Norfolk Journal and Guide,* the Black newspaper known to most people of color from Tidewater as the *Guide.* The route I delivered had been in the Sears family for years. It covered Washington Avenue, Proescher Street, Johnson Avenue, Lexington Street, the Bottom, Dungee Street, Galt Street, and a few other side streets. Every place I went was poorly lit. There were dogs to contend with and customers who would not pay. Often, I would walk up to a door, knock, and say, "*Guide.*" I could see people turning off lights inside to pretend that no one was home. I would repeat, "*Guide.*" No response. I would leave the paper on the stoop or inside the screen door. Almost as soon as I turned my back, I could hear someone opening the door to get the paper. It happened all the time.

Often my customers would pay me in pennies. The newspaper cost fifteen cents; people would give me fifteen pennies, which would quickly overload my pockets and make noise as I walked. The hoodlums could hear me coming. I was robbed more than once. One of the buildings I had to enter was a three-story apartment building on Washington Avenue. It had a solitary 20-watt bulb in the ceiling on the top floor struggling and failing to illuminate three tiers of stairways. It was dark and spooky. It was easy for a hoodlum to wait in the shadows in the hallway, then jump out, punch you, and take your money. That is precisely what happened to me. It pretty much made taking the *Guide* a losing proposition. But the family would not let me stop because they were caught up in the fact that the Sears family had one of the oldest *Guide* routes in the city. I hated it.

One part of my paper route went through what folks in the neighborhood called the Bottom. It was a narrow path between two houses whose property lines did not meet. There was a fenced yard on each side of the path, which provided a short cut from the side of Huntersville that was near Lexington Street to the side where Avenues A, B, and C were located. A family of really tough poor kids lived near the Bottom. It was as if they controlled the pass. The boys could often be seen wearing pants without belts, shoes without shoelaces, and no shirts. They were mean. And when you came through the Bottom, they would try to rob you.

I came that way one day delivering the *Guide* with a pocket full of noisy change. They confronted me. I took off running. I ran up Galt Street to Washington Avenue to Proescher Street and into my house. One of them chased me inside my house. My mother heard the commotion, saw this shirtless kid trying to rob me, and got a frying pan, which she hit him with to make him retreat. He finally ran out of our house. After that I would walk several blocks out of my way to avoid going near their house.

Because of racial segregation, our neighborhood was a hodgepodge of homes. In the 1950s and '60s, no matter how much money a Black person made, he or she had to live in the Black neighborhood. The result was that a big, well-built brick house would be next to a rundown, dilapidated clapboard house. The Black doctor would live next door to the Black trash collector. The most prominent family in the community would live next door to a prostitute. There also was no zoning in the Black community. The brewery at the corner of Church Street and Washington Avenue was right across the street from some of the most substantial houses in the neighborhood. We were just all crammed into one area. Mr. Dinkins's big house on the corner across from my grandparents' house had a long flight of front steps that ascended to a big shaded porch. His house looked like half the neighborhood could fit inside. But just down the block was a row of long, narrow brick apartments that seemed to be less than eight feet wide. These cramped apartments held families of five and six people.

Just as the houses and apartments were a mishmash of size and quality in the Black neighborhood, so were the cars that people drove.

On the streets of Huntersville, you would see a Cadillac or Chrysler Imperial next to a Studebaker or Dodge or Chevrolet. In the Black neighborhood, you did the best you could to live the life that you could afford. But one result of us all being thrown together was that the young children could see what successful Black people looked like. The doctors and the dentists dressed a little better, lived in bigger houses, drove better cars. So the older folks would tell us things like "You can be like Dr. Jones if you work hard."

One day, I had to ride the city bus downtown. I don't remember where I was going, but it had to be a very long way for me to be riding the bus and not walking. As usual, I didn't have much money. Not far from where I lived, a little girl got on the bus. I didn't know her, but though I was only about ten or eleven, she looked younger than me. She went to put her money in the till and missed. The coin fell to the floor of the bus, rolled down the steps, and into a storm drain. The white bus driver told the little girl to get off the bus because she had not paid. She broke into tears. There were grown Black people on the bus. No one moved. No one went to help her. I sat there wondering why the bus driver wouldn't let the little girl on the bus since obviously it had been an accident that the money had rolled away. I also wondered why one of the adults who saw what had happened didn't try to help. The bus driver said again, "You have to get off the bus." I walked up, young as I was, with the few coins I had in my pocket, and said, "How much is it?" When I was told the amount, I paid it. No one said anything to me on the bus. I never saw her again.

I am not sure why I did that except that it seemed so unfair to me to put this young girl off the bus because her money had accidentally rolled into the sewer. I thought that the Black adults on the bus should have spoken up and tried to help this child because I believed that part of what grown people did was to help younger people, the way my aunts and uncles did for me. I didn't think at that time that the Black adults on the bus might have been worried that if they confronted the white bus driver, it might have caused them trouble. But in hindsight I can see that that could have been a problem. Maybe they were just trying to survive.

Another function of the poverty that we lived with was the food that we ate. I cannot remember in my childhood buying a fresh loaf of bread. We bought day-old bread from the Mary Jane Bakery because it was cheaper. There were two kinds of day-old bread. One kind was still in the wrapper that you would find in a grocery store; it was just a bit older and not so soft to the touch. If you toasted it, you might not be able to tell that it was not fresh. But then there was the kind of day-old bread that was no longer in a store wrapper. It was just dumped into a big plastic bag, all twisted and bent up. This was the cheapest kind of day-old bread, and it was the kind my family could afford. We would pick through the twisted slices to find the most nearly regular ones to make sandwiches. We would put the really bent-up pieces into a kind of bread pudding with skim milk, margarine, sugar, and maybe a raisin or two.

Our sandwiches were invariably potted meat mixed with the cheapest brand of mayonnaise. There was usually much more mayonnaise than there was meat, so what we were really eating was cheap mayo with a hint of potted meat. Other times we ate military rations sent home by our uncles. The peanut butter in those military tins was almost always like solid rock, with some oil in the can. It was impossible to mix the peanut butter and oil back together, so we would take a lump of hard peanut butter, put it between the day-old bread, and try to chew it. Usually the bread tore apart and the lump of peanut butter got stuck in your teeth.

If we were lucky, we might get a baloney sandwich. We didn't have enough money to buy a whole pack of baloney from the big grocery store, so we would go to the corner store and buy one, two, or three slices of baloney at a time for a few pennies. We always had to ask for our baloney sliced thin. This meant that the slices were almost translucent. But that was all we could afford. At that same corner store, you could buy one egg at a time, one cigarette at a time, and so forth. We also could buy one of our childhood favorites, two-for-one-cent cookies and candies. There were big jars on the counter near the cash register filled with sugar cookies and other sweets. One penny would get you two cookies. Even for a poor kid in segregated Huntersville, that was a deal. We would buy a couple of cookies, break them into quarters, and have enough for our group of cousins. That and some barely sweetened Kool-Aid was nearly a party for us.

People in the neighborhood paid the corner store owner in different ways. Some people ran tabs that the shopkeeper kept in a grimy little notebook with worn pages. He would say to someone, "You already owe me sixty-nine cents; you have got to pay me something or you can't charge anything else." Other people paid for small purchases with pennies, nickels, and dimes. Hardly anyone in our neighborhood ever seemed to have paper money. You had to be prosperous to have paper money.

I went into the store one day, and no one was at the cash register near the door. I called out for the store owner, but he did not answer. The store was small and long. It had a center display case that effectively created two aisles. In the back of the store was a cooler that held meats. I headed to the back. I heard a low groan, then I looked around the meat cooler and there was the owner with a woman from the neighborhood with her dress hiked up above her waist and her legs all exposed, up against the wall. I was about ten years old. I didn't know exactly what he was doing. He saw me and said, "Get out of here! Come back later." As I got older, I guessed that was how that woman had paid for her food.

When we were little, we could hardly ever have any seconds on food, surely not a second piece of chicken or pot roast. There was only one food that we could have more of, a type of fish called "spot." It was a sweet-tasting, very bony fish. There was a white-owned fish market on Church Street near Virginia Beach Boulevard. They would routinely throw away any spot that they found among the fish that they sold. Many a day my grandma would tell me to take a bucket and go see if there was any spot. And often the answer was yes: "Here, you can have this." I never really knew why that white man would give us the fish. It seemed to me that if someone wanted something bad enough to ask for it, the person who had it could charge for it. But this man didn't. When there was spot, there was plenty. But you had to be careful not to get a bone stuck in your throat. It hurts now just to think about it.

Because of the way my father carried on, he did not have much to do with my upbringing. As a member of the merchant marine, he would be gone for long stretches. Then he would return and things would get as bad as they had been before. I learned early that it was better when he was not around.

So, the men who tried to guide me were my uncles, my mother's brothers. Uncle Tom and Uncle Charles both gave me lectures and pep talks from time to time. They didn't live in Norfolk. As army officers they were stationed all over the world, and I would see them only a few times a year, usually around Christmas or in the summer. They would ask me how I was doing in school and express pride in my grades or my school activities. They would tell me that I had to be the man of the house, or that I had to work hard to make money to help my momma, or that I had to be responsible for my brother and sisters. They started with these little lectures when I was eight or nine years old and kept them up until I was grown. I tried to heed their advice. They really were a strong, positive influence in my life.

I also looked up to and learned from men like my scoutmaster, my schoolteachers, deacons in my church, men in my neighborhood. I paid attention to characters in novels, to historical figures, to my friends' fathers, to the few Black men on television when I was young. Basically, I was attentive to the way different men carried themselves.

And regarding my own father, it is not that he did not influence me at all. It is just that he showed me what not to be. There are many reports of the sons of alcoholic, abusive fathers who themselves become alcoholic, abusive men. But I never wanted to be like my father. I did not want to be violent and drunk and unreliable. I did not want people to avoid my company. When I looked at my father, it was clear to me that he was the model of what not to be. He had hardly any meaningful relationships with his children; I have tried to know my children and be part of their lives. He hardly ever had a steady job and almost never provided for his family. I have tried to be steady and constant in my work and in taking care of my family. I am not trying to apply for sainthood; it is just that I have been conscious all these years of my father's broken life.

During the summers in Norfolk, before I became a teenager, my mother sent me to vacation Bible school. But it was not just one vacation Bible school, like it was for most children. For me it was back-to-back Bible schools from the start of summer to the end. It was my summer camp. During any given summer, based on the schedules of the various Black churches in Norfolk, I would attend vacation Bible school at my home church, First Baptist Bute Street, as well as Bank Street Baptist Church, Grace Episcopal Church, and St. John's AME Zion Church, up Bute Street from First Baptist. Going to vacation Bible school was my full-time job.

At the Episcopal Bible school I learned to genuflect and to recite the Nicene Creed, and their lunches were rather good. At the Baptist Bible schools I recited all the books of the Bible and all the great Bible verses. I do not remember what I did at the AME Zion Bible school, but I know I was there. I learned the Beatitudes, the definition of faith—that faith is the substance of things hoped for, the evidence of things not seen—and that there is a "time to be born and a time to die." But all the time I was in Bible school I was wishing that I could be like most of the other children I knew who were outside playing and goofing off.

The pastor of my church, Reverend Simms, knew that I was a good student who came from a difficult home environment. He wanted me to keep doing well in school, so he often gave me words of encouragement. He also gave me a book about some schoolchildren in the Midwest whose school had burned in a fire and had to be rebuilt. The children sold lemonade and did other things to raise money for their new school. I don't remember the name of the book. I know it was a hardback and that it was mine. I was so proud to have my own book. And I read it over and over.

In the summers, if we were lucky, we would get to go to City Beach. This was the beach set aside for Black people near where the Atlantic Ocean and the Hampton Roads Harbor meet. There was a long man-made barrier of huge boulders that ran along the right boundary of City Beach. It was a rite of passage among children from my neighborhood to run the rocks to the farthest point in the water. But the rocks were irregular and uneven and sometimes wet or sandy, so if you were not careful you could easily trip and fall among the huge boulders and break an arm, a leg, a back, or worse.

I ran the rocks, but it was scary. Even now I wonder how I managed to keep from killing myself. We would get out of the water barefooted, walk through the sand and get it all over our wet feet, then climb up on the rocks, damp feet and all, and start running. We would even race each other down the rocks. From time to time a navy warship would sail by. We could see the sailors busy at work preparing to tie up at the pier a short distance away.

We had many a picnic at City Beach. We would bring charcoal and grill hot dogs and hamburgers and have the best time. My cousins and I learned to swim at City Beach. We learned to hold our breath and swim under water to surprise each other out in the deep water.

When it was really hot it seemed that everybody we knew in Norfolk was at City Beach.

City Beach was divided between whites and Blacks by a fence that started on land and went out into the water. We did not much care. We were just happy to be at the beach. But there is a story in the Sears family about one of our uncles who was at City Beach with the Boy Scouts from First Baptist Church who were vying for their swimming merit badges. One of the boys got into trouble in the deep water and went under. I was told that one of my uncles went in after him. He too was overcome by the rough waters. When they pulled the two out of the water, the young boy was dead and my uncle was gasping for air but still alive. There was some kind of life-saving device leaning up against the fence on the white side of the beach. But the white people on the other side refused to hand over the equipment to be used by Black people. My cousins and I were told from the time that we were young that our uncle had died because white people refused to let his rescuers use a piece of public life-saving equipment. That story was one of many that we were told or that we experienced about the mistreatment of Black people. It reinforced the idea that white people in general did not seem to care about the fate of Black people.

Speaking of the Boy Scouts, while we were in elementary school my cousin Bucky and I decided that we wanted to join a Scout troop. When we signed up we were told what uniform to buy, what insignia, what kind of camping equipment. When I told my mother all the things I needed to be a Boy Scout, I heard something I had heard most of my life: "We can't afford it." Instead of buying a new uniform, she found an old one. It was a genuine Boy Scout uniform but from years earlier and had been worn by one of my uncles. It was not the dark green of the newer uniforms; it was brown. But that was my uniform, and it was all I had to wear. I had to get used to the fact that it was not the same as the other boys'. Instead of a backpack, I had a duffel bag that one of my uncles had used in the army. I had odds and ends, but I was in the Boy Scouts and I tried to make the most of it.

At our Scout meetings we recited the motto and the oath, and we had to pay dues of ten cents each meeting—basically ten cents per month. I did everything I could to raise that ten cents. I was already taking the *Journal and Guide,* running errands for my grandmomma, doing all a little boy could do to pick up some small change, but ten cents per meeting was more than I could afford. I fell behind in my dues. A big camping trip was coming up. The scoutmaster announced that those who had not paid their dues could not go on the trip. We were going to hike from downtown Norfolk to out near Southern Shopping Center. It was exciting. Still, I didn't have the money to pay the back dues, and my mother didn't have it to give to me. It might have been forty cents, but for me it may as well have been a thousand dollars. I was cut from the trip.

On the day of the hike, my cousin Bucky was dressed in his uniform with his gear and ready to go. His mother, my Aunt Evelyn, asked him where I was. Bucky replied, "Charles can't go. He didn't pay all his dues." Aunt Evelyn took Bucky to the church where the troop was meeting to start the hike. Then she came to our house and found me sitting in the front room crying. "Charles, what's the matter?" she asked. "I can't go on the hike," I said. "I don't have money for the dues." Aunt Evelyn said, "Stop crying and get your stuff. I took care of your dues." "But Aunt Evelyn," I said, "I don't have a sleeping bag or a backpack or the right socks or a canteen or anything." "Let's see what we can do," she replied. She gave me some change. I got a blanket to sleep in. I put on my old brown uniform. I got a tin plate and a fork and put it all in the duffel bag. Then Aunt Evelyn drove me to the point where the troop had already walked. I got out of the car and joined the other guys. I was always grateful to Aunt Evelyn for the help she gave me as I was growing up.

We hiked to the campsite. We cleared the ground. We found stones to encircle a fire. We pitched the tents. We set up a small grill. We played and talked and laughed and were Boy Scouts. My tentmate was a friend I had known all through elementary school, Henry Tucker. He had all the new gear. He shared what he had with me. When time came to cook the food that we had brought, Henry shared his with me. He knew that all I had was peanut butter and crackers. I had a good time on that camping trip. I have never forgotten the kindness of my friends along the way. Small acts of kindness can lift your spirits and give you just enough hope to keep going.

❖ 6 ❖

Real Jobs, Life Lessons, and Humiliation

My first real job was working for the Southeast Tidewater Opportunity Project (STOP) when I was eleven years old. It was a program to help poor, inner-city children like me find summer jobs, to teach us the importance of work and responsibility, and to stop poverty. The jobs were basically manual labor in sites around Norfolk. I wound up with a group of guys I did not know cleaning up litter at the Norfolk naval base. Our supervisor was an older white man who would drive us in a van to our worksite and tell us what to do. On our first assignment, he gave us canvas pouches and wooden sticks with spikes on the end and put us on Admirals Row at the naval base to pick up trash. The homes were beautiful. They sat on a curving street that ran along the water looking out over the Hampton Roads Harbor. Walking down that street picking up litter was not a bad place to be. It was open, so all the boys could be seen by people driving by or living in those beautiful houses. There was not a lot of opportunity for mischief on Admirals Row.

But not all the places where we worked were in the open. One day our supervisor took us to an isolated place where small boats were stored and told us to clean up the area. Then he drove off. As soon as he was gone, the other boys headed for a secluded place to shoot dice. One of them told me that I had better be on the lookout for anyone approaching, and that I'd better warn them or they would whip my ass. I kept working—raking leaves, pulling weeds, sweeping, picking up soda cans, and tidying up the place. When I heard the truck coming, I yelled. The other boys quickly picked up their tools and acted like they had been hard at work the whole time.

After a week or so of these assignments, our supervisor chose one of the boys and told us that this kid would be the leader of our group when he was away. As a result the kid would make more money than the rest of us. Now mind you, we were not being paid much, probably less than a dollar an hour. So, the difference in pay might have been a nickel or a dime, but to us it was real money. I was upset because I knew that the kid who had been chosen was off shooting dice whenever the boss turned his back, and this did not seem fair to me. But I was afraid to say anything because I knew these guys would attack me. I held my tongue and stewed about it to myself.

About a week or so later—with me being upset every day about how these other guys were getting away with not working while I was doing all the work and having to be their lookout—something happened. Our supervisor left us at a site with the usual instructions to clean it up, then he drove off. As soon as he was out of sight the other boys scurried off to find places where they could shoot dice. I went on working. Suddenly, our supervisor appeared out of nowhere and surprised everybody. He had driven off, parked his truck, and walked back. He caught all the other guys gambling beneath an overturned boat. Some of the boys lost their jobs, and others were assigned to other work crews. I got a raise.

In the end, I felt that justice had been done. I had been so upset, but out of fear I had remained silent. I knew that what was going on was wrong, but I felt helpless to do anything about it. I had been praying for a solution, and it came in the guise of a supervisor who demonstrated that you never know when someone is watching. It is a lesson that I had heard from my grandma all my life: "The night has a thousand eyes. Whatever your little hands find to do, do it well." That episode reinforced in me the point that when you have a job to do you get it done, whether or not someone is standing over you watching your every move.

Several summers later, on a different job, I learned another important lesson about human nature, labor relations, and how people think about work. I had gotten a job at a sporting goods store in Norfolk. The store sold football equipment to high schools, it supplied wrestling mats, and it even built bleachers in football stadiums, the kind with steel frames on risers with wooden boards to walk and sit on. When we had a construction job, the store manager and I would ride around certain corners in Norfolk looking for day laborers. I had not known that in certain places in the Black neighborhoods, men would gather in the hopes of picking up short-term work, what people called casual labor. And if you had a job of any duration, you tried to pick up the same guys each morning. So, the guys who had been chosen to work a job would wait together, hoping that they would get to stay on that one job. It was a limited kind of job security.

We were working on the football stadium at Cox High School in Virginia Beach. We had stacks of pre-drilled steel risers. The concrete footings had been poured. It was our job to erect the bleachers. We had blueprints, hard hats, wrenches, pliers, screwdrivers, metal-cutting snips, and all the things you would need for a small construction job. For me it was great fun. Because I was employed by the store, even though I was just a teenager, I was something like second in command at the job site. The old guys thought I was pretty savvy, and they would encourage me to do daredevil things like walking up the steel risers by putting my boots on either side of the beam, standing on the flange of the steel, and walking upward with the uprights for attaching the seats passing between my legs.

As on every worksite, there were times when the boss would leave to pick up supplies. When the boss was around, these old guys all worked quite hard and seemed eager to volunteer for anything that needed to be done. But as soon as the boss left, I noticed that they slowed down. They didn't stop work and go off to shoot dice as I had seen at my job on the naval base, but they did slow down. Someone would say, "Why don't we knock off and sit in the shade till the boss gets back?" or "Why don't we just take it a little easy till he comes back with the rivets?" But I would say, "Look, I can read these blueprints myself. We don't need him to tell us what to do. Why don't we get this done while he is gone and surprise him when he gets back with how good we are?" The old guys never wanted to do it my way. Then one day, one of them pulled me aside to explain the facts of life. He said, "Thomas, you work at the store. When this job is over you will still have a job. But all we have is this job. So, when this job is over we won't have anything. So, we see no reason to try to rush this job along."

What he said made perfect sense to me. It was a lesson in what motivates people when it comes to work. If you are living job to job with no assurance of work the next day, you want your job to last as long as possible. So, you don't rush your work; you sit down when you can in order to prolong the job. I never forgot that. These old guys were not bad. They just wanted work. And though their behavior at first reminded me of those boys who had gone off to play games whenever the boss was gone, I quickly realized that they had far different motives. They were doing the best they could to hold on, to survive in a world where having a job from one day to the next was not assured. I have never forgotten what they taught me.

In the summer of 1962, I was still eleven years old. I wouldn't turn twelve until September, after I started junior high school. In that summer I had to contend with a humiliation that I have never forgotten and with being beaten in my face by a hoodlum who robbed me for less than a quarter. It was a tough summer.

When I needed a haircut, I went to Mr. Bitty's barbershop on St. Julian Avenue near Tidewater Drive, up the street from Calvary Cemetery, where Black people in Norfolk were buried. Mr. Bitty's real name was Alfonso Carney Sr. Bitty was a nickname acquired when he was an itty-bitty skinny little boy, and though he grew to be a big man, his peers—who included my mother—still called him Bitty. And following the customs of the Black community, because I was a child, I had to call him Mr. Bitty.

Going to the barbershop was a twice-a-month event for me. Haircuts cost fifty cents. You got your haircut on Saturday to be ready for church on Sunday. My prescribed haircut was a "skinny with a part." This meant that every two weeks all my hair would be cut off close to my scalp, leaving me with an almost bald head. And then the barber would use a straight razor to cut a part into my hair and to cut a line across the front of my hairline and the back of my neck. The idea was that when hair started growing back it would have a neat hairline and a part. The hope was that hair could grow for two weeks without becoming too unruly. Typically, I went to Mr. Bitty's for a skinny with a part every other Saturday.

All the Black men and boys went to the barbershop: teachers, preachers, principals, deacons, doctors, everybody. A television set would usually be showing some sporting event. There were sodas to be bought, bags of chips, oatmeal cookies with cream fillings. The old men would talk politics or sports: local athletes, Dr. King, Roy Wilkins, all were on the agenda. It was an exciting place to be.

On this particular Saturday, I went to the barbershop and asked for my ritual skinny with a part. This time Mr. Bitty said, "Charles, you are a big boy now. You are too old for a skinny with a part. It's time for you to get a big boy's haircut." I thought to myself, "He's right. I have finished elementary school and I will soon be going to junior high school, so I am a big boy." I said, "Yes, sir, what should I get?" Well, the popular haircut at that time was called the "quo vadis." It looked something like the Roman haircuts in the movie by that name. Mr. Bitty said, "You ought to have a quo vadis." I was so proud. The idea of being a big boy was great. And the thought of not having a skinny with a part was even better. I was so happy to get my first big boy haircut.

My euphoria lasted only until I got back home. When my mother saw me, she said, "What happened to your haircut?" I said, "Mr. Bitty told me that I'm a big boy now and that I ought to have a big boy's haircut." She replied, "Well, Mr. Bitty ain't paying for your haircut, I am. You go back to that barbershop, and you tell Mr. Bitty to finish your haircut." "No, Momma, I can't do that." "You go back right now and don't come back here until you have a skinny with a part." I relented: "Yes, ma'am." Off I went, downcast and sad. The thought of standing before all those men in the barbershop and having to give up the idea of being a big boy was frightening. I just knew that the older boys would tell everybody.

When I got back to the barbershop, I had to tell Mr. Bitty in front of everyone that my momma had sent me back to get the rest of my haircut. You cannot believe the ridicule I had to endure. One moment I had been a big boy worthy of a big boy's haircut, now I was a momma's boy sent back to get all my hair cut off. I was mortified. But there was nothing I could do. I got back in the chair. Mr. Bitty took the clipper guard off so the bare metal would touch my scalp, and the last of my hair was gone. I continued getting a skinny with a part until Afros came in. Years later, when I was over twenty-one years old and had finished college, I went back to the barbershop for a haircut. Mr. Bitty told the man who was cutting my hair, "Before you do anything you better call his momma, 'cause if she don't like what you did she's going to send him back." I never lived it down.

That same summer I had a run-in with one of the worst hoodlums in Huntersville. He was known for snatching purses, beating people with brass knuckles, cutting people with switchblades. I am sure that if he had had a gun, he would have shot someone.

In the summer of 1962, as in all the summers I could remember, there was a Fourth of July parade through our neighborhood. The parade started at Booker T. Washington High School, proceeded down Princess Anne Road to Church Street, turned right, then proceeded to Washington Avenue, where it passed right by my grandma's house. One of the units in the parade was the Excelsior Band. It was made up of old army veterans. There were not many of them. And to us they were really old. Their bass drum was on wheels and was pulled by one member while another member played it. The band needed two boys to carry their banner in front of them in the parade.

My cousin Bucky and I were at Booker T. dressed in our Boy Scout uniforms, ready to march with our Scout troop. Someone from the Excelsior band asked us to carry their banner, and we said yes. We marched all through Huntersville at the front of the band of old soldiers. When we got back to Booker T. the old guys wanted to give us fifty cents apiece, but they did not have any coins, so they gave us a dollar bill.

Bucky and I decided to go across the street to a little store to break the dollar bill by buying candy and soda. When we approached the store, a group of older guys was outside. One of them said, "Do you have any money?" Bucky and I said, "No." Then we went into the store and made our purchases. When we came back outside, the roughnecks were still there. One of them said, "You lied to us. You said you didn't have any money." One of the guys grabbed me in a full nelson. That's the wrestling hold where you come up behind someone, stick your arms under their armpits, then lock your hands together behind their neck. It is a difficult hold to be put in. It hurts. And it is almost impossible to get out of. The person who has you in a full nelson has almost total control over your ability to move. When I got caught, Bucky ran. I was alone and trapped.

The leader of the thugs got in my face and said, "We have to punish you." He ripped the pockets of my Boy Scout uniform and took the pennies, nickels, and quarter that I had. Then he punched me in both eyes. I felt blood on my face. I saw stars and felt searing pain. My face started swelling up. The thug who hit me then lit a cigarette, and while I was still being held by his minion he blew smoke into my face and said, "If you come around here again, we are going to kill you." They let me go. All of this had occurred in broad daylight on a major street in the old Black neighborhood in Norfolk, right across from Booker T., but no one had come to my aid.

I staggered up Princess Anne Road heading toward Tidewater Drive. I was leaning against buildings and telephone poles, feeling my way along because I could hardly see. Cars drove by but no one stopped to help. I staggered all the way from Princess Anne Road to Chapel Street, then down Chapel Street to Proescher Street to my house. When I got home, everyone was in an uproar about what had happened. My momma got into a big argument with Aunt Evelyn about Bucky having run off and left me. My momma said that I would have stayed to help Bucky. Aunt Evelyn said that Bucky was smart to run and that I should have run too. It was an argument no one could win. Hardly anyone can know what they will do when in danger.

Because Aunt Evelyn was a guidance counselor at the junior high school, she knew the kid who punched me. He had not long been released from reform school, and apparently he was sent back for attacking me and others. Though I have no way to know for sure, I later was told by some of my childhood friends that this hoodlum was shot and killed when he was older.

❖ 7 ❖

Segregated Schools, Role Models, and Leadership

I n September 1962, I was off to Jacox Junior High School. It was down the street from Globe Iron Works, a block or two away from Princess Anne Road and Booker T. Washington High School. It was one of two all-Black junior high schools in Norfolk. The other one was Ruffner, our rivals. I was at Jacox until June 1965. Much happened in those years: I became a teenager, I fell in love, I learned lessons that I remember to this day. And, it was the last time that I was at an all-Black school.

At Jacox, I continued to be a good student. I made the Junior Honor Society, and I was inducted into the Quest Club (Quality Understanding Education Scholarship and Talent). Back in the '60s, the name "Quest Club" was particularly cool since there was a popular TV cartoon figure named Jonny Quest. We were the kids who attended the science fairs, the kids who were asked to lead the morning devotionals on the school public address system, the kids who ran the student government. Today they would call us nerds. Back then they called us names like "egghead" and "four eyes" since several of us wore glasses.

In March 1964, the *Norfolk Journal and Guide* interviewed six members of Jacox's Quest Club about their idea of a dream job. The *Guide* spoke to Josephine McDaniel, Deborah Matthews, Henry Tucker, Constance Jordan, Clayton Ramey, and me. My answer was: "To be the top scientist in the country and head a chemical division in some big company would be it. I can't think of anything more exciting than to have other scientists refer to you as a scientist's scientist."

Back then, in the midst of segregation, the Black schools around the state worked together to promote excellence in math and science by creating the Math Science Conference. It included Black students from junior high and high schools all over Virginia. We started with regional competitions, and the successful students moved on to the statewide competition. Our teachers pushed us to excel. They viewed achievement in the rigorous disciplines of math and science as a way into the fullness of American society. This was the age of Sputnik and the space race. President Kennedy was talking about Americans going to the moon. As young children we were excited to be part of the effort.

Because I had good grades in science and math, my teachers expected me to participate in the math and science competitions. Our regional competitions were held at Norfolk State College. Usually, I participated in the math competition. They would hand out an exam, put us in a room, time us, then retrieve our papers. Whoever got the highest score in the allotted time was the winner. I won the regionals more than once, and once I won the state competition.

In one of the years that I won the math regionals, the student who was supposed to compete in the general science quiz did not show up. The teachers turned to me as a substitute. I had not prepared for this quiz, but because of my grades the teachers thought I could handle it. Earlier that day I had won first place in the math quiz, which made you pretty famous in that crowd. So, when my classmates heard that I was going to compete in the general science quiz, most of them thought I would win.

All the quiz participants were called on stage. As I came down the aisle in the main auditorium at Norfolk State, I handed my coat to one of my classmates, a very pretty girl, and asked her to look after it. I was expecting to return triumphant. I walked on stage and got in line. When the moderator asked you a question, you had to provide the right answer in thirty seconds or he would say "ring the bell!" and you had to leave the stage to the annoying sound of a big hand-held bell.

The first person answered their question. I was second. My question was a math problem: what is 11/23 plus 13/18? I had to do this in my head standing in front of an audience filled with classmates and competitors from across my region. I struggled to find the least common denominator, but I just couldn't. The answer I gave was wrong.

The moderator said "ring the bell" and I was done. I was the first person to go down in flames. I had to walk off the stage and up the aisle facing everybody, reach across a few people to get my coat from the prettiest girl in school, and walk out of the auditorium while everybody marveled that John Thomas, the math champion, could go down so swiftly—and on a math question, of all things. I felt terrible.

I left the auditorium, turned down a hallway, and walked as far away as I could. Then I waited for everybody to go home. I walked home by myself later that day. I did not want to see anybody. I was kicking myself for having missed a math problem, but even as I mulled over that problem on my walk home I still couldn't do it in my head.

One thing about life at our all-Black schools was that we were subject to serious discipline almost all the time. Our teachers and principals were part of our communities, so they knew our families and they would not hesitate to contact someone at home if they saw you acting up at school. The principal at Jacox, Margaret Gordon, was known for running a tight ship. She was Miss Gordon to us; behind her back we snickered and called her Warden Gordon, but we knew that we'd better never let her hear us say that. When students changed classes at the bell, they walked in one direction on one side of the hall and in the other direction on the other side. There was no running or pushing or shoving, at least not much. Miss Gordon would walk the halls during class change, and if she caught you out of order you were in serious trouble. As people say, the tone is set at the top, and because Miss Gordon demanded that we be on our best behavior and be serious about learning, the whole environment at Jacox responded to her leadership.

When we were young we did not appreciate Miss Gordon, but when we got older we understood that the way she ran Jacox helped instill in us a sense of scholarly discipline. By her example, she taught us that education is a serious thing not to be taken for granted.

Years later, on a return visit to Jacox, I talked to Miss Gordon about how I had come to appreciate the way she ran our school. She told me that back then the school board had sent a team to review the school, and that she was criticized in the report for creating what the reviewers called "a repressive environment." But she said to me, and I agree, that if she had not run our school the way she did, our students would not have learned as much and as well as they had.

One of the great teachers at Jacox was Miss Dorothy Keeling Joyner, my English teacher, a legend who was famous for her efforts to push her students to achieve. She made us stand and recite Shakespearean soliloquies and portions of famous speeches. We had to read our papers aloud. We had to recite poetry, including classics like "In Flanders Fields" and "The Prisoner of Chillon." We had to perform *Julius Caesar*. I played Caesar, so I got to say, "Et tu, Brute?"

In those days, if you wanted to leave the classroom to use the restroom, you had to have a hall pass. Most teachers kept the hall passes in their desks, which meant that you had to ask for permission to go to the restroom. Miss Keeling said, "Look, you are young men and young women; you don't need to be asking permission to go to the restroom. I am going to put the hall pass right here, near the door, at the blackboard. If you need it, take it. Go to the restroom and come right back. If I find out you are abusing this privilege, I will take it away. But, as long as you do what you are supposed to do, we will do it this way." We were flabbergasted. No teacher had ever treated us like that before, putting responsibility on our shoulders to do the right thing, to comply with the rules and thus gain a measure of independence. We liked it. Not one of us abused the privilege.

Miss Keeling demanded that we be attentive while she was teaching. When she caught someone talking in class, she had some choice phrases to get your attention. She would start with a general warning like "Child, you better shut up over there and listen to what I am saying." If a child had the nerve to talk back, she might move to "Boy, you better shut up before I come over there and smack the grease out of you." That would usually be enough to restore order, but if a kid was really being disruptive, she might move her warnings up a notch or two. For moments like that she would reserve one of her most famous lines. Miss Keeling was not a small woman. Her famous line to a loud-mouthed kid was this: "If you don't shut up, I am going to climb up on top of this desk and leap into your lap and you better catch me." That would just about break the class up. And the smart-mouthed kid would be outdone and would always back down.

We loved being in Miss Keeling's class, and we learned a lot. That one woman taught the first Black Supreme Court justice in the history of Virginia, the first Black judge of the Court of Appeals of Virginia, the first Black woman director-counsel of the NAACP Legal Defense Fund, the first Black female judge in the city of Norfolk, the first Black corporate secretary of one of the ten largest companies in America, one of the first two Black students from Norfolk to be appointed to the U.S. Naval Academy, and the first Black woman tenured professor in retinal surgery. We were not all in her class at the same time, but we spanned about a ten-year period, which showed that Mother Keeling, as we came to call her, consistently demanded excellence from her students. If she thought that her students were not living up to their potential, she would show up at their homes and talk with their parents. If she couldn't catch you at home, she would catch you at church. She was relentless in pushing us to do the best we could. She would tell us that when we left Jacox and went out into the white world, nobody was going to give any of us a break, and that in order to survive we had to be better than the best in whatever we did. That was our Mother Keeling.

Other teachers at Jacox also taught me important life lessons. One year I was nominated to be homeroom representative to the student council. My longtime friend Henry Tucker was also nominated. When the time came to vote, Henry voted for me and I voted for him. I do not recall the overall vote; all I remember is that our homeroom teacher, Mr. Thomas Newby, who also taught science, said, "Neither one of them deserve to be homeroom representative." Everybody, including me and Henry, asked, "Why?" Mr. Newby explained: "Because if a person will not vote for himself, he does not deserve anyone else's vote." What Mr. Newby said that day struck me as true, and I never forgot it. You must vote for yourself.

We had limited resources at Jacox. As a segregated, all-Black southern school, we were treated as an afterthought by the school system. Our books were old editions that had been used by white students then passed on to us when the white students got newer editions.

The hand-me-down books that we got from the white schools were in bad shape. They had other children's names written in them and on the edges of the pages. The spines were often nearly ripped off. The books were almost in tatters. We had to first tape them back together with masking tape then cover them with brown paper from grocery bags.

But oddly enough, those hand-me-down books taught us something that the white school administrators never would have guessed. The blank spaces on the homework pages had been filled in. When we looked at what the white students had written, we could see that some of the answers were wrong. Sometimes my classmates and I might look at a written answer and say, "Hmm, will you look at this! We thought everybody knew that answer." We realized that the white children did not know everything, that they were not infallible. In the segregated world that we lived in, this was an eye-opening discovery. We had heard all our young lives that the white students were smarter than we were, that we lagged behind them, that we could never compete with them because we weren't good enough. That message was amplified on television, in books, in movies. That message permeated our society. And so, discovering wrong answers in the books that were handed down from the white schools taught us something surprising.

The other thing about always getting used books is that it made me remember the first time I got a brand-new book while at Jacox. The city of Norfolk had started teaching the "new math," based on set theory. Because it was a new course, they had to distribute new books citywide. I was in the highest-level math class at Jacox, and I got one of those new books. It was the most amazing thing for me to open a book that no one else had ever used, that no one had written in. It smelled new. It looked new. It is a pity that it should have been such a big deal for me, but that was the first new book I had ever received.

In those years, team teaching was in vogue. For certain classes like civics, an entire grade level was brought together in the cafeteria with TV sets around the room and several teachers there. We got some instruction from the TVs and other instruction from our own teachers. Something happened in one of those classes that caused one of the teachers, Miss Lucille Olds, to think well of me, and I learned another lesson about dealing with people.

President Kennedy was assassinated in November 1963. In early 1964, the team teachers in our civics class taught a session about his death and burial. During that class, Miss Olds said something that I thought was wrong. But I did not challenge her in class. I went to her afterward and told her that I had read something different from what she had told the class. I told her where I had read the information. She thanked me, and later she corrected her misstatement in class without mentioning me. But from then on, she told people that I was a thoughtful, well-mannered young man, and she was one of my biggest supporters. That episode taught me that it is sometimes better not to call out a person's mistakes in the presence of others. It was a useful lesson.

Again, in the segregated schools we never had much of anything. During recess at Jacox, we usually had one football to toss around among hundreds of children. Since we didn't have enough footballs to divide into teams and to play real games, we improvised. The person who caught a long pass would take off running around the field "profiling," as we called it—striking poses, trying to look like a pro running back who was dodging tacklers. Nobody tried to tackle the runner, and the runner did not try to run into anyone. It was just a chance to show off in front of the girls, who usually were on the side of the playground playing "bobby jacks" or jumping rope.

One day at recess, one of the big boys from the ninth grade caught the ball and started running with it tucked into his arm. Everybody got out of his way. We knew he was trouble. He was old enough to have been in high school, but he was still at Jacox. With everybody scurrying out of his way, there was no one for him to duck or dodge or look good against. So, he didn't have a foil for his showboating.

I was walking away from the field, with my back turned. This guy hit me hard from behind. I had no chance to brace myself. The tough kid with the football had decided to make mayhem since nobody would play with him. When he ran into me, I was near a concrete boundary marker beside the service road to the cafeteria. It stuck up from the ground. My right knee smashed into one of its sharp corners. My knee exploded in my pants leg; it swelled so fast that it was constricted by the material in my pants. I could not walk. They brought out a stretcher, and when I got on it the dry, rotted canvas tore open and I fell through to the ground. That was the kind of substandard equipment we lived with every day at segregated southern schools in the '60s.

They took me to the emergency room at Norfolk General Hospital, where I was just another poor colored kid from one of the Black junior high schools in the city. After a long wait I was examined by someone who said that I had sprained my knee. They drained fluid off my knee, put an elastic wrap on it, and sent me home. But my knee was not just sprained. There was torn cartilage and bone fragments and other injuries caused by the concrete marker.

From that day forward, I could feel loose debris inside my knee that stayed there and continued damaging my knee from the inside. That knee would sometimes give way and I would stumble. Other times that knee would lock when it was straight, and I had to move the debris with my fingers to get it to bend again. That injury at Jacox and the treatment I received that day would affect me for the rest of my life. As with many other things in my life, I had no choice but to learn to live with it. I used braces and elastic wraps from then on. When I finally had that knee replaced in 2014, the surgeon said that it was both injured and deformed. But I had hobbled around on that knee for almost fifty years from when I was blindsided at Jacox.

While I was still at Jacox, a local Black lawyer named Joe Jordan created a program to inspire young kids like me to achieve. On Saturday mornings we would go to his law office and listen to a speaker. He got Black soldiers, sailors, marines, police officers, lawyers, and doctors to come talk to us about what they did and what it took to enter their careers. Joe Jordan's idea was that the Black community could not truly be free unless young Black people were motivated to become part of the struggle to change the world. He tried to make these little weekend meetings interesting. At the end of each meeting he would serve us punch and sandwiches. I have never forgotten what Joe Jordan did. He was in a wheelchair. He had been injured in World War II. But he remained active in the battle for justice all his life. He and his law firm defended many of the Black students who were arrested for sit-ins at lunch counters in Norfolk during the civil rights protests. He became a judge in the Norfolk court system. Years later, after I myself had become a lawyer, Joe Jordan and I were on a program together. I was honored to hear him say that when he looked at the little children of today, he had to keep in mind that they too had the potential to become a John Charles Thomas, who had come from Norfolk and helped break barriers.

During our junior high school years, there were several male social groups that would organize parties, sell tickets, and sponsor events. But getting into these groups was always hard. You had to be from a certain neighborhood, or know certain people, or attend a certain church, or have gone to summer camp, that kind of thing. Whatever the criteria, I did not fit it, nor did most of my friends. So, we decided to start our own group. One of the guys, John Spruill, loved cars; he suggested that we call ourselves the BonneVilles, which we did. My mother agreed to be our sponsor. I was leader with the title of Baron of the BonneVilles. I designed a patch that we had made and put on the pockets of our burgundy blazers, which we wore with gray slacks and blue shirts. I created our motto: Tenacity, Grit, Determination. These were my words. They did not come from a poem or any other source. I cannot remember how I settled on these words. But I am sure that they expressed my view of the world when I was a teenager. "Tenacity" expressed my sense that you had to just keep at it, stay on mission. "Grit" expressed my sense that you had to suck it up even if it hurt, that the effort would not be easy. "Determination" expressed my sense of a long haul, a near endless struggle.

I also found words of wisdom from a philosopher named Sir William Drummond, who said, "He that will not reason is a bigot; he that cannot reason is a fool; and he that dares not reason is a slave." These words spoke to my belief that reason and logic when applied to the problems of the world should make the difference. At the time we were only thirteen and fourteen years old, but that was how I saw the world.

There were not many of us: John Spruill, Henry Tucker, Willie Harris, Calvin Mitchell, Robert Lee, Randolf Biddle, Raymond Hopkins, Wesley Peace, Bucky Taylor, Rodney Selden, Philip Robinson, and James Wilkins. As I was working on this book, I talked to one of the guys about how I ended up being the leader of group. He said that it was because the other guys thought that I was smart and would get the job done, but that they also thought I had a kind of street sense that made me able to communicate easily with everybody.

Most of the groups had their parties at the Charlotte Street Recreation Center, which was in the middle of one of the housing projects. But the BonneVilles decided to come out with a splash by having our first event at the Golden Triangle, a new hotel in Norfolk. We pulled it off. We had a deejay, we had flowers for the girls, we had a great time. We got a lot of street cred from our peers for holding this big splashy party.

The March on Washington was in the summer of 1963. I was still twelve years old. I did not attend. But I sat with my then seventy-three-year-old granddaddy, watching the TV coverage of that day. Everybody was waiting to hear Dr. King. He had never let us down, and we were sure he would not let us down that day. The other speeches seemed to drone on. Then, after a long while, there he was. My granddaddy and I perked up. I had heard Dr. King before. I was ready. And, boy, did Dr. King deliver. He just went for it. He started in his slow, preacher-like way. He built up and up and up, and then, "I have a dream." I looked at my granddaddy and he was near tears. We kept quiet. Dr. King said, "It is a dream deeply rooted in the American Dream." As young as I was, I still knew that Dr. King was saying something special that day. In the end, it was clear that Dr. King had done it again. He had blown the whole thing wide open. He had said what everybody was waiting to hear him say. We thought we could just lift off from the earth and fly. When Dr. King told us that we could change the world for the better, we believed him. We were profoundly inspired. I will never forget.

I was not at school on November 22, 1963, the day President Kennedy was killed. The Lions Club had given me a voucher for my first pair of eyeglasses, and my mother and I were at an optometrist's office near Norfolk General Hospital to pick them up. I had started getting headaches when I read books; sometimes I would get dizzy trying to do my homework. My mother did not believe me at first, but when the headaches got so bad that I couldn't eat she had my eyes checked, and the answer was that I badly needed glasses. We could not afford them. Somehow, the Lions Club stepped in to buy those glasses. I remain grateful to them to this day, because without their help I would have had to struggle without eyeglasses.

When we left the optometrist, we walked to a nearby grocery store. A man with a transistor radio in his hand came running into the store shouting, "The president has been shot! The president has been shot!" Many of the people ran to the front of the store and gathered round the man with the radio, who repeated what he was hearing. Soon we left the store and went home to see what was on the television about what had happened in Dallas. Kennedy was dead.

The grief that I saw in my community on the death of President Kennedy rivaled the grief I had seen when Uncle Dukie died. All up and down the streets people were in tears. Members of my own family cried aloud. I cried too, for this was the president I had touched with my own hand. Kennedy had inspired hope in the Black community, and his death felt like the end of that hope. It was as if anything that might lead to a better life for Black people was always taken away.

But even after Kennedy's assassination, the push for integration and racial equality continued. There were small changes here and there: the integration of lunch counters, the integration of shopping centers, and two years after Kennedy's death I was caught up in the integration of the schools.

I finished Jacox on June 15, 1965, No. 2 in my class. My commencement speaker was a young guy from my neighborhood, Alfonso Carney Jr., Mr. Bitty's son. Al had finished Jacox two years ahead of me and was a student at Booker T. Washington High School, Norfolk's old Black high school. He swept floors and cut hair in his father's barbershop. I was amazed that someone I knew was standing on the stage in front of a big audience giving a speech. It had never occurred to me that someone my age could give an important speech. I don't remember what Al said; I just remember being impressed. What Al did that day showed me what I might do one day.

In September 1965, southern school systems were set to implement what they called the Freedom of Choice school desegregation plan. It was their answer to *Brown v. Board of Education of Topeka,* the Supreme Court decision that struck down "separate but equal" schools as unconstitutional. Under the plan, any white student could choose to leave his neighborhood school and attend any formerly all-Black school, and any Black student could choose to leave his neighborhood school and attend any formerly all-white school. With that, the southern states declared the schools integrated and argued there was no need for federal oversight or busing or for any other kind of "outside interference."

But our teachers in the segregated all-Black schools were having none of this. They could see that the plan would not lead to meaningful integration. What white child from a better-built, better-equipped, better-funded school would choose to come to a Black school? It did not seem likely. Nor did it seem likely that many Black students would want to isolate themselves by volunteering to leave their friends and neighbors to attend a white school where they would be strangers.

Ultimately, this scheme failed to pass muster at the U.S. Supreme Court because the justices concluded that it did not result in meaningful integration of the schools. The flaw that was obvious to our teachers at Jacox was the flaw that led to the end of that scheme and the start of court-ordered bussing.

Our teachers had an idea about what needed to be done. One day in June 1965, not long before graduation, we heard an announcement on the public address system directing several students, including me, to go immediately to a room in the science wing of the building. We recognized most of the names. They were all the high-achieving students with honors grades. We were sent to Mr. Newby's classroom. He and some of our math teachers, science teachers, and sponsors of academic clubs were there. There were about twenty of us in the room. One of the teachers went to the front of the classroom and said, "You all have to go to white school next year." We replied, almost in one voice, "Why?" The teacher said, "Because we are fighting for integration, and if you all don't go it is going to fail." Then another teacher said, "Who's going to volunteer? Raise your hands. Raise your hands right now, we need volunteers." All of us raised our hands. But that summer I did not stay in Norfolk, and my absence would have a profound effect on me when school started in September 1965.

After my graduation in June, there was more of my father's violence in our house. My mother decided that we needed to escape, to physically pack up and leave. She wanted to get as far away from my father as she could, so she decided that we were going to go to California.

Norfolk was and is a navy town. Back in the '60s, when the navy moved a great vessel, like an aircraft carrier, to a new home port in another city, the sailors would leave their personal cars with consignment companies. If someone had a valid driver's license and enough money to buy gas, they could take a car from Norfolk and deliver it to the sailor in his new home port city. My mother found a car that needed to be delivered to Los Angeles.

One day while my father was either in a drunken sleep or was away from the house, my mother packed us all up. I was fourteen, my brother, Clarence, had just turned eleven, my sister Estelle was seven, and my sister Jerrie was two. We left Norfolk in a hurry with the idea of going west and starting a new life in California, far away from my father. We did not want to drive through the Deep South in the summer of 1965 because things were dangerous there for Black people, so I plotted a route to California that took us north. We drove through Virginia, West Virginia, Ohio, Illinois, Indiana, Missouri, Oklahoma, Texas, New Mexico, Arizona, and then to California. We traveled over much of the old Route 66. It was a long drive. I was still fourteen and would not turn fifteen until September, so all I had was my learner's permit, but I drove many miles on that trip.

When we came through St. Louis, the Gateway Arch was under construction. Both of the long, curving sides were in place, but the keystone was missing. It looked to me as if two long arms were reaching up to the sky. The arch without the keystone reminded me of someone praying.

In Oklahoma I remember the oil derricks right on the grounds of the state capitol. And in other parts of the Midwest, I remember how straight and long the roads were. There were places with almost no elevation. As far as you could see there were fields and plains. It was an amazing sight for someone from Virginia.

In New Mexico we stopped at a roadside rest area that sat on a slight elevation above the interstate highway. My brother and I decided to sit on the rocks and watch the passing cars and trucks. Apparently, our mother had either called us and we did not hear her, or she decided to play a prank on us. As we were sitting above the roadway, we saw our car passing by. Then it pulled to the side of the road and our mother got out and told us to come get in the car. We had to scramble down the rocks; I did not think this was funny.

From New Mexico we went to Phoenix, Arizona. My mother's sister, Aunt Lucy, and her husband, Uncle Bob, lived there. We stopped at their house for about a day as we prepared for the final leg of the trip to Los Angeles. While there, I heard for the first time the jazz album by the Dave Brubeck Quartet called *Time Out*. It is the one with "Take Five" and "Blue Rondo à la Turk." I still love that album.

When we got to Los Angeles, we first stayed at the house of a woman who claimed to be a former television actress. If she was, I didn't recognize her from anything I had ever seen on TV, and she was living in frugal circumstances. We stayed with her until my mother found a job as a night-duty nurse at one of the Los Angeles hospitals. Then we moved to a room at the Hayes Western Motel on Figueroa Street. We had a sterno stove and two single beds. While my mother worked nights, I kept an eye on my brother and sisters. We cooked on the sterno stove and bought day-old groceries from the local supermarket.

We were living that way when the 1965 Los Angeles riots broke out. We were not far from the center of the riots, which had started at the corner of Imperial Highway and Avalon Boulevard as the police were arresting a Black male and his mother tried to stop them. One of the officers knocked this woman to the ground, and the watching crowd attacked the policemen. From there the Watts riots started. Back at the motel we got word that there was shooting and burning and crowds in the streets.

The next night of the riots we were with friends of my mother's who had also moved to Los Angeles from Virginia. Everybody wanted to see the place where the riots had occurred. No one could have known that it was the beginning of a week of rioting. We all got in a car and drove to the intersection where the riots had started the previous night. As we got nearer, the crowd got larger. When we got to the intersection, we were the only car on the street and the traffic light was red. People were chanting, "Burn, baby, burn!" The man driving the car stopped at the light. His wife screamed, "Get out of here or they are going to kill us." He then drove through the red light and across the intersection. People were everywhere, but no one bothered us. We gave the peace sign that people were flashing to each other.

After we crossed the intersection, we drove about two blocks then turned onto a side street. As we did we saw the blue lights of several police cars coming our way. We all ducked down in the seats. The officers were shining flashlights into parked cars as they drove by. The beam of a flashlight passed over our heads. The blue lights moved off in the distance. When we dared lift our heads, we could tell that shotguns were protruding from the windows of the police cars as they moved in groups of three or four, cordoning off an area around the riot zone.

When we saw that the blue police lights were well beyond us, my mother said, "This is history; I think we should see this." So, we all got out of the car and walked back to the brightly lit intersection where the riots had begun, where the buildings were still burning, where people were shouting and chanting. My mother and her four children stood at that intersection, amidst that crowd, on the second night of the Watts riots. I do not remember feeling scared; I remember looking around, watching people yelling and taunting the police, who were gathered about a block and a half away.

As we stood there, a white family in a station wagon drove into the intersection. I figured that they had been following a route and that they did not know where they were. The mob surrounded their station wagon and began rocking it violently from side to side as if to turn it over. The police saw what was happening and mounted a foray. A wedge of police cars and motorcycles came toward the imperiled station wagon, surrounded it, and helped the family escape. All the while, rocks were flying and insults were being hurled. We turned, walked back to the car, and left.

A day or so later we were driving down a street in Los Angeles that intersected with an exit ramp from the freeway. We were the first car in line at the stoplight. As we sat there, a convoy of soldiers drove off the freeway and turned in front of us. The convoy stopped all traffic. We sat for a long time as truck after truck of soldiers wearing helmets and carrying rifles poured into Los Angeles. Some of those soldiers were Black. As I sat there, I wondered whether one of those Black soldiers would shoot a Black person who was demonstrating in the streets. I figured that a Black soldier in that situation would have to do what he was ordered to do.

Not long after the troops poured into Los Angeles, machine gun nests began to pop up on corners near our motel. Mounds of sandbags were positioned to make an area where soldiers could crouch down with their weapons. They were stopping cars to check them for guns and explosives. I remember the story of one woman who ignored shouted orders to halt and who tried to speed past one of those gun embankments. The machine gun rounds came through the midsection of her car below the doorknobs and cut her off at the knees.

Our mother was still working nights while we stayed in the motel room during the riots. We did not know from day to day whether she would make it back safely. We spent those days afraid and locked in our room.

What I remember most about the riots is that they smelled like a cookout. Grocery stores were on fire and the meat in the stores was burning, so the smell of bacon, beef, and chicken was in the air. At some point—with buildings burning, with soldiers pouring into Los Angeles, with the smell of burning meat, with bodies being found in buildings—I said, "Momma, we've got to get out of here or we might die, and no one will know who we are."

We had escaped to Los Angeles to get away from our broken home, but we also thought that we would escape the racism of the South. We had thought that life in California was better than life in Virginia, but we had walked into the very thing that we thought we were escaping. Even in California, more than two thousand miles away from where I was born, the divisions of race and inequality still existed. I learned that there was no paradise in America, no utopia, no perfect place. And so, we may as well go home and work on the problems where we were born.

Not long after I told my mother that we needed to go back to Virginia, she found another sailor's car that was waiting to be delivered to Norfolk. We had our ride back home. We left Los Angeles in early September and started the long drive back to Norfolk. We still didn't dare drive through the South, so we retraced our northern route back to Virginia. The little car was so loaded down with our possessions that its frame dropped dangerously close to the road surface.

Because we hardly had any money we could not afford to stop in motels, and because we were Black some hotels would not take us anyway. As a result, we drove as long as we could during the day then pulled off the road and slept in the car most nights.

As bad luck would have it, we had a flat tire on a two-lane bridge on a truck route. It was almost evening. The car was so loaded that when the tire went flat, the chassis went all the way to the pavement, leaving no room for the jack to fit under the bumper. We were in serious trouble. We got everybody out of the car and put them in the road waving at the approaching traffic to warn of our predicament.

With adrenaline flowing for fear of being hit by a big rig and killed, my mother and I grabbed the car's bumper and together we lifted it high enough to get the jack in place. In the midst of the traffic jam that we had caused, we changed the tire then drove off the bridge. It started raining so hard that we could barely see. We found our way to the parking lot of what looked like an abandoned drive-in where there was a metal covering under which customers once parked. We stayed there all night through the downpour. The next morning we resumed our trip back to Norfolk.

When we got to Norfolk, school had already started. I was in for a surprise. Many of my classmates who under the prodding of our teachers had said they were going to go to the white high school had changed their minds and instead signed up for Booker T. Washington High, the old Black school. But it was too late for me to change. I had no choice but to go to Maury High School. I was on my way to what we called white school.

❖ 8 ❖

White School and Surprises

W hen I reported to Maury in September 1965, I was met
with another surprise. The car that we had driven back
from Los Angeles was parked in front of the school. I recognized the scrapes and scratches on the top and trunk where we had
tied luggage. Small world. Apparently the sailor who owned that car
had a child at Maury. I always thought that the presence of that car was
a sign from above, but I never figured out what it might mean.

My mother could not find a job in Norfolk, so she decided to move
to New York. Since I was in high school and doing well, she decided to
leave me with my grandparents. She took my brother and two sisters
and moved to the Far Rockaways on Long Island. She got a job as the
night nursing supervisor at Park Nursing Home in Rockaway Beach.

Thus, at fifteen I was essentially living alone, upstairs in the house
where I had been born. By 1965 my grandfather was seventy-five and
in failing health; my grandmother was seventy, and after a life of child-
birth and struggle, she showed her age. There was no way they could
have kept up with me had I wanted to run wild. But that was not my
nature. I could easily have come and gone without them knowing, because I had a key to the front door that led directly up the stairs to the
room I lived in. Yet all I did with my freedom was study, read books,
complete my homework, walk to and from school, and stay out of
trouble.

I was on the academic track at Maury, rather than in auto mechan-
ics, machine shop, or chorus. Most of those classes were held in the

basement, so at Maury there was a real "upstairs, downstairs" divide that was markedly along racial lines. I was upstairs in government, advanced English, Spanish, and chemistry. Maury was the first time I had been around white kids on a day-to-day basis. Although it was eleven years after *Brown v. Board*, it was still the early days of school integration in Virginia.

I well remember Spanish class because Miss McCloud called all of us by the Spanish version of our names. Because my name is John Charles, she could not resist calling me Juan Carlos, the name of the king of Spain. I had never been called by two names before. At home I was Charles. At the schools I had previously attended I was called John. But at Maury, the Juan Carlos that I was called in Spanish class soon spilled over to other classes, and my white classmates started calling me John Charles. The two-name designation stuck, and now even some of my Black friends call me that.

In Spanish class at Maury, I soon learned that my white classmates were ahead of me. Miss McCloud saw this and volunteered to meet me early in the mornings to help me catch up. She was wonderful. I accepted her offer and made my way to Maury many a morning to meet with her. Before long, I caught up. I never became the top Spanish student, but I could get by. I was surprised that this white teacher had gone out of her way to help me, but I appreciated it.

Between tenth and eleventh grades at Maury, I decided to try out for the football team. I attended twice-a-day practices starting in August. I went through the drills, the push-ups, the leg lifts, the dashes. My injured knee hurt, but I kept going. But one day I was holding a blocking pad when one of the veterans came charging down the field. He came at me from my right side, the side with the bad knee from Jacox—bam! right into that knee. Any thoughts of playing football were gone. My knee puffed up again.

The team trainer, a student, put an ice pack on my knee and wrapped it. As I returned each day to the locker room recovering from my injured knee, I started helping by taking out the balls and tees and pads for morning practice, distributing salt tablets, and setting up the projector to look at game films. Coach Sazio saw that I was reliable and asked me to be the team's assistant manager. I agreed. So, although I was not a player, I was part of the team. I went to all the practices, attended all the games, went to the sports banquets, and was awarded a Maury letter.

Soon, I learned to tape ankles, thumbs, and knees. The Cramer Athletic Supply Company, which made sports products, had a course for trainers. I took their course and learned about hydration, sprains, head trauma, and other ailments. The players started calling me Doc. Dr. Ben Casey and Dr. Kildare were characters on television; I decided to wear a white doctor's jacket, like they wore, while on the sidelines of the football games.

When I became head trainer and manager for the football team, Coach Sazio gave me a key to the locker room so that I could come early to prepare for practice. The key to the locker room was essentially the key to all of Maury, because once you got into the locker room you could get into the whole building. I didn't think much of having the key, but my mother was proud that the coach trusted me that way. She would say, "They gave you the key to the building, to the whole building." I never misused it. Indeed, I found out there was a way to jimmy the lock on the outside door to the locker room. I showed Coach Sazio, who had it fixed.

When I took the trainers course, I learned that any blow to the head is a concussion, and that the severity of a concussion is measured by things like whether the person lost consciousness. I learned that a person who had lost consciousness must never be allowed to go back into a game until seen by a doctor. In one game, one of our fullbacks was hit hard and lost consciousness. He was down on the field. We ran to him and I broke an ammonia capsule under his nose. He woke and staggered to his feet. As he left the field our fans roared. He took a seat on the bench and soon was telling the coach that he wanted to go back into the game. I said, "No." The player insisted that he was good to go and that he had only had his "bell rung." I told the coach: "He has had a concussion. He can't play again until he is checked by a doctor, otherwise he could be seriously injured." The coach listened to me. After the player saw a doctor who diagnosed a problem, the coach thanked me for my advice.

I went on to become the head trainer for the basketball and baseball teams. I attended all the games. I taped injured joints. I provided the ice packs, and I ran the whirlpool therapy sessions.

The baseball team played at City Park. I was there with the team one day when my father showed up drunk. He walked around saying to people, "That's my son. That's my son." I said, "Daddy, please get out of here." He finally left.

One day in homeroom during my second year at Maury, the teacher announced that it was time to elect the representative to the student assembly. She asked if anyone wanted to serve. I raised my hand. A white student raised his hand as well. The teacher said, "Okay, looks like we are going to need to vote." The other guy and I had to stand up and tell the class why we thought we should be elected to the student government. I don't recall what either one of us said that day. To my surprise, I won the election. Since my homeroom was mostly white, obviously a majority of them had voted for me. It had not occurred to me that a majority of white students might vote for a Black guy who was running against a white guy for anything. It caused me to reassess my thoughts about race relations in my life. I took it as a hopeful sign.

I joined the Key Club that year as well, along with another Black guy. The Key Club was sponsored by Kiwanis International to promote civic awareness and public service. By tradition, the local Key Clubs would go downtown to Norfolk's Monticello Hotel for the periodic Kiwanis luncheons. The problem was that in the '60s both the hotel and the Kiwanis were segregated. Nevertheless, I was told one day that I should come to school in a coat and tie because the members of the Key Club were going to attend the Kiwanis luncheon. We went to the Monticello Hotel. We were apprehensive. The hotel was historically off-limits to Black people, so we did not know what to expect. There were probably only three or four Blacks in the room. But nothing untoward happened. We sat down. We had lunch. We heard speeches. We left.

Later, I invited Maury's Key Club to worship at my church, First Baptist Bute Street. They came. The visit made the news: "White Group Attends Negro Church" was the headline. The newspaper even ran a picture of us standing outside the church. My white classmates did not say much about how they felt attending my church. But it had to have been one of the few times in their lives that they were in an overwhelmingly Black setting immersed in the Black experience.

I soon realized that what I thought were routine events others thought were newsworthy because they involved race relations. It was as if everything we did was the first time it had been done. I was at Maury when we first played Booker T. Washington High School: "White School Plays Negro School" was the headline.

While at Maury, I learned about prejudices among white people. Prior to being there, all white people were just white people to me. I did not know of divisions among them. The only white people I had previously encountered were the merchants who owned corner stores throughout the Black community in the '50s and '60s. I had never stopped to think about whether a white person was Jewish or Catholic or Polish or any other subgroup, but at Maury I learned about these differences.

I was in the locker room one day treating minor injuries at the end of football practice. Some of the white players were talking about going out on dates. One of the guys asked another, "Why don't you take Patsy to the party?" The other guy replied, "I can't take Patsy. You know that." I was thinking there must be something wrong with Patsy, but I sure thought she was cute. The first guy said, "No, I don't understand. Why can't you take Patsy?" The other guy responded, "Because she's Polish." I thought, "What's wrong with being Polish?" I didn't realize it was a problem. At other times I heard players say, "I can't go out with her because she's Jewish" or "I can't go out with her because she's Catholic." I remember thinking, "Boy, white people have a lot more rules than I ever imagined."

There was a girl in several of my classes who I thought was simply beautiful. She was smart and funny. I decided that I was in love with her. She was white. We would talk in the halls and in the cafeteria. She was also a cheerleader, so I would see her at football and basketball games. I even went to her home one time so that we could work on a class project together. Imagine: Norfolk in the 1960s, a Black guy visiting a white neighborhood to study with a white girl. It was unheard-of. Her parents were cordial. Nothing happened. I was there for a while then I went home.

Later, at school, one of the assistant football coaches came to me and said, "I understand that you like one of the cheerleaders. I just want to warn you to be careful. This could be dangerous for you. Nobody needs any trouble around here, so you need to be very careful about who you say you like. Do you understand?" I said, "Yes, sir." I learned to keep some things to myself, to not express all my thoughts and feelings. I am sure that the coach thought he was doing me a big favor by warning me to be careful about who I paid attention to, but he was enforcing the racial prejudices of that era.

I turned sixteen in September 1966. On my birthday I was called to the living room of my grandma's house and was surprised to see several of my Maury classmates, four or five of whom were white. My mother, who had come back to Norfolk for my birthday, had contacted one of my Black classmates, who gave her the names of people with whom I was friendly at school. My mother invited these kids to my party, and here they were in my grandmother's living room. I was a bit embarrassed because the place was old and rundown, and I was not sure I wanted these kids to see how we lived. What if one of them had to use the restroom? They sang "Happy Birthday," ate cake, and left. All the white kids had ridden together in one car. Later, one of them told me that they had been scared to death to come into the heart of Huntersville. The way things were in the '60s, the most a white person would do was to drive on the streets that skirted the edges of the Black community. Only someone like a white merchant with a store in the Black community would come into the heart of the Black neighborhood. Yet, a few of my white classmates had decided to venture into unknown territory for my birthday. I thought they had been brave.

Despite the small steps toward better race relations, I continued to encounter prejudice. During my junior year I was the only Black student in the advanced English course. One of the course requirements was to write either a poem, a short story, or an essay. Because I was the only Black student in the class, and because neighborhoods were still strictly segregated, I did not see any of my white classmates outside of school. Nor did I talk to any of them on the phone. This meant that I had no one who might remind me that the assignment was due.

I went to school one Monday not realizing that the assignment was due that day. I had study hall just prior to the English class and was sitting there reading when I noticed that my white classmates all were perusing typed papers with covers on them. I thought, "Oh, my God, the assignment is due today." The clock showed that I had twenty-five minutes to the end of study hall. I said to myself, "I guess I have to write a poem."

Since I had been raised to recite poetry from the age of four, the sound of poetry was not alien to me. On top of that, at Jacox Miss Keeling had taught us the formal rhyme schemes used in writing poetry, so I knew the structure of a poem. And, as grace would have it, in church the previous day Reverend Simms had preached about a man who had a very expensive watch, which he would carefully wind up each night as he went to bed. But the next day the watch would lose time. The man took the watch to several jewelers, all of whom told him that there was nothing wrong with his watch. Finally, a jeweler told the man: "Your problem is that you are starting your watch on a weak spring each day. Don't just wind your watch at night, wind it in the morning when you get up." The point of the sermon, of course, was that we should not just pray at night but also in the morning to start the day. All this was in my head as the time ticked away to the end of study hall.

In just a few minutes I wrote a poem. It came easily. I finished the poem so quickly that I had time to print it again in a neater hand on another sheet of paper, which I would hand in to satisfy the course requirement. I felt surprisingly good. I had written "The Morning."

The bell rang. Everybody left study hall and headed to class. When I got there, my white classmates were putting their themes in a box on the teacher's desk. I went in and handed my one sheet of paper to the teacher, who was standing near the door. While the class assembled, I saw her reading my poem to herself. Once everybody was there, she called the roll, walked over to my desk, held my poem by the corner in front of my face, and said aloud in front of the whole class, "I reject this. I do not believe a colored child could write this." I said, "Yes, ma'am, I did. I just wrote it in study hall. You can see my first version." She said, "I don't believe you."

Here is what I had written:

THE MORNING

The Morning is the time for man to rise
Review the things that formed his past
Make all his disappointments and mistakes quite clear
So they will be his last

The Morning is the time for man to think
Of all the things to come
To plot, to plan, to try his best
To be ahead when day is done

The Morning is the time for man to dream
Of things not yet conceived
To gather his thoughts and ideas round
The things that he alone believes

The Morning is the time for man to rise
And think and dream and see
That all the world depends on men
Who with thoughts of hope the day begin

When I wrote that, I was seventeen years old.

My mother was back in Norfolk from New York, so I told her what had happened. She came to school to tell the teacher that I was not a liar and that if I said I wrote the poem then I had written it. I was given some credit for my poem but not much. I think I got a B. But my poem was never entered into the citywide poetry contest and never held up as an example of a student's creative ability. After that experience I kept writing poetry but kept it largely to myself.

While I was doing my best to cope with life at Maury, the problems in the rest of society continued unabated. Marches, protests, lawsuits, and the full range of efforts to secure justice and equality were in the news in the late 1960s. Dr. King went to Memphis trying to secure better wages and more rights for the sanitation workers. He was assassinated there on April 4, 1968, during my senior year at Maury. I was still living upstairs at my grandma's house. Granddaddy had already died. I heard on a transistor radio that Dr. King had been killed. When I told my grandma, she did not want to believe it. She said, "Oh, don't say that. That's terrible." I said, "I know, Grandmomma, but it's true."

Dr. King was killed on a Thursday. When I got to school on Friday, one of the two Black teachers at Maury came to me and said, "You have to do something today. You are a leader around here, and you cannot let this day pass without doing something to remember Dr. King." I said, "Yes, sir." I went looking for all my Black classmates to talk about what we should do. We decided we wanted to lead a march around the school and then return to the auditorium for an assembly. I went to see the principal, Mr. Steckroth. He did not object. I think he even made sure that some teachers would follow the march to be sure that it was orderly. And then, to my surprise, as we passed the word about what we were going to do and the students who wanted to march gathered in the front hall, many white students showed up. From somewhere we got a few candles. We walked down the great front steps of Maury, went to the right, turned the corner, walked around an exceptionally long block, and came back to the school.

When we got back we went to the auditorium, where I made a speech. I still have that speech written in my young handwriting in a little red-covered spiral notebook. It was the first speech that I had written by myself and delivered to an audience. It was my first effort to respond to a public event at a public forum. I was still only seventeen.

At Maury, I was in the top 3 percent of the class, which meant I was one of the top twenty students. I was the highest-ranked Black student in the class. I had honors grades. I was in the National Honor Society. I had 95th percentile SATs. I was a National Merit Semifinalist and a National Achievement Scholar. In the November 18, 1967, edition of the *Norfolk Journal and Guide,* they wrote about the Black students from Tidewater who had won National Achievement Scholarships: "Four students from Norfolk, Portsmouth, and Chesapeake were among 1,028 finalists in the 4th National Merit Scholarship Program for Outstanding Negroes. The finalists were selected from 35,000 students from more than 4,500 schools across the nation. Included in the finalists were: Marsha Rene Jones, Josephine Armenia McDaniel, and John Charles Thomas, from Maury High School."

When it came time to apply for college, most of my white classmates with grades and test scores like mine were looking at places like the University of Virginia and Virginia Tech, some even at Harvard and Princeton. But when I went to see the counselor—an older white woman—she said that she would not encourage me to apply to any of the white schools. She said that she thought I would be more comfortable at a Black college, and she urged me to apply only to historically Black colleges. There it was again, a white person who probably thought she was doing me some kind of favor but who was really re-inforcing racial prejudices and stereotypes that she believed in.

I might have taken her advice were it not for three things. First, during my junior year at Maury, the basketball team had made it to the state finals in Charlottesville at the University of Virginia. As head trainer for the basketball team, I was on the trip. I had never seen or thought of the University of Virginia, but there I was walking the grounds. I remember walking up a sidewalk and turning to see the Lawn for the first time. I thought it was beautiful. And there were the students walking to and from class wearing coats and ties. Their ties were orange and blue. Maury's colors were also orange and blue, and the school tie we wore at Maury was the very same tie worn by the students at UVA. I thought, "This looks wonderful." We lost the state championship in a close game. But I remembered being at UVA, and I liked the thought of it. That was the first reason I did not take the counselor's advice.

Second, when I became a National Merit Semifinalist and a National Achievement Scholar, I won a $2,500 per year scholarship that I could use wherever I went to school. With that money in hand, I got letters of interest from hundreds of colleges around America, great and small. I heard from Brown and Dartmouth and Williams and others. But I did not get a letter from the University of Virginia. I wondered why they had not asked me to consider coming to UVA. Their failure to invite me made me more interested in going. I am sure that sounds odd, but I think I felt something didn't make sense for so many other schools to invite me to apply while my own state's university remained silent.

Third, as I was thinking about going to college, many things were happening in America. Dr. King had been killed. There were riots in the streets of many cities. And the memory of the Watts riots was fresh in my mind. Integration was more hope than reality. The need to press for change that had been repeated to me all my life was still in my head.

I applied to UVA and was accepted. When word got out at Maury that I had made it into UVA, I got pats on the back from my white classmates. They knew how hard it was to get into UVA. I actually had not known that it was a big deal to be accepted at UVA. I had applied in part because I did not want to be ignored by the beautiful school in the mountains of Virginia.

As part of the graduation ritual at Maury, we had class night. There we announced such familiar titles as "Most Likely to Succeed," "Shyest," and all that. I was chosen "Best Personality." And I was runner-up for "Most Likely to Succeed." The girl who was chosen as "Shyest" was a Black girl who really was the shyest, so much so that I was surprised my white classmates knew she existed. She was so quiet and shy she was almost invisible. And although I can't be completely sure, I don't believe that her shyness was a reaction to being at white school. I think it was just her natural personality. The class picked the right person.

Shortly before graduation, Maury's senior class decided to have a beach party down at Virginia Beach. Black people still did not frequent Virginia Beach. We had our own beaches, and that was how it was. But my cousin Bucky, who was a senior at Norview High School—another white school in Norfolk—agreed to go with me to the gathering at Virginia Beach. Two things happened that day that I will never forget. First, as Bucky and I walked across the sand toward the ocean, the white people looked up, saw two Black guys approaching, and started scurrying out of our way. It was like the parting of the Red Sea. As crowded as the beach was, as Bucky and I walked through, white people picked up their blankets and towels and moved. We thought this was strange, but we did not much mind because it made it easier for us to get where we were going. We reached my classmates without any real problem.

Second, once Bucky and I were with my classmates, we found out that some of the white guys were passing out cans of beer. Bucky and I got one can to share. But no sooner than I had taken my first sip of beer—which I really did not like in the first place but was sipping to be like my classmates—I realized that a white police officer had walked up and was standing slightly behind me near my shoulder. I thought to myself, "Oh, no, I am about to be arrested." To my surprise the police officer said, "Young man, why do you have to drink the beer out of the can in the open like that? Why can't you put it in a paper cup or something, so it is not obvious what you are doing? If you drink it out of a can in front of me like that, I have to arrest you." I said, "Yes, sir, I understand." I promptly dropped the can to the sand and let the beer run out.

The policeman gave me a bit of a smile then walked on down the beach. It was a powerful moment for me. This white man would have been well within his rights to arrest me. I was underage and had a beer can in my hand on the beach in public. Never mind that several of my white classmates were doing the same thing. But instead of being arrested, I got a lecture that I never forgot. If you flout the law in front of a policeman, you are asking for trouble. But if you recognize that by not getting into a policeman's face he might be able to give you a break, then you might avoid a hell of a lot of trouble. Later, when I was a lawyer and then a Supreme Court justice, it was clear to me that had I been arrested that day, none of the other things would have happened. If that officer had arrested me instead of giving me advice, my whole life would have been upended. And in all likelihood, becoming the first Black Supreme Court justice in the history of Virginia would not have happened, and no one would have known what might have been.

Just days before graduation, the senior class was at school signing yearbooks and getting last-minute instructions from our class sponsors. I was standing on the front steps of Maury with a group of my classmates. A white kid said something to me about the graduation ceremony. I am not sure exactly what he said, but it had something to do with where I was going to be in the line of march. There was another Black student standing nearby; I recognized him as one of the tough guys to be avoided when walking to and from school. To my surprise, when the white student asked me about where I was going to be in the line-up, the Black guy took offense and came to my aid, saying, "He is going to be at the front of the line with a gold tassel just like all the other honor graduates, and if you don't like it I'll knock your ass down these steps." Well, this was new. One of the hoodlums was speaking up for me. As I thought about it, I took it to mean that this Black guy whom I really did not know was still proud of what he had seen me accomplish at Maury, and when he thought a white guy was doubting my achievement, he got upset.

Graduation was held at the Norfolk Arena. Friends and family were in the bleachers around the walls. Chairs were on the main floor for most of the class. But the seats for the honor graduates were on the stage; my seat was there. We marched to Elgar's "Pomp and Circumstance." The piece has a long introductory section that leads up to the famous melody that almost everybody can hum. I will never forget that

I came so early in the procession that I had walked all the way into the arena, down the aisle, and up on the stage to my seat while the introductory portion was still playing. When I came into the arena that day, I was the first Black student in the line of march. As soon as the crowd saw me there was a thunderous roar. It was as if the place had exploded over the fact that a Black kid had made it through with honor. To this day, when I hear the opening section of "Pomp and Circumstance," I remember the resounding reception I got that day.

9

UVA and Isolation

I got to Charlottesville in early September 1968; move-in day was September 8. I was assigned to room 113 Lefevre, part of the Lefevre-Metcalf Association, as it was called. I was the only Black guy on my hall. My room was directly across from the resident advisor's room; I noticed that right away and did not think it was a coincidence.

I didn't have one of those big trunks to bring my things to school, so I brought what little I had in whatever I could put things in, including that old military duffle bag from one of my uncles. I scurried about picking up towels, pillows, and bed linen. My scholarship money had been enough to cover most things. I was on the meal plan, and I had money for books and school supplies.

Soon after I arrived I met the two other Black guys in our all-male class of fourteen hundred: Lunzy Britt and Willie Perkins, both from Suffolk, Virginia. We introduced ourselves, said where we were from, what high schools we had gone to, and the dorms we were in. In those first few hours at UVA I also met the few other Black guys who were already there: George Taylor from Hampton, Roland Lynch from Newport News, and Lem Lewis from Lynchburg. The number of undergraduate Black students at UVA was less than ten. We all knew we were isolated in the mountains of Virginia.

My roommate was from Memphis, where Dr. King had been killed in April that year. My hallmates were from far and wide: New York, Massachusetts, Pennsylvania, Arizona. They all were white. One or two were Jewish. Most were WASPs—White Anglo-Saxon Protestants. All of us were acutely aware of recent major events in the news, like the Chicago nominating convention for the Democrats, the assassination of Bobby Kennedy, and the riots following Dr. King's death. We were fully aware of the Vietnam War and the fact that some of our high school classmates were on their way to the war. We knew we were starting college in the midst of a rapidly changing world.

On the first night in the dorm, we sat on the floor in the hallway with our backs against the cinderblock walls and introduced ourselves. "I'm John Charles Thomas from Norfolk, Virginia. I was an honor graduate at Maury High School. I came to UVA because I want to learn enough to change the world." The personal introductions went from one person to the next. When we had completed the intros, to everyone's amazement one of the guys who was sitting there flawlessly repeated what each of us had said in our introductions: "You are John Charles Thomas from Norfolk, Virginia. You were an honor grad from Maury High School." We could not believe it. I thought to myself, "Good God, how can I compete with guys like this? If this is what my classmates at UVA are going to be like, this is going to be too much." After that dazzling display of recall, we just sat there and talked into the night.

One of the guys was from Newport News; his father was a distributor for the kinds of cakes and chips that were sold in small stores like barbershops and corner groceries. In his dorm room he had a large red tin can filled with oatmeal cakes, spice cakes, potato chips, bags of nuts. He also had fried chicken and other food from home. He shared his food with us and told us that we were welcome to come into his room and take cookies or peanuts out of the tin can whenever we needed a snack. Then another guy said that he had a bottle of gin he had "liberated" from his home. Someone else had paper cups. We went looking for cold sodas to mix with the gin.

The soda machines in the basement of the dorm had been turned on, but the sodas were still warm. But we did not know that when we put in our quarters and bought several cans. We wound up sitting on the floor drinking gin and warm ginger ale out of paper cups. I had never had hard liquor before. I had only ever had a sip or two of Colt 45 or of a beer. I sat there, joining in with my hallmates, trying to be one of the guys, talking and drinking warm gin and ginger ale. Soon my head was spinning. And then I felt sick to my stomach. And so, on my first night in the dorm at UVA, I ended up crawling down the hall, hugging a toilet, and being sick. It took me years before I could drink gin again.

All my hallmates seemed to come from much more money than I had ever seen. One guy had so many clothes that he went up and down the hall looking for someone who was not using all their closet space. I was with that same guy one day early in our first year when he was at one of the men's clothing stores on the Corner at UVA. I watched him buy two pairs of shoes, some shirts, some ties, some sport coats. I asked him why he needed all those clothes when he already had more clothes with him than could fit in his closet. He said, "Those clothes are not the right style for UVA." He explained that to fit in at UVA he had to buy the clothes that the stores near the university were selling. As I sat there owning one sport coat, three pairs of pants, and two pairs of shoes—one black, one brown—I thought, "Wow, I have never seen such money."

Another hallmate came with a mattress and box spring to go on the bed in his room. The dorm beds consisted of a spring base with a thin mattress on top. This guy claimed that the dorm beds were not good for his back, so he had to have his own stuff. The result was that his bed was about two feet higher than his roommate's. It looked laughable.

A day or so after moving into the dorms, we had to go to Memorial Gymnasium to sign up for courses. For most of the students it was a mad dash to choose first-year electives. But, my choices were very limited because I had signed up for the bachelor of science in chemistry program. This meant that whereas most of the other students would take two years of electives then decide on their major for their third and fourth years, I was in my major from the first day.

The reason that I chose chemistry had to do with racism. I had been a good science student all through school in Norfolk. I had participated in the science fairs, and at Maury I had an A in chemistry. As a teenager facing a segregated society, it seemed to me that because science had right and wrong answers, if you could figure out the right answer you could excel in science despite racism. Thus I thought that being a chemistry major was a hedge against the subjective judgments that a hateful person might be able to make concerning my work in a non-science discipline. I thought I had it all figured out.

And so, as I made my way through Memorial Gym on registration day, I picked up the required English course, but also the required calculus course, the required physics course, the required German or Russian course (I picked German because at least some of the alphabet was recognizable to me), the required chemistry course, and the required five hours of chemistry laboratory. It was quite a load, especially since I had never had calculus, which had not been offered at Maury. Once you chose your courses you had only a few days in the add/drop period to switch to other courses. In hindsight, I should have dropped the bachelor's program in chemistry, but I didn't, despite having gotten a warning of what was to come.

That warning came on the first day of chemistry class, which was still within the add/drop period. We took our seats. The professor called the roll. Then without further ado he said, "Gentlemen [we were all male and wearing coats and ties], I assume that all of you know your stoichiometry and that all of you are familiar with oxidation reduction reactions, so we will begin by integrating the Heidegger wave equation through all space." "What?" I thought to myself. "Good Lord, I haven't had calculus. What am I going to do?" If I had to do it all over again, I would have left that class and immediately dropped the chemistry program. But being young and strong-willed, I thought that I could just study hard and make it through this very tough course, which had left me behind with the professor's opening words on the first day of class. I had not been raised to quit.

When I went to physics class things got worse. The professor had a very thick accent that was almost incomprehensible to me. I believe that he was Austrian. The story was that he was a great scientist who had worked on the atom bomb, so he was highly esteemed, but I could not understand him.

Then I went to my German class. Our teaching assistant was a graduate student. She was very slight and had a meek voice that I could hardly hear. To make matters worse, the class had several football players in it who constantly gave the instructor a hard time. I did not learn much German. Partway through that course, all the students had to take the German departmental exam. It was a standardized test with an answer sheet on which you blackened a box to select your answer. I knew so little German that I made random marks on the test sheet. I got a C by pure luck.

Within our first couple of weeks at UVA everybody in the first-year class had to go to the gym to take a test that consisted of running around an indoor track; doing sit-ups, pull-ups, and push-ups; and swimming the length of the pool in the basement of the gym. If you failed the test, you had to take "body building." I failed the test. I swam fine, but I couldn't do enough pull-ups in the requisite time. So, I had to go to the gym several days a week to work out until I could meet the minimum requirements. Finally, I passed body building.

One night after we had been at school for a few weeks, one of the guys on my hall said, "Let's all go out to dinner." I had never been out to dinner before, other than to a buffet at a sports banquet in high school or a fish fry at church. I had never been to a restaurant, nor had I been to a dinner outside my home. Nor had I ever heard of anyone just going out to dinner for no particular reason. And I didn't have any money. I was on scholarship, on the meal plan, and I had just enough money for books and supplies. The idea of spending money to go out to dinner was unheard-of in my world. I said I couldn't go because I was busy. My hallmates insisted that we all go out together. I said, "Look, I don't have any money." One of them replied, "Ah, come on, Thomas, we've got you covered." I went with them. I had a steak and a salad. It was great. I did not know quite what to say. I said thanks. I have never forgotten that small act of kindness from a group of white guys I was just getting to know.

Things were not always so harmonious. My roommate was from Memphis. One day we were sitting at our desks studying when I wondered to myself what it must have been like in that city the day Dr. King was killed. I put the question to my roommate, expecting him to say something like "All of a sudden, sirens were wailing everywhere, and they were blocking off streets and interrupting the television shows with news reports." I was just trying to get a firsthand description, but the response I got was totally different. My roommate said, "I don't know, and I don't care."

I was stunned. This white guy was telling me that he did not care that Dr. King had been assassinated in his city. I ran toward him, leaped on him, wrestled him to the floor, and started shaking his shoulders. "How could you say that? What the hell kind of attitude is that to have?" Soon a hallmate came running into the room and pulled us apart.

Our resident assistant came in. "Thomas," he said, "you know it is a judiciary violation to start a fight. I ought to turn you in. They might send you home." But I said, "You didn't hear what he said to me. All I did was ask him how it was in Memphis on the day Dr. King was killed, and he comes back with a nasty, bigoted comment. I don't think I have to take that from him." I was told to stay away from my roommate until the resident staff members decided what to do with me.

Later I was called back to the R.A.'s room, where he told me that they had decided to put me in a room by myself at the end of the hall. In other words, I was to be punished by being given a private room, as if that would hurt me. Although it was permissible for one person to occupy a room that was meant for two students, that one person had to pay the full room rent. But because they were putting me by myself as a matter of discipline, I got the whole room and only had to pay half the rent.

I loved that room. I promptly put the two single beds side by side and tied them together. Then I laid the mattresses across the two frames and made up the bed in a way that it felt like a king-sized bed. I took the two metal desks and made them touch at right angles so I had a wrap-around desk. I created a great private room. That cinderblock room in the old dorms at UVA was the nicest physical space I had ever lived in. It was sturdier and warmer than the rooms at Grandma's house or the projects or the house on Proescher Street. I quickly fell into a pattern where on holidays I stayed in the dorms until they were closed to all students and came back to the dorms as soon as students could return.

The room was the first one that you came to when you entered the main doors of Lefevre House then pushed open the swinging door to the hallway on the right side. The room was next to the bathroom that served the two halls on either side. Thus, it was easy to slip into my room without anybody seeing you. My room became the meeting place for the few Black guys who were at UVA in 1968. We would gather there just to talk, or we would buy food at the Castle and bring it back there to eat. It was like a private breakout room.

During my first two years, UVA was all male. If you wanted a date you had to find a girl from town, or you had to date someone from one of the nearby girls' schools. And the way you met girls from those schools was at a mixer.

I had never heard of a mixer. But, one day my hallmates started talking excitedly about going to a mixer. I had no idea what they were talking about or why they seemed so excited. One of the guys explained it to me and said, "Get dressed. You have to do this. They are going to bring all these girls to the Newcomb Hall ballroom, and all you have do is pick one you like and take her out on a date." I put on my coat and tie and went along with the guys.

Just as they had described, the ballroom was filled with girls, all of them white. I remembered the warning I had gotten in high school about the dangers of liking one of the white girls in my class, and I thought, "This isn't the place for me." So when my white hallmates came back to the dorm with excited tales of romantic walks along the Lawn and plans for future dates and parties, I was in my room studying.

Not long after that mixer, I got to thinking about how hard my courses were and how different I was from the other guys in terms of wealth and having a social life at UVA. It seemed that UVA was just not the place for me, and that I needed to withdraw and return to Norfolk. I told the guys on my hall that I could not take it anymore and that I was leaving.

I packed a bag and went down to the Trailways station to go back to Grandma's house. After I got to Norfolk I sat thinking about whether I could really make it at UVA. My trip was over a weekend, so I did not miss any classes.

I got a call at Grandma's house from one of my hallmates. He said, "John, come on back to school. We miss you, man." And then I heard a loud chorus of voices behind the person who was on the phone. The voices were shouting, "John, come back! John, come back!" I asked who was doing the shouting. The guy on the phone said, "It's all of us. It's all the guys on the hall. We really hope you come back, John." As I thought about it, I liked almost all those guys. We got along pretty well. We talked and played together. Several of us had similar hopes and dreams. These were the guys who had insisted that we all go out to dinner. These were the guys who—for the most part—treated me like I was a friend. I had never heard any of them use a racial slur in my presence. I didn't really want to quit; I was just at a low point. But I knew that low points come and go in life. And that phone call made me smile. So, I went back.

The few Black guys at UVA complained about the lack of Black girls to date and the problems of the mixers with the white girls from the surrounding schools. By our second year, the Office of Student Affairs had found the names of all the Black girls at the nearby girls schools and given those names to us. UVA also let us borrow a car from the motor pool to drive to those schools to pick up dates. UVA even gave us money for the movies and other incidentals. We would drive to Sweet Briar or Hollins, go to the dorm, and say, "We are from UVA and we are looking for . . ." A Black girl would come down with her luggage and we would return to Charlottesville. I appreciated UVA's efforts to help us cope with the problem of interracial dating in the 1960s, but I think that we only did this once or twice.

Usually when the handful of Black students socialized, it was at Dr. Wes Harris's house. He was a professor in the engineering school who had attended UVA himself. He was the only Black professor at the university. He mentored us and held study halls for us; he encouraged us to stick it out; and he often invited us to his house just so that we could relax and talk about what we were experiencing at UVA. Wes made a real difference in our young lives. When we got together at his house it was not just the few of us who were undergraduates. There were also Black law students, Black medical students, Black doctoral candidates. We ranged in age from seventeen to thirty-something. It was an amazing group to be part of. We would eat together, play cards together, dance together, and talk about events of the day. It is rare for a first-year undergraduate student to be regularly exposed to people who are so much older, wiser, and more mature. We learned a lot just being in that group.

We met some interesting people at Wes's house. Muhammad Ali came to speak at UVA during that time. After his speech he visited with the Black students at the house. UVA was still all-male. So there Ali sat, surrounded by about a dozen Black students, telling us about his *Sports Illustrated* cover stories and his interviews with the likes of Howard Cosell. He joked us for being book-smart college boys who did not know anything about the real world. He made a fist and compared it to ours. His fist was huge; it seemed to me that my two fists—one on top of the other—were barely as large as his single fist.

He continued to rib us about being book-smart college kids until one of the guys said, "Well, if you so bad, why don't you come outside and shadowbox with us?" To our amazement he said yes. All of us poured out of the house onto Wes's front yard under the streetlight. Wes lived in a largely white neighborhood in Charlottesville. We took turns pretending to box the great Muhammad Ali.

Soon a police car drove up. The officer said that a neighbor had complained about a group of Black men congregating out on the street. Wes Harris—who was strong, Black, and vocal—stood in military fashion at parade rest, and all of us immediately adopted the same stance with Ali there surrounded by us. Wes then said, "Officer, you can see that there is no disturbance. This is my home, this is my front yard, and we are just standing here talking." Wes was talking to a white police officer from Charlottesville, and Wes was talking with authority. We were rooting him on inside, thinking to ourselves things like "You tell him, Wes." We thought that we might have to fight the police that night. But the officer, who saw Ali there with the group, simply said, "Okay, just be sure you don't create a disturbance." With that he drove off. We thought we were some kind of militants, having stood down the police.

On another occasion, the great tennis star Arthur Ashe visited us at Wes's house. But we were not happy to see him. After a lot of hard work, the Black Students for Freedom had created and sponsored a program to focus on Black culture, with the hopes of raising the awareness of the broader university community to problems that Black students faced at the university and in the city. We were proud of our fledgling effort. We put up posters and announced the program on UVA's student-run radio station. Then we learned that the university was bringing Arthur Ashe to Charlottesville to play an exhibition tennis match on the same day and at the same time as our program. To the Black students, this was obviously an effort by the university to sabotage our program. We were angry.

A week or so before our program, we tried to get word to Ashe about the conflict between his exhibition match and our cultural awareness program. We weren't successful. On the day of the program, when we knew Ashe was in town, we sent a delegation of Black students to ask him not to play the tennis match. He told the delegation that he was sorry, he had a contract, and he had to play. But he said he would come visit with us after his match.

We went on with our program. We had a small turnout, which we were sure was the result of the university's having scheduled Ashe against us. When we left the program, we gathered at Wes Harris's house to lick our wounds.

As we sat there listening to music, laughing a little, blowing off steam, in walked Arthur Ashe—big square Afro, long tan leather maxi-coat, looking just like he did when we saw him on television. The great Arthur Ashe was standing right there with us. But our leader, Professor Harris, greeted Ashe with a cold stare and arms folded across his chest. When Ashe held out his hand to Wes and said hello, Wes did not take it but continued with his cold glare. We adopted the same stance. So, Ashe walked around the room saying hello, and we pointedly ignored him. We were proud to express our anger at the way he had betrayed us by playing tennis at the very time of our Black culture program. Ashe wrote us a check for a hundred dollars and then left. In truth, all of us had really wanted to shake his hand and get his autograph and have our picture taken with him, so it was hard to try to play tough and to ignore him. After all, he was just about as famous as a person could be. He was known all over the world. But he had had the temerity to play tennis at the very time of the Black culture program. How dare he. And how dare UVA ignore the hard work of the Black students who were trying their best to teach the community about the importance of diversity. It made us feel at odds with the university.

A little more than twenty years later, I played a role in a tribute to Ashe. The city of Richmond had agreed to erect a sculpture in his honor. The question was where to put it. Some people thought it ought to go on the Boulevard near the tennis courts where Ashe was not allowed to compete when he was young and living in Richmond. Another group thought that the sculpture should go at the intersection of the Boulevard and Robinhood Road in front of the Ashe Center. But a great number of people thought that the sculpture should be on Monument Avenue. As that last idea was discussed in the news media, out came some who argued that Monument Avenue was for the Confederate statues only, and thus Arthur Ashe did not belong there. One person wrote a letter to the editor contending that to put the Arthur Ashe statue on Monument was like putting a commode in your living room. Tempers flared.

There was division among the people in the city who had authority to decide where to put the statue. One of the skills that I had acquired over the years was that of a mediator. I asked for the warring factions to meet at my home on Monument to find out whether they could reach an agreement. We met, we talked, I asked questions and made a comment here and there. In the end the decision was to put the statue on Monument Avenue. The sculptor, Paul DiPasquale, liked the resolution and thought it was fitting that the statue go on Monument Avenue. After it was erected, he told me that to thank me for the role I played, he had etched my name in the underground foundation of the statue that fits down into the pedestal on which it rests. I have often wondered what people will think hundreds of years from now if someone sees that inscription, for they will surely have to wonder, "Who is John Charles Thomas?"

10

Leadership and Conflict at UVA

Because I had not dropped my B.S. chemistry program, I was suffering through those classes. Often my hallmates would say they had finished studying and were going out to play, but I was never finished. For my first semester at UVA as a B.S. chemistry major, I got a 2.0, the lowest grade I had ever gotten in my life. I decided that I needed to get out of that major. But to do that I had to have a C average or better at the end of my first year. Given my poor grades in my other classes, it turned out that I needed to get a B on the last chemistry exam in order to reach a C average. I did it. My second-semester average was a 2.2, but I was free of B.S. chemistry. Given all the unrest around the nation on questions of justice and equality, I decided to major in American government.

In my first year George Taylor, who was president of the Black Students for Freedom (BSF), introduced me to the organization. The point of the group was to push for a more diverse university community: hiring Black faculty and administrators, teaching Black studies courses, pushing for pay equity for Black staff members. The whole group was about four or five people, and even with the new guys from my class the size of the group did not even double. George asked me one day, "Do you want to be president? I've been president for a long time, and it's time for somebody new." I said, "Okay." Quick as that, I was president of the Black Students for Freedom. I took office in the second semester of the 1968–69 school year. Because of this, I was invited to the Mountain Lake Retreat at the beginning of the 1969–70 school year.

At the start of each school year during my time at UVA, the president of the university, Edgar Shannon, along with his senior staff, members of the board of visitors, and student leaders retreated to the mountains of Virginia to discuss issues facing the university in the coming school year. Issues like expanding enrollment, parking problems, classroom space, and minority recruitment were all on the table. We held small-group sessions, ate meals together, and attended plenary sessions where the president and other senior leaders spoke. It was quite a place to be for a young Black kid from Norfolk at the very beginning of his second year of college.

In one of the nighttime plenary sessions, we were in a large room with a roaring fire. It was cold in the mountains, and everybody was huddled together. I had signed up to speak. I saw it as my mission to help increase minority enrollment and the number of Black faculty at the university.

When my time came to speak, I stood in front of the fireplace and argued for increased efforts to recruit Black students. I talked about the fact that UVA belonged to all the people of Virginia, and I described how I had not heard from UVA even though I had heard from hundreds of other colleges and universities based on my high school record. I argued that UVA simply had to do a better job of attracting all high-achieving Virginia students. I just laid into the administration about the low number of Black students at UVA. President Shannon must have felt like I was putting all the blame on him. When I sat down the room was still.

President Shannon then stood in front of the fireplace. With emotion in his voice, he said that he wanted the University of Virginia to be open to all the people of Virginia, and that he wanted more Black students and Black faculty members. The more he talked the more you could hear the emotion. He said, looking in my direction, that he was not a bad man and that he wanted the university to be more integrated. He said that he was working hard to make that happen. The longer he stood there, the more choked-up his voice sounded. I got up from my seat, walked to the front of the room, put my arms around President

Shannon, and said, "Dr. Shannon, I don't think that you are a bad man. I think we can work on this together." He embraced me in turn. And the room broke into sobs and quiet tears. Dr. Shannon and I developed a strong friendship after that, so much so that years later I was a speaker at his memorial service.

One of the administrators attending that Mountain Lake meeting was Monrad Paulsen, the dean of UVA's law school. Following the emotional moment between me and Dr. Shannon, Dean Paulsen came up to me and said, "Young man, if you ever want to go to law school, I want you to come to mine."

At the beginning of the school year in 1969, I went to see Ernest Ern, dean of admissions, whom I had also met at the Mountain Lake Retreat. I asked for a job helping to recruit Black students. He hired me as an assistant to the dean of admissions. George Taylor already had a similar job. Both of us would travel around Virginia recruiting Black students.

My focus was Tidewater. I visited the historically Black high schools in Norfolk, Portsmouth, Newport News, and Hampton. I talked first to the school counselors, then I spoke at assemblies for interested students. I explained that though Charlottesville was a long way from home, and though there were not that many Black students, we had a vibrant community and that we were making a difference in the fight for integration. When I was not out recruiting, I was in the admissions office helping to think of programs and events to attract minority students.

My second year at UVA was my first full year as president of the Black Students for Freedom. That year I lived behind the Corner in an apartment building that was very near the train tracks. It was so close that when a train passed by you could feel it as well as hear it.

One of the white guys from my first-year hall, Bob Golding, and I shared an efficiency apartment. Bob had a great record collection of jazz, folk, and soul music. He was the first person I had ever seen who had so many albums that he had to arrange them in alphabetical order just so that he could find the album he was looking for. We had become good friends our first year because of our love of jazz.

Bob was as smart as could be. He was the first person I ever saw sit down and read a massive tome in one sitting. He had to read *Crime and Punishment* for one of his classes, but he had put it off. So, one day he got out the book, sat in a chair, put a blanket around his shoulders, and stayed there for hours until he had read the whole book. I had read plenty of books, but it had never occurred to me to read a whole book nonstop. Later that school year I found myself in the same situation Bob had been in, behind on reading going into exams. I followed Bob's example: I read several books in one sitting. Sometimes you do not know what you can do until you see someone else do it.

As president of the Black Students for Freedom, I knew that UVA had a policy against funding racially exclusive student organizations. I got Bob to join the BSF. He would come to meetings, sit through the opening, and then get up and leave.

My second year at UVA, 1969–70, was a time of increasing militancy in the Black community around the nation. It was the time of the Black Panthers, of Black power, of Afros, of dashikis, of Malcolm X Liberation University, and of students toting rifles at Cornell. The Black guys at the still all-male UVA wanted to be part of the militancy.

Two of the guys decided that they were my bodyguards; they went with me wherever I went around the university. Their presence caused me to act differently on at least two occasions. On the first occasion, they were with me when I went to a second-year class being taught by a visiting professor from Boston, a woman, a rarity at UVA in those days. I was rushing to get to class. I reached the room in Cabell Hall a few minutes late, and class had started. The classroom had a front and a back door. I came in the front door with my two bodyguards. Though we tried to be quiet, we made a bit of noise. As we took our seats, a white guy who had been one of my first-year hallmates said, "John, why did you have to come in the front door of the classroom making all that noise? Why didn't you just come in the back door and be quiet?" If I had been by myself I probably wouldn't have said anything, and I might have been able to ignore the "front door, back door" remark. But I was with my bodyguards, and I had been called out. I thought I had to say something.

I turned to my old hallmate and said: "The days when a Black person has to slip in through the back door are over. I can come in the front door just like you. And I am not going be sorry for it." There was a stunned silence in the classroom. And then, to my surprise, the professor—the woman from Boston—said, "You need to apologize to Mr. Thomas." Although I haven't named him here, I remember the person who made those remarks. He never spoke to me again. I liked him. He had been one of the guys on the phone saying, "Come back, John." But in the racial environment of the late '60s, I could not remain silent in the face of what sounded too much like an old-fashioned racial putdown. At the professor's urging he finally said, "I apologize."

On another occasion, my bodyguards were with me in a sociology class on the Black family. The big classroom had a sharp incline, and the professor stood at the bottom lecturing. He made some comment about the Black family and I said, "Bullshit." The professor said, "Mr. Thomas, I guess you disagree with me." I said, "Yes, sir, because you don't know what you are talking about." He then said, "Well, Mr. Thomas, would you like to teach the class?" to which I replied, "I may as well, since you don't know what you are talking about." I got up, walked down the steep incline to the front of the room, and taught the class. It was about the role of the Black woman in the structure of the Black family. As if I had not lived what he was trying to describe.

At exam time, I got a perfect score on the objective portion of the test. But on the essay I got a 99. There were no negative marks on the paper. There were no corrections of grammar or usage or anything else. There was just this 99. But the effect of the 99 was that I got an A in the course and not an A+, which was the highest grade that a student could get at UVA. I might not have thought more about the matter except that I went to where the grades were posted and saw that another student had gotten an A+. Since I was the only Black student in the class, this meant that a white guy had gotten an A+ and I had not, even though I had confronted the professor, challenged some of his assertions, and lectured to the whole class. I went to see the professor. I made all the points about my class participation and my performance on the exam and essay. Later, my grade was changed to an A+, what we called a bullet.

In November 1969 the commonwealth of Virginia elected a new governor, Linwood B. Holton, a Republican. His election was a shock because the powerful, conservative Democratic machine had long run Virginia, and it had been thought unlikely that a Republican would win a statewide election. During his campaign Holton had talked about being inclusive. The word "diversity" was not in vogue then. The idea of including more people in the government of Virginia was looked at by some as almost radical. Not only did Holton say he would include Blacks and whites in the government, he also said he would include young people as well. I decided to write this new governor.

In my letter, which I sent in January 1970, I told the governor that I had heard he wanted to include young people, and I told him that I was young, that I was a government major at UVA, and that I wanted to be in the government. To my surprise, Governor Holton responded positively to my letter. He appointed me to the Virginia Commission for Children and Youth. I was a member of a state commission, and I was under the age of majority, which at that time was twenty-one. This was my first appointment in government. It made me one of the youngest government officials in the United States. I was sworn in by a judge in Norfolk.

My appointment made the news in Tidewater. On August 1, 1970, the *Norfolk Journal and Guide* published a story with the headline "Stimulates Own Appointment; Norfolk Youth Picked For Gov.'s Youth Panel." The story reported that I had written Governor Holton asking to be made part of the government of Virginia. It also said that at Maury I had received offers from eighty colleges and universities but not from the University of Virginia, and that in working my way through school I had been "a waiter, a construction worker, a clerk for Norfolk Senator Peter K. Babalas and . . . a warehouseman at C&P Telephone Company."

The Norfolk *Virginian-Pilot* also published a story about me:

> John Charles Thomas wants to help Gov. Linwood Holton communicate with young people.
>
> A couple of months ago, Thomas, 19, a dean's list pre-law major at the University of Virginia, wrote Gov. Holton urging him to include young people in the decision-making process of the Virginia Commission for Children and Youth.
>
> The commission, the governor's youth arm, is interested in unrest on college campuses and the new life style of many young people.
>
> Holton wrote Thomas and said he would keep the Maury High

School graduate's ideas in mind. On Friday, Holton went even farther than Thomas expected. The governor named Thomas a member of the commission.

"I thought the governor could do a more efficient job working and communicating with students if he actually had young people within the commission's program," Thomas said. . . .

"I would imagine the governor's choosing me had some political angles as well. What with the possibility of 18-year-olds voting this November, he probably wants it known he favors young people," Thomas said, breaking into a smile.

Acting as a liaison between young people and their elders will be nothing new to Thomas. At the university he is a student assistant to the dean of admissions and last year traveled around the state talking with Negro high school seniors about entering the university.

As a senior at Maury, where he was an honor student and trainer for the school's football and basketball teams, Thomas received offers from more than 80 colleges and universities. U.Va. was not one of them. . . .

Thomas is going through the university on a National Achievement Scholarship and a student loan. He is partially paying back the loan by earning money from summer jobs.

Typically, the commission met in Richmond, but from time to time we would meet elsewhere in the state. We considered problems affecting children and youth in Virginia and made recommendations for remedies. One meeting convened in Richmond during a time when there was unrest among students at Norfolk State University. The students were protesting that they did not have the same degree of personal freedoms, including the freedom to visit each other in the dormitories or leave the campus, that students at majority-white state colleges in Virginia had. The problem at Norfolk State was discussed at one of the commission meetings, which I remember because the governor himself was there. It was rare for a governor to attend a commission meeting; he was free to do so if he wanted to, but he was usually too busy.

I wound up sitting beside Governor Holton. He told me, "I am getting phone calls from my friends all over the state urging me to send in the state troopers to put down this unrest." I asked whether there was some other approach that could be taken. After a bit of back and forth, the governor said, "Look, not one of those students voted for me. Not many of them vote at all. Why should I be concerned about what they want me to do when they do not vote? I am going to pay attention to the people who voted for me and are asking me to end this trouble." His words were a lesson in political reality. The governor taught me in an instant that if people don't participate in government, then they leave themselves on the sidelines; if people don't vote, they lose their voice within the government.

Many years later, when I was serving on the Supreme Court of Virginia, I saw Governor Holton and passed him a note saying, "You know you started all this, don't you? You gave me my first appointment in government, and that led to all this." He smiled and put the note in his pocket. Not long after that brief encounter, Governor Holton was named a lecturer in residence at the Kennedy School of Government at Harvard. He invited me to come to Harvard to join him in lecturing about the changing South. I accepted his invitation.

As the newspaper articles quoted above mentioned, in the summer of 1970 I was working for the Chesapeake and Potomac Telephone Company as a warehouseman at its Lynn Street supply depot. I helped unload the big trucks that brought new telephones, junction boxes, and cables. I stocked the shelves, filled orders for the repairmen and linemen, swept floors, and ran errands. I was just this invisible young Black kid working in the warehouse. Nobody paid much attention to me. There was the typical pecking order that people fall into in places like that. The office workers were almost all white. The guys who worked in the warehouse and the storage yard were almost all Black. The white people typically wore coats and ties; the Black people usually wore overalls and work boots. The two groups barely interacted. The women in the office secretarial pool hardly spoke to the guys who worked in the yard.

But one day, one of the women from the office came into the warehouse asking for me. She had an odd tone in her voice. "You are John Thomas, right?" "Yes, that's me," I said. And then she said in a voice that suggested she did not believe what she was saying, "The White

House is on the phone for you." She said this loudly enough that every-body could hear and thus join her in wondering why the White House would be calling John Thomas, a mere floor sweeper and stock boy. I put down the broom and followed her into the office.

Indeed, it was the White House on the phone. I was told to come to Washington in a few days to talk about my appointment by President Nixon as co-chairman of the National Task Force on Education for the 1970 White House Conference on Youth. I immediately said, "How am I going to get to Washington?" The woman on the phone said, "Just go to the airport and there will be a ticket waiting for you at the airline counter." I could hardly believe my ears. I did not know what was go-ing on. No one had told me anything about this. I was on my way to Washington for what I did not know.

When I got to D.C., I was taken to the Executive Office Building next door to the White House. I was told that President Shannon of the University of Virginia had proposed my name to President Nixon to serve as co-chairman of this national task force. The 1970 White House Conference on Youth was set up in a way that there were twenty task forces covering subject matter areas like education, economic de-velopment, and on. Each task force had a youth co-chair and an adult co-chair. My co-chair was Robben Fleming, president of the University of Michigan. We hit it off immediately. I had always loved Michigan because that's where my Uncle Dukie had studied and I knew he had loved it. Dr. Fleming was a commanding figure in the world of higher education, and he seemed to know everybody on earth. The story of that appointment also made the local news. It was getting to the point that I was not surprised anymore to be mentioned in the news.

It was the job of the task force to hold hearings around the country in order to explore the main issues in education affecting young people. Because we were a national task force, we had members from all over the U.S. and could meet almost anywhere in the country. Dr. Fleming let me pick the meeting places. Though I had driven cross-country and back, I had not really been to many of the great cities of America. I set the first meeting of the task force in San Francisco. We stayed at the Hyatt Embarcadero, which had a revolving restaurant at the top. San Francisco was the most beautiful city I had ever seen. I love it to this day.

On another trip we went to Boston; we stayed at the Lenox Hotel and ate at Joyce Chen's Chinese restaurant, where I embarrassed myself. I had never eaten at an upscale Chinese restaurant. All I had ever had was Chinese take-out food from corner stores in Norfolk. At Joyce Chen's they first brought out a tray of various appetizers. I recognized the egg rolls. I put one on my plate, cut it with a fork, and proceeded to dip the entire forkful into the little bowl of mustard that had been given to me. I was sitting beside a beautiful Asian woman who was on the staff of the White House conference. She said to me, "Are you sure you want to do that? The mustard is hot." I kind of drew myself up in my seat, feeling challenged, and said, "Yes, I like Chinese mustard with my egg rolls. Isn't that what it's for?" My dinner partner shrugged and said, "Okay." When I put the mustard-covered egg roll in my mouth, I thought my head would explode from the heat of the mustard. I was trapped. I had ignored the warnings of this beautiful woman, and now I had to try to save face. I felt like steam was coming out of my ears. I tried to keep the egg roll in the middle of my mouth as I reached for the water. I drank the water almost in one gulp, trying to dilute the mustard. No good. I drank more water. Not much help. And then, with the egg roll still in my mouth, I got up and went to the restroom. No more mustard on the egg roll after that. Later I said to my dinner partner, "Those egg rolls were really good, but that mustard sure was spicy." She smiled.

As part of the National Task Force on Education, I was invited to be a guest on ABC's *Issues and Answers* with Edward P. Morgan. We talked about student unrest, the Vietnam War, and other issues.

The 1970 White House Conference on Youth convened in Estes Park, Colorado, in the spring of 1971. It was an eye-opening experience for me to be involved in the conference. I was just nineteen when I was appointed to the task force. I met leaders of great institutions around the country. I was placed in situations where I had to learn about and discuss complex issues in the world of higher education. But the opportunity came about not because I had been shy and afraid to speak up; it came because at places like the Mountain Lake Retreat I had stood up and said what I thought the right answer was. It makes a young person strong to debate his elders and to get to know them in the process. But to successfully engage in those debates you have to do your homework, read the reports and position papers, exchange ideas with those around you, and listen with care.

In my third year at UVA, I lived in an apartment on Brandon Avenue with Willie Ivey, a Black guy from Newport News who had attended a New England prep school. Willie was a deejay at one of the university's radio stations. He and I loved jazz, and together we had a great collection. Our apartment became a gathering place where Black students would come to debate issues, play cards, drink wine, and chill out.

The first class of undergraduate women arrived in September 1970. There were only a few Black women in that class. The total number of Black students in the class exceeded the number of Black students in the preceding two classes, which meant the first-year class of Black students could out-vote all of the Black students who were senior to them. This was the era of increasing militancy, and the first-year Black students had their share of wanna-be firebrands. At meetings of the Black Students for Freedom, demands that we take over buildings or confront the school's leadership or storm the board of visitors meetings soon were on the rise. But I said no. I took the position that we did not need to resort to such tactics to get what we needed. I gave several examples of programs at UVA that benefited Black enrollment. Nevertheless, the new arrivals were itching for a confrontation, and before long they got what they wanted.

I heard through the grapevine that at the next BSF meeting I was going to be ousted by the first-year students. I went to the meeting prepared. I did not wait to be ousted. I walked into the South Meeting Room, went to the front of the group, and said, "I have heard that some of you think you are going to get rid of me tonight. Well, you are not going to get the chance because I quit." I then took a letter of resignation from my pocket, threw it on the floor, and walked out of the room with several of the guys who had been with me from the early days of the BSF.

It did not take long for the new leaders to demonstrate their control. But they did not understand the problem of having an avowedly racially exclusive organization. They announced that they were Black-only and made sure no whites were members. Quick as that they lost university funding, lost the right to hold meetings on university property, lost the right to use the copying machines and such. The BSF was essentially run off the grounds. I stayed away from the organization in those days. I was coming up on my fourth year and was working hard to post honors grades in all my courses because I had decided that I wanted to be a lawyer. I had realized by then that not being the leader of the Black Students for Freedom gave me more time to study.

That year I ran into some local prejudice, the kind that can pop up almost any time when you are Black in America. During my third year, one of the most popular places to go to dinner in Charlottesville was the Japanese Steakhouse for the Four Seasons. Its tables included cooking surfaces around which several people would sit to watch the food being prepared. If you were with a large enough group, you could have a cooking table just for yourselves. But if you were by yourself or with a date, you had to sit with strangers.

One weekend, after I had scrounged together all the money I could come up with, I took my date to the Japanese Steakhouse. We were the last people to be seated at a table that was occupied by several white people. As soon as we sat down, all of the white people got up and walked out. They did not say anything to me and my date. They just left. When they got to the front door, I could see a few of them scolding the person in charge of seating the guests. Soon that man came over to me and my date and said, "I am so sorry for what just happened here. Your dinner will be on the house." Though I knew that I had just been a victim of racial prejudice, I did not care; in truth I was quite delighted. I had not wanted to be seated with other people anyway. I was happy to sit just with my date. So, the fact that all the other people left suited me fine. On top of that, I hardly had enough money to buy the cheapest thing on the menu, and the fact that the meal was suddenly on the house was a thrilling development. We had a great dinner, and I came away thinking about the way that racism can have unintended, even ironic consequences.

11

Going on Television, Graduating, and Law School

During the summer after my third year at UVA, I got a job working in Norfolk at WTAR News, Channel 3. I was hired to pick up lunch for the newsroom personnel, run errands, and clean up around the teletype machines. Jim Mays was the news director at Channel 3. Betty Ann Bowser and Ed Hughes were the six o'clock anchors. Stan Garfin did sports. For me, it was the most amazing place to work, no matter what my job might be. Because I was born in Norfolk, I had watched Channel 3 all my life. It was the CBS affiliate, so it was the channel that carried Walter Cronkite, the most trusted newsman in America, and the *CBS Evening News*. When I was working at Channel 3, being on television was a very big deal. To know a television celebrity, even a local one, was like knowing a movie star. Just working in the newsroom was enough to make your friends starstruck.

I was fascinated to see the news coming across the teletype machines. There was a machine for the Associated Press, for United Press International, and for Reuters. The machines would sit idle for a while, then suddenly they would spring to life. When all of them started clattering at the same time, it was a good bet that a big story was breaking. I had to make sure that the paper rolls did not run out; and as the stories came across the wire I had to find the end of one story and the beginning of the next, tear the paper to separate the stories, then deposit each story in the collection box with the latest story on top. And I had to sweep the floor around the machines where little pieces of paper would fall from ripping the roll of paper. I did not mind any of this because I got to see the news before it went on the air.

Because I have always been an avid reader, I didn't just rip the stories and stack them in the box; I would read them as they came in. One day I saw a story that caught my attention. It was about a Staten Island ferry in New York colliding with a pier and injuring several people. I ripped the story from the news wire, walked to Jim Mays's office, stood in his doorway, and said, "Mr. Mays, listen to this story." I started reading from the wire service report. He listened to me read then said, "Can you do that again?" I said, "Yes, sir." He said, "Don't read it standing there. Come with me into the sound booth. I think you belong on the air." We went to the recording booth. He told someone in the control room to run a tape, and I read the story in earnest. Jim then turned to me and said, "You are going on the air."

In a flash I had gone from a gofer to newsman John Charles Thomas, WTAR News, Norfolk, Virginia. I could not have been prouder. I came to work the next day dressed in a coat and tie and ready to go on assignment. I was twenty. I was a newsman. This was amazing. I did not care what the story was, I was willing to do it. There were only one or two Black people on the air in Norfolk in those days. This was a big deal.

Oddly enough, even though I was the most junior reporter in the room, I had the longest name. Everybody else went by a nickname—Ed, Betty, Stan—but my mother had never wanted me to have a nickname. I was never Jack or Chuck or Charlie; I was always and only John Charles Thomas, so that is how I was announced on the air. You would have thought that I was John Cameron Swayze, me with the three first names who used all of them in my news stories.

One of my first stories showed me the perils of not knowing how to edit news film. There was a big charity horse show in Norfolk to raise money for the Children's Hospital of the King's Daughters. Because I was a complete novice, I did not know what a reporter needed to do to get the A and B rolls of film to work together in presenting a news story. The A roll had the sound strip on it and would show the film of an interview or a standup (when the reporter is in the shot talking to the camera). The B roll was for silent film that depicted parts of the story. The trick was to use the B roll to illustrate what you were say-ing on the A roll, or else your story would just be what newspeople called a "talking head" on the A roll. When I filed my story about the charity horse show, I had no idea what images were on the B roll, and I didn't know that I should have told the cameraman that I needed to look at what he had shot. As a result, when I chose the sound bites that I wanted from the A roll, my only instruction to the cameraman was for him to use thirty seconds of B roll twelve seconds into my A roll segment. When the story ran, I got a big surprise. I was talking about the importance of the work being done by the hospital, and just at that point a horse's rear end filled the screen and stayed on screen as I finished talking. I was ridiculed by the veterans. I learned right away to be in close communication with my cameraman.

I saw a great deal of human drama in my two summers as a tele-vision newsman. One story was about a child who had drowned in a borrow pit from which construction crews were taking sand to use building a highway in Virginia Beach. When I got to the scene, the fire and rescue crew was pulling the young boy's body from the pit. Standing nearby and heaving with sobs was the boy's mother, cradling a shirt, socks, and pair of tennis shoes. Her anguish was heartbreaking.

On another occasion a man had drowned in the Lafayette River but his body had been missing for days. The Channel 3 News helicopter spotted a body in the river. We called the police, and I went with a cam-eraman to the area where the body had been seen. It was floating in the middle of the river nowhere near the shore. The helicopter had pon-toons so it could sit down on water. The Norfolk police asked our he-licopter crew to help them recover the body. A police officer straddled the pontoon on the passenger side, linked his left arm through the seat belt, and then was flown over the body. The police officer reached down and grabbed the clothes on the body, then the helicopter stayed low and moved towards the shoreline. The body was in bad shape. I had not known that police officers had to help retrieve dead bodies. My appreciation of the work they do reached a new level.

Another story involved a house fire up the street from Jacox Ju-nior High. The dilapidated wood-frame house burned to ashes. We got to the scene while the fire was still burning. The police allowed me and my cameraman to get close enough to get shots for the story.

My parents' wedding day, February 14, 1948. *Left to right:* King Edward and Estelle Thomas, John and Floretta Sears Thomas, and Eunice and William Harvey Sears.

With my older cousin Howard Waddell Sears, ca. 1954.

At Aunt Lula Sears's graduation from Hampton Institute, June 1963. *Front row, left to right:* me; my cousin Bucky Taylor; my brother, Clarence Thomas; my cousin Pat Taylor; and Aunt Henrietta Childs. *Middle row:* Uncle Bill Frazier; Aunts Eunice "Toppie" Frazier and Kathy Sears; Grandma Eunice Sears; Aunt Lucy McCray; Aunt Lula; and my cousin Eunice Taylor. *Top row:* Uncle Charles Sears; Aunt Evelyn Taylor; my mother and father, Floretta and John Thomas; and Uncle Bob McCray.

At UVA law school, 1974.

Black members of UVA law school class of 1975. I'm fourth from left.

Pearl Walden Thomas, 1982.

Wedding day, October 9, 1982. With Pearl and me are her parents, Frank and Ruby Walden, *left,* and my parents, Floretta and John Thomas.

With my Hunton colleague Tim Ellis, "the Taz," 1984.

With Virginia governor Charles Robb at the press conference announcing my appointment to the Virginia Supreme Court, April 1983.

Calling dignitaries to announce my appointment to the Virginia Supreme Court, April 1983.

With Pearl at the Virginia Supreme
Court on the day I was sworn in,
April 25, 1983.

With Aunt Evelyn Taylor Peevy, *left,* and my mother, Floretta Thomas, April 25, 1983.

With Dayna Matthew in chambers, ca. 1987. Dayna was a member of the UVA law school class of 1987. In 2020 she was named dean of the law school at George Washington University.

On the Virginia Supreme Court, mid-1980s. *Front row, left to right:* Richard Poff, Harry Carrico, and Chris Compton. *Back row:* Me, Roscoe Stephenson, Charles Russell, and Henry Whiting.

My portrait at UVA law school.

At a graduation ceremony at William & Mary with Chancellor Robert Gates, former U.S. secretary of defense, *right,* and Provost Geoff Feiss, ca. 2006.

With civil rights activist and U.S. representative Andrew Young, *second from right,* at Monticello, July 4, 1998. (© Thomas Jefferson Foundation at Monticello)

With Mikhail Gorbachev at Monticello, 1993. (© Thomas Jefferson Foundation at Monticello)

With Margaret Thatcher at Monticello, 1996. (© Thomas Jefferson Foundation at Monticello)

As I looked inside the structure, I saw the remains of a chair. At first, I did not understand what else I was looking at, but as I looked more closely I saw a charred skeleton in the chair. Someone had burned to death sitting right there.

From time to time a story would be assigned to me because none of the other reporters wanted to do it. In 1971, Norfolk was building its downtown convention center and concert hall known as the Norfolk Scope. The building was nearly complete, and workers were putting a waterproof coating on its dome-shaped roof. In that process, an acetylene torch ignited the coating. Thick, acrid black smoke started billowing from the top of this new building and could be seen for miles around. After the fire was doused, Jim Mays wanted a reporter and cameraman to go up on the roof of the building to shoot the story. The older reporters were worried that the roof had been weakened by the fire and that if you walked on it, it might collapse. I had no such fears. I wanted to see what the roof looked like up close and what the city looked like from the top of the building. I climbed up a ladder to the roof. I will never forget the panoramic view I had of Norfolk from the top of the Scope. I could readily see the steeple of my church, First Baptist Bute Street, and I could see the top of Maury High School. I was glad I did the story.

During the summer of 1971, I remember seeing a young Larry Sabato in the newsroom at Channel 3. Jim Mays told me how much Larry knew about politics in Norfolk and around Virginia. That summer Larry was statewide youth coordinator for state senator Henry Howell, who had decided to run for governor of Virginia. Larry went on to become a professor of government at UVA, but his love of politics was with him even in his youth.

One of the really great things about working at Channel 3 was that they would let me come back to work when I was home from UVA for the holidays. Thus, I worked there on and off from the summer of 1971 to the summer of 1972. In January 1972, I covered a story that made the national news. A navy frigate broke loose from its moorings in a storm and collided with the Chesapeake Bay Bridge-Tunnel, knocking one of the road sections out of alignment and closing the whole bridge-tunnel for a month and a half. The day after the storm, Jim Mays wanted to send a cameraman and reporter to fly over the site, land close by, and do a story. But the weather was still blustery, and none of the full-time reporters wanted to go up in a small plane in such conditions. I did not care. I was a young kid from the housing projects. I had never been near a small plane, so I wanted to do the story. Off we went, flying over the wrecked roadway with the ship still nearby. Because the bridge-tunnel was closed, we were able to land on the roadway and shoot the story. The story went out over the news feed for other stations to pick up. It got picked up nationally, and I was paid a hundred dollars, which seemed then like the most money in the world.

On another story, I got help from a very prominent public official in overcoming racial prejudice. The story starts with the christening of a new navy ship at the Newport News Shipyard in the summer of 1972. It was a grand event with sailors in uniform, admirals in braided hats, and high officials from the Defense Department, including the secretary of the navy, John Warner. Not long before the christening ceremony, a story had broken that the navy was considering putting women on fighting ships. Navy wives in Norfolk were in an uproar. I was assigned to try to interview Secretary Warner about women on fighting ships.

There was a reception following the christening at what was then the racially segregated James River Country Club. My cameraman and I shot film for the ship launch and then headed to the country club to intercept Secretary Warner. We got there before he did and set up the camera. There were gates around the private club. To my good fortune, Secretary Warner parked outside the gates and walked toward the reception. I caught him on the walkway and said, "Mr. Secretary, I am John Charles Thomas from Channel 3 News. Would you let us ask you a few questions about the navy's idea to put women on fighting ships? This has caused a stir in Norfolk." As we walked, we were nearing the gates to the private club. A man approached me and said, "You can't come in here. You need to go back to the parking lot." I said, "But I am interviewing Secretary Warner." I did not know what would happen next, but I knew our cameras were rolling so if they pushed me back it would be on film. To my surprise, Secretary Warner put his arm around my shoulder and said to the person who had tried to shoo me away: "I am being interviewed. Please step back." And then he carried me with him right into the country club. I got the story. I also recognized that Secretary Warner could have allowed me to be shooed away, but he did not. I have always appreciated what he did that day. Years later I reminded him of what he had done and thanked him.

I also interviewed the captain of the aircraft carrier *John F. Kennedy* in his quarters about that great warship. The *JFK* was a flagship of the fleet, which meant that it carried on board a captain, who commanded the ship itself, and an admiral, who commanded the fleet. It was an impressive sight to turn down a corridor and see at the end two black doors facing each other. One door, the captain's quarters, had an eagle on it. The other, the admiral's quarters, had stars on it.

The captain's quarters were impressive. When we first came through the black door to the captain's suite we saw a small bedroom on the right side very near the door. I thought, "That's nice, but it sure looks small." Those were the sleeping quarters for the captain's steward. We entered another room and there was a rocking chair with pads on it, just like the one President Kennedy had been seen in during his time in the White House. We learned that it was an authentic Kennedy rocker. Also, there was a huge map table with papers strewn about. Through another door was the captain's sleeping quarters with a canopied king-sized bed. It was an incongruent sight to see on board a fighting ship. We sat down in the captain's wardroom for the interview. He talked about what it was like to command a vessel with thousands of people on board. He said that it was much like running a government, with him as mayor, governor, chief of police. He said he loved his job. He talked about being at sea for months at a time. I was left with the impression that part of what he had to contend with as skipper of the JFK was loneliness.

During my fourth year at UVA, 1971–72, I lived in room 30 East Lawn. I had been smitten by the beauty of the Lawn on that high school trip to Charlottesville back in 1967. I loved the colonnades, the rows of trees, the pavilions that looked similar from a distance but up close revealed distinctive details. To apply for a room on the Lawn I had to demonstrate leadership as a student. I had to have good grades. I had to explain why I wanted to live there. I was elated to be selected. I was the only Black person living on the Lawn that year and was possibly the first Black to live there ever. I had one of the best rooms on the Lawn. The rooms on either side of mine were occupied, which meant my walls were warm. In addition, the men's restroom was below my room, which meant that my floor was warm, too, and that I did not have a long walk to get to the restroom.

When you lived on the Lawn you had to go outdoors then downstairs to the restroom and showers. Typically, we would wear hooded terrycloth robes to and from the showers. When you saw someone walking along the colonnades on the Lawn in a bathrobe, you knew that person had to live on the Lawn. But when I walked outdoors in my robe, white people walking along the Lawn would say to me, "Do you live on the Lawn?" I would say yes. But I was always thinking, "No, I just took off my clothes and put on a robe so I could walk up and down out here pretending to live on the Lawn."

There were rocking chairs in the rooms on the Lawn. On warm days I would put my rocker out under a tree near the door to my room, put my stereo speakers in the doorway, and sit there reading a book while listening to jazz. I would play jazz greats like John Coltrane, Miles Davis, the Modern Jazz Quartet. Often, white students walking along the Lawn would come over to me and say, "What kind of music is that?" All I could figure was that they had never heard jazz before. I thought it was a strange question, but I tried to be civil about it.

There were many secret societies at UVA. I came to my room one day and found an envelope strung on a thread across my door. Inside there was a letter with a ticket. I was told to go to a certain place and sit in the designated seat at a certain time. I did not do it. I was not sure what was going on, and I was not curious to find out.

The rooms on the Lawn had doors that opened directly onto the sidewalk. There were louvered shutters in front of the doors that could be closed and locked. That way you could safely leave your door open and get a breeze. And if someone came to your door you could talk to them through the shutters without letting them in. I always closed and locked my shutters at night.

One night I heard a knock on the shutters. I opened the door and asked, "Who is it?" The response was, "John, open up and come outside." But the person would not identify himself, and I did not recognize his voice. I asked again, "Who is it?" This time he said, "John please come outside." I shut the door. I found out later that had I unlocked the shutters I would have been pulled outside into an initiation rite. Over the years I have been a little curious about what might have happened had I opened the shutters, but not that curious. I guess that growing up the way I had made the idea of opening a door to a stranger something that just was not tempting.

By the time I was fourth year at UVA, my overall grade point average was closing in on finishing with distinction, UVA's equivalent of cum laude. But in order to do this, I had to ace my last exam, which was in formal logic. That effort reminded me of what I had had to do to get out of the chemistry program in my first year. Here I was again trying to overcome an academic hurdle. And I did it; I aced the test. This meant that my grades at UVA were 2.0, 2.2, 2.8, 3.2, 3.8, 3.8, 3.8, 3.8, which added up to taking my degree with distinction. Every time I look up on the wall in my office and see that "distinction" on my diploma, I think how hard it was to get it and how much better my average would have been had I not signed up for chemistry. Years later I told the provost of UVA the experience I had had in the chemistry program. He said my story made him sad because when he was at MIT, his instructors made it so much fun to go to class that he and his classmates were excited to learn science, and thus he lamented the fact that I had not been encouraged more by my professors to love science and make it a career.

I applied to law school. Although I had enjoyed being a television newsman, I found out that the salary for a local news reporter was less than the salary for a schoolteacher, and I knew that schoolteachers were woefully underpaid. And, as I had traveled around the country and served on governmental commissions, I learned that lawyers played a crucial role in the life of the nation.

As mentioned earlier, Dean Paulsen at UVA Law had long ago told me that he wanted me to come to his law school. When he heard that I was interested in law school, he called me to his office. He asked what other schools I was looking at. When I said Harvard and Michigan, he said, "Thomas, you can go to those other law schools if you want to. But if you want to be something in Virginia you ought to come to this law school. If you come here, your classmates will be governors of Virginia, attorneys general of Virginia, leaders in Virginia." I said, "Yes sir."

When I looked more closely at Harvard and Michigan, I saw that the disclosure requirements called for information from both parents. Because I did not know where my father was, I figured it would not be easy to apply to those schools. At UVA Law, because the undergraduate school had my financial information, the disclosure requirement was different and my father's absence did not present an obstacle. In the end, my sole application was to UVA Law. I scored in the ninetieth percentile on the LSATs. I had a 3.8 average in my major at UVA and an overall average of 3.2. I had been a student leader as an undergraduate. I had significant public service experience, like co-chairing the education task force of the White House Conference on Youth. Not long after I submitted my application, I learned that I had been accepted at the law school.

When I graduated from UVA in May 1972, there was a huge turnout from my family. I was the first in the family to finish the University of Virginia. The Sears family, my mother's side of the family, is large. I knew that all the hotel rooms in the area had long been booked, and that even if some were available my family could not afford them. So, I went to the resident staff office and asked if I could get dorm rooms for my family. They said yes. I wound up with a whole floor of rooms.

About forty family members came to graduation. They brought grills and had barbecues on the grass in front of the dorms. I led them on a walking tour of UVA, ending up on the Lawn near my room. Some of my classmates were having elaborate catered parties on the Lawn in front of their rooms, and I showed up leading a large group of Black people along the colonnades. One white guy made some wisecrack. I don't recall what he said, but it made me get in his face and tell him, "Shut up. This is my family. We have just as much right to be here as you do." One of my uncles grabbed my arm and said, "Charles, come on now, come on." We walked away from the brief confrontation and headed to the Rotunda.

My family had never seen a scene like the one on the Lawn at commencement. They were used to the graduation ceremony at Hampton University, where many of them had gone to college. There, the students dressed in coats, ties, and dresses, and they treated graduation with great formality. But at UVA the atmosphere was quite different. Some students wore shorts and sandals under their robes. Others wore bathing suits. Some wore clown paint on their faces. And instead of a dignified procession of the graduates, there was whooping and shouting and a bit of chaos. When they called our names for our degrees, they did not call our full names. Rather, they went in rapid fire, like a machine gun: "Mr. Smith, Mr. Stith, Mr. Swartz, Mr. Tate, Mr. Titus, Mr. Thomas, Mr. Thompson." Even so, when my large family heard them say "Mr. Thomas" and saw me walk to the front, they roared. It was probably the biggest single sound that day. They were proud, and so was I.

Later in the day, after the ceremony was over and everyone was packing up to leave, I was walking around the grounds with my Uncle Tom—Lt. Col. Thomas E. Sears—and his wife, Aunt Onnye. He said to me, "So, what do you want for graduation? Do you want me to give you something cute or something substantial?" I said, "Give me something substantial." He reached in his pocket and gave me a crisp new hundred-dollar bill. Well, that was the first time I had ever seen a hundred-dollar bill. I thanked him.

12

Studying Law and Being a Law Clerk

I entered law school at the University of Virginia in September 1972. When I started, the law school was still housed on the main grounds near the Greek amphitheater. When you came through the front doors of the law school you walked into Mural Hall, where the walls were painted with nude and scantily clad classical images. The room had big sofas and chairs where the law students would congregate between classes.

On that first day, there was all the coming and going one would expect when students are trying to find classrooms, restrooms, professors' offices, and suitable places to study. There were not many Black students in that entering class, but as we looked across Mural Hall we quickly spotted each other. Soon we had formed a small group. There was Dennis, just back from Vietnam; Joel, who had finished Virginia State University; Kester, soon called K.C., who had finished business school; Ron from Yale; Henry from William & Mary, whom I had grown up with in Norfolk; Godfrey, who had attended Hampton; Jan, who had also attended Hampton; Delores from Alabama; Sheila from New York, who had also attended Yale; Charles from Delaware, who had also attended Hampton. We were the new kids on the block. Later we met some of the upper-class Black law students, who gave us dire warnings of how hard things were in some of the classes. We were all on edge, not knowing what to expect but hoping we were ready.

Back then, each class was divided by alphabet into what were called small sections. The small sections were where they taught legal writing and legal research. In the small sections you were meant to get to know your classmates and your professor in a way that went beyond the typical classroom experience. The small sections socialized together and tended to build friendships that lasted through the years. But the odd thing about them was that you only got to know people in a small slice of the alphabet. My section went from St through Z. But the Black law students in my class formed what amounted to another kind of small section.

Almost all my Black classmates and I got a rude awakening on the first day of class. We went to class expecting to meet our professors, see who else was in the class, get our assignments, and return the next time to start class. Not so. We all had to take Torts, Civil Procedure, Legislative Administrative Law, Constitutional Law, Contracts, Property, Criminal Law, Legal Research, and Legal Writing. In the first class on the first day, the professor said, "Welcome, this is Contracts. Fill out the seating chart that I am passing around. Now turn to the first case and raise your hand if you can state the issue in the case." I went, "What?" I did not have books. I did not know that assignments had been given out or how. I was taken by surprise. So were all the other Black students in that class. What we had not known was that the professors had posted on the door to their classrooms the books that were required for the course, where the books could be purchased, and what the first-day assignment was. Nor did we know that we were supposed to have found our classes, gone to the room, read the assignments on the door, and been ready to start class on that first day. So, we were immediately up against the wall, as people used to say.

As soon as class let out, we all went running to the bookstores on the Corner, directly across the street from UVA. We hurriedly bought books, legal pads, pens, ink, erasers, highlighters, bookmarks, and went running back to our rooms to study in preparation for class the next day. We were sure that we had been the victims of a conspiracy against us. We whispered to each other, "Mighty funny that all the white students seemed to have known the assignment. How come we were the only ones left out?" But we got going and hit the books.

The first-year law professors seemed to make it their business to be tough on us. They saw it as their job to mold us into lawyers. If they saw you slouching in the last row of the class in the back of the room trying to look inconspicuous, they were sure to call on you. And if they called on you, it was not enough to say that you did not know the answer. The retort would be something like "Don't you ever come into my class unprepared again. And that holds true for all you. And now, since you don't know the answer, sit here right now and find it." So, if you got called on you were pretty much caught until the professor decided to let you go.

That teaching style led to an early casualty among the Black students in my class. There was one Black guy from Mississippi. I remember him because I had never met a Black person from Mississippi. He got called on in class that first week of law school. The professor asked him a question. He replied, "That's a good question." The professor shot back, "Well, that is not a good answer. You are going to sit here till you give me a good answer." The poor guy was caught out. He had nothing to say and did not know what to do. He quit. We did not see him again after the first few weeks of law school.

When I learned that I had been accepted at the law school, I applied to be a graduate advisor in the undergraduate dormitories. Indeed, I asked for and got the slot as the graduate advisor in my own first-year dormitory, Lefevre. I was graduate advisor for the Lefevre-Metcalf Association and had a small apartment on the first floor of Lefevre. It was a bit strange to return to the same dorm where I had first lived at UVA. But by being graduate advisor I did not have to pay rent, I had a phone, and I was paid about fifty dollars per month. I had a bedroom, a bathroom, a small kitchen, a living room, and an office at the front door to the little apartment. It was my job to counsel the undergraduates, to back up the resident advisors on each floor in their dealings with the students, and to be the voice of reason and authority in the dorms. Thus, as I was starting law school, I was dealing directly with young students who were just starting college.

Law school was brutal. There did not seem to be enough time to get everything done. The first-year professors seemed to delight in giving us impossible deadlines. Several professors used materials in their classes that were not in the textbooks. They would put a certain number of copies of the materials on reserve in the library, but they never had as many copies as there were students in the class. The Black students soon found out that we were at another disadvantage. Our white classmates would rush to the library, check out all the available copies, and pass them around to the various study groups that they had formed. None of the Black students were in study groups with our white classmates, and we had not immediately created our own study groups. As a result, we were usually the last people in class to see what had been placed on reserve.

We felt like we were grinding it out all the time. Study, study, study. No time for anything else. No holidays, no breaks, no vacations, nothing. My law school classmates both white and Black soon realized that we were living in a world that was difficult for outsiders to understand. It was hard to explain that the difference between day and night, weekday and weekend just didn't mean anything anymore. You worked on what you were doing until you were finished, then you plopped down on the bed for a while, got up, and went on to the next thing that you had to do. And there was always something to do.

Because of the pressures that we were living with, the Black law students formed very close bonds. It did not really matter what year you were in law school; what mattered was that we were Black people trying to be lawyers in an environment that we did not think was welcoming.

One thing we did was to organize a chapter of the Black American Law Students Association, BALSA. The organization was founded in 1968 at New York University law school to articulate and promote the needs and goals of Black law students and to be an agent of change in the legal community. Our newly formed chapter at UVA Law gave us a reason to meet and to work together on issues that concerned us. It also gave us a link to Black law students at other schools. As we communicated with other BALSA chapters, we could see that what we were experiencing in Charlottesville was similar to what other Black law students were experiencing around the country. It helped us feel a part of something bigger than just our small group.

The other thing we did was to start gathering on weekends to have potluck dinners and play cards. We often went to Godfrey's apartment because he had a great stereo system and he enjoyed cooking. Other times we were at Joel's apartment. His wife, Ollie, made great casseroles and the best pound cakes, and she didn't complain when we played cards and talked late into the night. It was our time to recharge and refuel.

During that first year I broke up with a girl who I had thought that I was going to marry. The next day I skipped class, drove up to the Skyline Drive, bought some cheap wine, sat on a hillside looking into the valley, drank wine, and threw the bottles down the side of the mountain. I missed class for a couple of days. I was despondent.

When I went back to the law school, I went to see Dean Paulsen to tell him that I was going to quit. I walked into the foyer of the law school and there he was. I rushed up to him saying, "Dean Paulsen, I've got to talk to you. I just broke up with my girlfriend, and I just can't do this anymore." I had thought that he was going to be sympathetic; after all, he had recruited me to the law school. But his response was entirely unexpected. In a brusque manner, as he kept walking away, he said, "John, every man must wrestle his own devil, and I have to go to class." His response left me stunned. I thought to myself, "These lawyers are cold-hearted. I need to be like them." I returned to class.

During the days that I had been sitting on a mountainside, my Black classmates did not know where I was. When I got back, I had fallen behind in all my classes. I told some of the guys where I had been. My Black classmates rallied round. They shared their notes. They offered words of encouragement. They grabbed hold of me and held on; they helped me to cope with that moment in my life. With their help, I got back into the swing of things. I hunkered down, studied like hell, and became a law student again.

In my job as graduate advisor in the first-year dorms, I soon found that the students in my two dormitories were acting just like you would expect teenagers away from home to act. They were pulling pranks, having parties, staying up all night, and doing almost anything but studying. They distracted me from studying the law, but they also forced me to develop some counseling and dispute-resolution skills.

One memorable example of my role as the oldest person living in the dorm occurred during a power failure. The power went out on a winter night when it was pitch-dark outside. The narrow hallways of Lefevre-Metcalf had no windows, so the halls were jet black. The students on one of the halls decided this was the perfect time to put furniture in their hallway to create an obstacle course. One of the resident assistants came to get me. The students who had packed their hall with furniture, suitcases, bookcases, and trash cans just would not listen to their RAs, but that is why the dorms had graduate advisors. We were meant to be the old heads in the room. And the fact that I was a law student—and probably the fact that I was a Black guy with an Afro— added a little bit more.

When I got to the offending hallway, I opened the door and could not see a foot in front of my face. I put my hands out and felt something directly in my path. I turned on my flashlight, pointed it towards my face so the students could see me, and said, "I am John Thomas. I am the graduate advisor in this building. You have five minutes to clear all this furniture out of this hallway or I am going to turn everybody on this hall over to the judiciary committee and let them decide what to do with you. Is that clear?" No one responded. I turned off my flashlight, turned around, walked out of the door, went to the landing, stood by the big window for a few minutes, then came back to the hallway and shone my flashlight down the hall. All the furniture was gone; the hall was completely clear from one end to the other. There was no way in that short time that they could have sorted out the furniture and put it back where it came from. I figured that they had just grabbed what was in the hall and pulled it into the nearest room. I was pleased with the immediate result of clearing the hallway. I have always wondered how long it was before all the things that had blocked the hallway found their way back to where they came from.

The students in my dorms never got into any serious trouble. They might drop a water balloon from the top floor or moon people from their windows, but that was about the extent of it. Many of them were curious about law school. I would often sit at my desk with my door open so I could see them coming and going and they could see me studying. Almost all law students in those days used *Black's Law Dictionary*. When the students in my dorm asked me what *Black's* was, I usually said it was the dictionary for Black law students. I always thought that was funny since it seemed to me that nothing about the law was for Black people.

I was one of those law students who took copious notes. I wrote down everything that was said in class. I looked up the words and wrote their definitions in the margins of my textbooks. I thought that the classes in law school were interesting. I often sat in class thinking, "So this is what they say Black people cannot understand." I intended to show any doubters that I could understand the law.

By a few weeks into the first semester, my Black classmates and I had formed study groups. We would meet to review our notes and discuss what we had heard in class. We would share copies of our notes from the classes that we felt most comfortable in. I shared my notes from Corporations Law. I thought that I really understood that area of law and that I was going to get an A in that course.

When exam time came, I thought that I had done quite well in Corporations Law, and the others who had used my notes thought they had done well too. After the exams, there was the long wait for the grades to be posted. In the main entrance hall to the old law school building, there was a bulletin board that the students called the Wailing Wall. That was where grades were posted with your social security number beside your grade.

I went to the Wailing Wall for my grade in Corporations. I looked up and down the list trying to find my social security number. When I spotted it, I could not believe what I saw. There was a D beside my name. The only D in the class, which meant that everybody else had outperformed me on this exam. I was certain that something was wrong.

I went to see the professor. I told him that there must have been a mistake because I was sure that I did not have a D on that exam. The professor said, "I don't make mistakes on my exams." I told him that I would go get a blue book like the one I had used, that I would write on it in the same ink that I had used, and that I would give it to him to compare with the blue books that he had so that he could see that there must have been an error. The professor said that I could do whatever I wanted but that he did not make mistakes. I went to my room, got everything, brought it back, went to see Dean Paulsen to tell him what had happened, and went again to see the professor.

A few days later, I came into the entrance hall of the law school and saw people standing near the Wailing Wall saying, "Can you believe they did that to him?" I went to see what the fuss was about. Beside one social security number a B+ had been marked through and a D was posted. Beside my social security number the D had been marked through and a B+ had been posted. But the white students standing there were upset about what had happened to someone they knew. They thought it was terrible that this other guy's grade had been reduced from B+ to D. No one had any idea of what it was like for me to have been given a grade that was not mine. The professor never said a word to me about this. All I know is that if I had not believed that I had done well in that class, I would have never challenged the professor or told the dean. And if I had gotten a D in Corporations, I probably would not have been hired by Hunton & Williams. And if I had not been hired at Hunton, then—all things being interrelated as they are—I probably would not have become Justice Thomas.

Another part of being in law school is landing a law-related summer job. A good summer job in the law is a learning experience because it can teach practical things that you would not usually learn in law school, things like dealing with the staff in a law firm or with the staff in a clerk's office, for example.

I had very good fortune when it came to my summer job following my first year. I landed a position in the Justice Department in Washington as an honors clerk in the Civil Rights Division, Race and Sex Discrimination. This job was in the very wheelhouse of my being. It put me in contact with some of the lawyers who had worked in the Deep South on lawsuits involving the integration of public transportation and school systems and such. Some of the lawyers I met that summer had litigated cases involving the freedom rides. I learned a lot that summer working on race and sex discrimination cases in places like Tennessee, Texas, and New York. It was an exciting place to work, and I was proud to have my Justice Department ID and my government-issued briefcase.

On one assignment, I was sent alone to a southern state to contact witnesses in a race discrimination case and to update and confirm their testimony. The Justice Department was preparing to take the case to trial and wanted to know whether the witnesses were ready to proceed. I was so proud to be on the road for the Civil Rights Division of the Justice Department.

When I got to town, I checked in with the U.S. Attorney's office and was given a place to work. I had never been to that part of the South, so I was a bit wary. I started calling the names on the witness list. When someone answered I would say, "This is John Charles Thomas with the Justice Department. I am here to talk to you about this case." To my surprise, one person after another hung up the phone. On the next series of calls, I began by saying, "Hi, I'm from Washington working on the lawsuit. Please do not hang up. There is no reason for you to be afraid. The Justice Department is working on this case." How naïve I was. I just did not understand the depth of the fears of the people who had filed a complaint that a big southern business was discriminating against them.

On one of the calls an older-sounding man said, "Give me your phone number. I'll call you when I can talk." I gave him my number. After that I drove around the city, found the Black part of town, got something to eat, then went back to my motel room hoping to get the return call.

Later in the evening my phone rang. It was the older man. He asked whether I had a car. I said I did. He gave me an address and told me to come there and then I could talk to everyone. The witnesses were so afraid of being retaliated against that they had gathered at one of their homes in the hope that there was some protection in being together. They were willing to talk to me face-to-face, away from the workplace, but they were not willing to say anything of substance on the telephone.

I found the address, a small, neat house down an out-of-the-way road. I sat in a room while the witnesses came in one at a time to refresh their testimony. There were about nine or ten people, men and women, Black and poor. Afraid. As I sat there with them, I felt as if I were the United States government come to help them. I had no thought that anyone would try to do anything to me because I was with the Justice Department. I finished that trip uneventfully. I submitted my report to the lawyers with whom I was working. I was not around when the case went to trial. Many years later I got scared thinking about that trip. It had dawned on me that those witnesses were afraid because they knew that some people might kill them to keep them from gaining their civil rights.

A civil rights case against the airline industry took me to New York City. The main claim in that suit was the airline industry was discriminating against Black women who had applied to be stewardesses. The Justice Department was conducting discovery against the airlines.

Thousands of boxes of personnel files had been put in a hangar near LaGuardia. FBI agents had set up cameras to photograph files that we thought were pertinent. A great many lawyers, paralegals, and summer associates were sent to New York to look through these boxes.

Of all the people looking through all those files, I was the one to find a smoking gun. We had been instructed by the lawyers to look for any evidence that a Black woman's file had been handled in an unusual manner. I opened a file to which was clipped a photo of an attractive Black woman. The first few pages gave test results; she had passed each test with high scores. Next there were evaluations from the people who had interviewed her. Then there was a note in the file that said, "This woman meets all the qualifications. I recommend that she proceed to the next class for stewardesses." And then I flipped the page and saw a note clipped to the back of the recommendation. It said, "Take no further action on this file until you see me." It had someone's initials. The next entry in the file showed that the woman had been hired not as a stewardess but as a ticket agent. I jumped up, ran to the senior attorney, and said, "Look at this! I found it!" The lawyers were excited too. You can spend your whole life in the law and never find evidence like that. I was not around for the resolution of that case. But I left the Justice Department knowing that I had helped secure someone's civil rights.

One of the things that a lot of law students tried to do with their summer jobs was to gain experience in different facets of the law so that when the time came, they could make an informed decision about what they wanted to focus on in their careers. After my first year, I got to see what being a government lawyer was like. For the summer after my second year, I wanted to see what the big law firm experience was like.

For that summer I landed a clerkship at Gibson, Dunn, and Crutcher, one of the great West Coast law firms. Their offices were in the ARCO Towers on South Flower Street in Los Angeles. I had never seen such beautiful offices. When I got to L.A. I did not yet have a place to live, so the firm put me up at the Century Plaza Hotel, which was not far from the backlot of 20th Century Fox studios. While staying at the hotel I met a man at the bar one evening who said that he was the rock star Alice Cooper. This man was dressed in a sport coat and slacks. He looked nothing like a rock star. But then it dawned on me that the makeup he wore onstage allowed him to be famous when he wanted to and incognito when he felt like it, a rather neat trick. As it turned out, Cooper was not the only celebrity I met that summer in L.A.

One of my high school classmates was a bunny at the Beverly Hills Playboy Club. She got me a celebrity key for that club, and I used it while I was staying at the Century Plaza. When I went to the club and they hung my key on the wall, everybody wanted to know who I was. The more I said things like "I'm from back East," the more interested the other guests got. Before I knew it, people were buying me drinks trying to get me to tell them who I was and what I was doing in L.A. It is amazing how curious people can become when someone is not spouting off about who they know and what they do. The more reticent I was, the more certain these people were that I was trying to keep something from them.

That summer of '74, Gibson Dunn was paying me about two hundred dollars per week. It was the most money I had ever made. It was a stunning amount of money for a poor Black kid from the housing projects of Norfolk. Back then you could buy a used car for that amount of money. One day I said something to one of the partners about my being paid that princely sum; the partner said, "Don't worry. You'll get used to it." Gibson Dunn was at the top of the heap. In addition to the offices in the ARCO Towers, they had offices on Rodeo Drive in Beverly Hills. I was working in that office one day and saw Liz Taylor step out of a car to go into one of the upscale shops.

One day a partner took me to lunch at a restaurant called La Scala, a very trendy spot in Beverly Hills. When we went in, there were movie stars and politicians all over the place. I remember seeing California senator John Tunney, the actor Louis Jourdan, and other notables. The lunch that day was not my usual burger and fries. But the thing I remember most had to do with a bottle of wine the partner ordered with lunch. When the waiter showed up with the bottle, the partner looked at it and without tasting the wine immediately said, "Take it back. Bring me another bottle, and bring the maître d.'" I had no idea what was going on. But I did not say anything. I just watched. Soon another bottle came, was opened, and we drank it with the lunch. Later I found out that the problem was that the waiter had uncorked the bottle before he brought it to the table. I learned that when you order fine wine it must be uncorked in your presence to ensure that an inferior wine has not been poured into the bottle. It was the kind of thing that I never had the chance to learn in my childhood, where all wine bottles seemed to have screw-off tops.

Gibson Dunn allowed its summer clerks to select special events to attend. You might go to a baseball game or a concert. For my first event I chose to attend the Hollywood Bowl to hear Yehudi Menuhin play Beethoven's Violin Concerto. It was not that I was a classical music devotee; rather, it was that I wanted to see the Hollywood Bowl, which I had heard about all my life. It was a beautiful evening, and I had a date who was quite surprised to find out that I was Black.

One of my law school classmates who knew I would be at Gibson Dunn for the summer told me that he had friends in L.A. and that he would tell them about me. He gave me their phone number. But apparently he never told them I was Black. And, given my TV reporter voice and my years of public speaking, I have been told that I don't always "sound Black" on the telephone. When I got settled in L.A., I called the number he had given me. I identified myself and had a pleasant conversation with a woman who said that she had heard that I would be working in L.A. and that she had someone nice for me to meet. It never occurred to me that my classmate had not told his friends that I was Black. It was pretty clear to me that she was white, and I guess she did not pick up anything from my voice. She asked me to call again when I had time and wanted to have somebody show me around Los Angeles.

I called her and told her that I had tickets to a classical concert at the Hollywood Bowl. Now that I think about it, that probably did not give her much of a clue that I was a Black guy either. She gave me a phone number and the name of the girl to call to be my date for the concert. I called. The young lady answered. I identified myself. She gave me her address. I found her apartment and knocked on the door. She opened the door. She looked shocked, but she recovered quickly and invited me in. We drove to the Hollywood Bowl. We pulled up to a sign that said "parking lot full"; we showed a special pass and the gate went up and we were shown to a parking place.

Then, we were escorted to a place where baskets of bread, wine, cheese, and pâté were being handed to those sitting in the box seats where we were. We picked up our basket, went to our seats on the floor of the Hollywood Bowl, and looked up toward the stage. We were in a perfect position, front and center. It was like being in the movies. Our area was roped off with red-and-white checked cloth separating the boxes. All around us were the rich and famous. We sat there talking, drinking wine, eating cheese. When the concert began, we sat together listening to Yehudi Menuhin. After the concert I took her home. We said goodnight. I never saw her or talked to her again. I always wondered whether my classmate got an earful the next time he spoke to the woman who had arranged my date to the concert.

My other firm-sponsored outing took me to a famous jazz venue, the Lighthouse Café at Hermosa Beach. I had seen that name all my life on jazz albums. Back in the '60s, when I learned about jazz, it seemed that all the great jazz groups played at the Lighthouse. The very idea that I could listen to jazz at the Lighthouse was almost beyond belief, but when I found out who was playing, I was almost dumbstruck. I was there for the last West Coast concert of the Modern Jazz Quartet, "live at the Lighthouse." I got to Hermosa Beach early in the day because I was so eager to be there. When the club opened, I was one of the first to go inside. I took a seat at a small round table right in front of the little platform that served as a stage. As I sat in my chair I could and did put my foot right on the edge of the platform.

To my surprise the Lighthouse was small. There was no backstage; indeed, there was no real stage at all. There was just this platform in a room with exposed pipes and beams. There was a bar running along the wall directly behind me and parallel to the platform. It was a truly intimate environment for jazz. The members of MJQ came in, set up their equipment, did sound checks, all while I was sitting there watching. Then the room filled up with people and the concert started.

For a jazz connoisseur, there is nothing better than to sit five feet from one of the greatest jazz groups of all time and to be awash in their music. Percy Heath, Milt Jackson, Connie Kay, and John Lewis: the Modern Jazz Quartet. When they took a break from the first set, there was no place for them to go. They just put down their instruments, stepped off the platform, and walked through the crowd to go wherever they were going. I took a small, plain white napkin from the table and asked each of them to sign it in one of its four corners. I have the napkin to this day inside the album from that last West Coast concert.

It was an unforgettable event. Whenever I listen to the Modern Jazz Quartet, I can still see them in my mind's eye.

When I left Los Angeles at the end of the summer of '74, I knew that I was not going back there to work. It was just too far from where I had lived all my life. I had clerked out there because I had been in Los Angeles during the riots about a decade earlier, and I was curious to see if things had changed with the passage of time. Also, I had heard that my father was in Los Angeles. I tried to find him but was never able to track him down. And when I drove to the part of town where I had stayed during the riots, it still looked rundown, as if time had done nothing to heal its scars.

13

Finishing Law School, Passing the Bar, and Working at Hunton

I returned to law school for my third year with the idea of getting a job somewhere on the East Coast. A new law school building was nearing completion on another part of the university grounds, far from the building where I had started in 1972. When school started in September 1974, first- and second-year students were sent to the new building, which was still surrounded by muddy clay rather than grass and sidewalks. The third-year students were left in the old building; we would attend class there for the first semester then move to the new building for the second semester. Thus, the third-year class of 1975 became the last group of third-year law students to study in the old building. It was eerie. The library books had been moved to the new building. Furniture, bookcases, and shelving were gone. The once-crowded hallways became echo chambers for the remaining students and professors.

That year I was in the job hunt in earnest. Everybody was scrambling to find work. Interviews for third-year law students started early, near the end of September. I signed up for Norfolk firms because that was home and I had decided that I wanted to work there. I told my friends at Channel 3 News that I was going to interview with the firm that represented the TV station. They put in a good word for me. I also signed up to interview with other big Norfolk firms. I got interviews with each firm. Not only did I visit with them when they interviewed in Charlottesville, but I was invited back to Norfolk for on-site interviews, which is usually a good sign. But not for me.

I was turned down by all the firms with which I interviewed. I was shocked. I had finished undergraduate at UVA with distinction. I had a 3.5 at the law school and three semesters with a 3.8. I had been co-chair of the National Task Force on Education for the White House Conference on Youth. I had been a local television reporter. I had helped to integrate the schools in Norfolk. I had been a high achiever all my life. But I couldn't get a job.

At one Norfolk firm the entire senior leadership interviewed me, in their library, at a big conference table surrounded by white men in suits, with me sitting at the end of the table. One of the lawyers, who had my transcript and other papers in his hand, looked at me and said, "Young man, you have a fine record at UVA law school. It is better than my record and better than the record for most of my partners. You have done well, but we are afraid to hire you. We believe that if we give you a job we will lose some of our clients, and we cannot afford to do this." I said, "But I am from Norfolk, and I want to come home." Someone else replied, "You ought to look for a job in Washington or up North somewhere. Or maybe one of the Richmond firms could take you." There it was again, that seemingly friendly advice from a white person that at its core worked to keep things as they were.

At the other Norfolk firms, the rejection was not face-to-face. I just received rejection letters. I called one of those firms to ask why and was told that it was apparent from my record that I had been active in politics, and that the firm's clients would "just gag" if the firm had a lawyer who was politically active.

If the Norfolk firms had been at the end of the interview season, I would not have had any further chance to get a job at one of the big firms. But, the rejection from the Norfolk firms came so early in the interview process that I still had time to sign up for some of the Richmond and D.C. firms, which I did.

I got interviews with some of the D.C. firms, but my heart was not in it. Although D.C. is just across the water from Virginia, it seemed a vastly different place to me, as well as very expensive and not what I really wanted.

I interviewed with several Richmond firms, but I did not sign up to interview with Hunton & Williams. I knew that Hunton had represented Prince Edward County in the school desegregation cases and that it had argued on behalf of segregation in the *Brown v. Board of Education* arguments to the U.S. Supreme Court. I thought it would be a waste of time to apply there. As things turned out, I was rejected by all the Richmond firms too. Notably, in 1974, when I was interviewing with the Norfolk and Richmond firms, not one of them had ever hired a lawyer of color. Three-quarters of the way through the twentieth century, the big white firms in Virginia were still racially segregated.

With all these rejections, I concluded that I was being discriminated against. I called my friends at the Justice Department in the Civil Rights Division, Race and Sex Discrimination. I told them what had happened to me in the interview process. They asked me to send them my law school grades. After they saw them, they called back and said, "John, we have had many complaints from Black law students over the years saying that they were being discriminated against in hiring by the white law firms in the South. But when we compared their records to the records of the students those law firms were hiring, we couldn't make the case. With your record, if you let us proceed we will lock up the state of Virginia in a consent decree." I said, "Let me think about it."

From my perspective I was a poor law student, with a lot of loans, with a family living in the grip of poverty, and without a job. What I really wanted was a job, not a lawsuit. I called Dean Paulsen. I told him how I had been rejected by all the firms with which I had interviewed in Virginia and the reasons I had been given for being rejected. I told him too about my call to the Civil Rights Division of the Justice Department and the request they had made of me.

Not long after I talked to Dean Paulsen, I got a call from Hunton & Williams inviting me to a dinner they were holding for some law students the night before their interviews in Charlottesville. They invited me to interview with them at the law school. But the call was a surprise; I had not applied to interview with them. What would make Hunton invite me to be interviewed when I hadn't applied? I accepted the invitation to dinner. And after meeting the interview team, I went to the interview the next day. Hunton offered me a job. It was the only job offer that I got from any law firm in the state of Virginia. I was the first Black lawyer hired to work at Hunton.

I found out later that after I spoke to Dean Paulsen he convened a conference call with the leaders of all the major law firms in Virginia and told them, "Somebody had better give John Charles Thomas a job or every one of you is going to be in litigation with the Justice Department and risk being subject to a consent decree." Hunton, the largest law firm in Virginia, apparently took the weight for Virginia's legal community by hiring me.

I had finished law school. I had a job. Now I had to pass the bar exam, move to Richmond, and get to work. The summer bar exam was administered in Roanoke at the Hotel Roanoke. Our classmates who could afford it simply booked rooms at the hotel and stayed there for the two-day exam. The Black guys in my class didn't have that kind of money. Yet, we had a plan. Our classmate Dennis was moving to Roanoke for a job. We loaded our cars with his belongings, took it all to Roanoke, and set up shop in his empty apartment. We hung sheets at the windows and slept on the floor in sleeping bags.

All of us were completely on edge the whole time. We didn't have money to go out to dinner. We were living on pizzas, potato chips, and Coca-Cola. During the day, we might get coffee and a snack at the hotel. We were quizzing each other about what might be on the bar exam, and we were drinking wine. We were not living under optimum conditions to get ready for the grueling bar exam. After the exam, we were exhausted. We would have to wait about four months to find out whether we passed. Passing or failing is the difference between becoming a lawyer or finding another line of work. We split up after the exam. Dennis stayed in Roanoke, Joel went to Lynchburg, Henry went to Chicago, and I went to Richmond.

I arrived in Richmond on August 9, 1975. It was a Saturday night. I had found an apartment on the Southside of the city that cost $150 per month. I lugged my belongings into my apartment and sat on the floor to regroup. I remembered that one of the partners had told me that he was having a cocktail party that night, so I drove to a pay phone to tell him I was in town. I told him that I was dressed in jeans, a sport coat, and an open-necked shirt. I asked him if I could come to the party dressed that way. He said, "I don't think you would feel comfortable over here dressed like that." I figured that it was best not to go to the party. I was surprised, though, to hear someone tell me that I might feel uncomfortable about how I was dressed. To tell the truth, I felt quite comfortable dressed as I was. I looked the part of the preppy. I looked like most of my classmates from law school looked when they were not wearing coats and ties.

I went to work on Monday, August 11. On that day I signed up as the 156th lawyer who had ever worked at Hunton. The way things worked at the firm in those days was that each new lawyer was given a unique, nonreusable number that was for that person alone. If the lawyer left the firm, the number was retired. It was a sign of seniority. The older the lawyer, the lower the number. That numbering system worked out for me when I left the firm for the Supreme Court of Virginia, then returned later. My old number was simply reactivated along with my seniority.

When I started at the firm, its full name was Hunton, Williams, Gay & Gibson. Eppa Hunton, the son of the founder, was still there. Mr. Gay and Mr. Gibson were also there. But my first briefcase from the firm was marked "Hunton, Williams, Gay, Powell & Gibson." Justice Lewis F. Powell Jr. of the Supreme Court of the United States had left the firm in 1972 to go on the bench, but the old briefcases were still in use.

I was assigned to work on what was called the Vepco team. These were the lawyers who worked on utility rates and other business matters for the state's largest electric utility. I had asked for this assignment because I had concluded that if I was going to be a Black lawyer at an otherwise all-white firm, I needed to carve out a niche for myself and make sure that I was not a fungible commodity that could be easily replaced. I thought that the arcane world of utility rates and finance would give me such a niche. Later I would change my mind.

The leader of the Vepco team in August 1975 was Evans Brasfield. He was not there the day I started work so I was met by Mike Maupin, another partner on the team. Mike introduced me around and showed me to my office. It was on a floor the firm had recently annexed that was not outfitted like the floors where the more senior lawyers were housed. I was in what amounted to a cubbyhole of an office with a sliding door like a broom closet might have. The size of my small office was further diminished by the presence of a support beam for the building that took up a quarter of the space. There was barely room for a desk with a chair behind it and a bookcase. In front of the desk was room for one wooden chair. It was one of the worst offices in the firm, but it was mine and I had to get used to it.

Early in my time at the firm I had two quite different conversations with older lawyers who were partners. One lawyer came to see me to apologize for the firm's role in *Brown v. Board*. He said that some of the firm's lawyers wished that the firm had not gotten involved in the case. I was a bit surprised, but I thanked him for coming to see me. The next year, in 1976, that lawyer helped me land a job as co-counsel to the Carter-Mondale campaign in Virginia, a job in which I advised the state campaign on the federal election laws.

Another partner came to see me after I had been at the firm nearly a year. He told me that his father had been raised in such a way that he would not even have spoken to me if he had encountered me. The partner explained that he was not like his father. He went on to say that in the time I had been at the firm, I had "hit the ground running." Basically, he told me that I was doing a good job and that I should keep up the good work.

I was not sure what to think of these conversations; they were not the last. It was as if some of the white lawyers saw my presence as a chance to get things off their chests, to unburden themselves on matters of race.

Soon I got my first major research assignment. Vepco was in the process of building the North Anna nuclear power plant. The Sun Shipbuilding Company was building the heavy welded structures that would support key components of the power plant. There had been construction delays, and equipment for the plant was sitting in crates on the site waiting to be installed. All this equipment had warranties that extended for a certain time period after purchase; the question was whether you could extend the warranties further on equipment that could not be put into service because of construction delays. It was my job to find the answer; millions of dollars were at stake.

During those early days, in addition to doing research on the construction dispute at North Anna, I also worked on utility rate filings at the State Corporation Commission (SCC) on behalf of Vepco. We had to develop the facts to support requests for rate increases by valuing and accounting for the depreciation of things like utility poles, power lines, conduits, coal-fired power plants, trucks, cars, and buildings. We often worked with economists and accountants. They spoke their own private language of finance and economics, but we had to put their words into plain English so that nonexperts could understand what they were saying. It was hard to do. But one of the very senior partners at the firm, John Riley, had the magic touch when it came to translating the jargon of experts into readable, understandable briefs.

It was quite a process in which to participate. The young lawyers would pore over expert reports to locate the most important parts. We would then quote what we thought were the pertinent parts of the experts' thoughts and put them in a very rough draft of a brief for the SCC. Then we would give the draft to Mr. Riley, and it would come back from him written in the most beautiful language. That process of drafting and editing has stayed with me ever since. I learned early that the language of the law need not be opaque and impenetrable; the law could be readable and accessible, but it took a deft hand to write it that way.

As a young lawyer, I paid close attention to the way lawyers talked. I recall asking a partner if I could see a memorandum he had written regarding an issue I had been asked to work on. He responded, "Well, yes, John, let's look and see what I have opined on this subject." I had never heard anyone use the verb "opined." It sounded so highbrow to me, but lawyers at the firm said things like that.

I noticed too that if you asked the old lawyers what they thought about something, they typically would not say, "John, I think this" or "John, I think that." Instead, they would say, "John, in my judgment, we ought to do such-and-such." I had never heard anyone say "in my judgment." But soon I started using it. It seemed to give more authority to the simplest things.

I also noted that there was a big culture of going to lunch. The older lawyers would often come by to take a younger lawyer to lunch. Nothing fancy. A barbecue place on the first floor of our building was a popular spot. I did not get many invitations from the older partners to go to lunch. Usually, I would either get food and bring it back to my office or go to lunch with a group of young associates.

In addition to the socializing at lunch, I learned that there were often dinner parties at various partners' homes to which associates were invited. For a long time, I did not get any of those dinner invitations. But then someone broke the ice. I can't recall who gave me my first invitation, but it led to an opening of the floodgates. It appeared that nobody had wanted to go first, that they did not know what would happen if they invited a Black person to dinner at their home. I guess they thought I might cause a disturbance. But after I went to one home and sat and ate and talked and laughed and was sociable and had interesting things to add to the conversation, suddenly it seemed that I had become the trophy guest. I got so many invitations in rapid succession that I thought everyone was scrambling to be able to say that they had had the Black guy over to dinner.

Human nature is funny; most people don't like to be the first. They want to have assurance that when they do something, it has a likelihood of success because it has been done before. It is hard to be on the leading edge, to be treading into new territories. For me, living that way had been a part of my life from at least when I went to Maury. But for my white colleagues, matters of race relations probably seemed like a whole new world.

My little office did not have much space to decorate, but I tried. I had a small potted plant, something hanging on the wall, a few pictures of family members on my desk, and a radio that was tuned to WRVA for news, weather, and sports. One day I had to be out of the office on business and got back after five o'clock when the cleaning crew was there. When I went into my office my radio was gone. I was incensed. I did not have much. I was working all the time. I was the only Black person at the firm, and I suspected that someone on the cleaning crew—which was all-Black—had taken my radio. The idea that a Black person would take something from another Black person who was trying to integrate our divided society upset me a lot.

I went into the hallway and asked the first person I saw who had cleaned my office that day. I got no answer. Then I asked to see the supervisor. I brought him to my office. I told him that my radio was missing and that I had better get it back. Then I told him to tell the crew that nobody was going to leave the building that night without having their bags checked. I didn't have authority to search bags, but I was upset and I said it anyway. After I talked to the supervisor, I went to the restroom. When I got back to my office, my radio was on the top of my desk with the cord around it. Nothing else was taken from my office.

One of the things that I had to do that none of the young white lawyers at Hunton had to do was to join not only the white bar associations but also the Black bar association. Basically, I had to live in two worlds. In a way, I almost had to have a split personality. There was the way I talked, dressed, and spoke while downtown with my white colleagues, and there was the way I lived and socialized with Black people.

The Black bar association in Richmond in 1975 was known as the Old Dominion Bar Association (ODBA); it existed because of segregation. There was the Virginia State Bar, the state licensing authority, which was integrated because it had to be under the law. Then there were the private bar associations, and they were not integrated. The Richmond Bar Association and the Virginia Bar Association had historically existed for white lawyers. By the time I got to Richmond, I could and did join these groups. But for years all the Black lawyers had was the Old Dominion Bar Association, a statewide organization with local chapters.

I joined the Richmond chapter of the ODBA and went to my first meeting. When I walked in, the first thing I heard coming from a Black female lawyer who I did not know was this: "Oh, look, here comes that Uncle Tom nigger from Main Street." I thought to myself, "Isn't this something? I get greeted like this by my own people, when here I am trying to do the very thing that Martin Luther King died for—to integrate our society." This comment was not the end of it. A Black judge chimed in: "Yeah, he must love those white boys because he has never been to see me." To which I replied, "F—you! Where I come from, the people who already live in town reach out to welcome the new people who have just arrived. So why haven't I heard from any of you?" When I turned on the judge, a Black lawyer named Jim Benton—who was also from Norfolk and who had been at UVA law school when I was an undergraduate—ran to me, pushed me away from the judge, and said, "Calm down, man, calm down." Which I tried to do. But I was hot.

From my standpoint I was putting it all on the line every day, and yet other Black lawyers responded not with words of encouragement but with criticism. It was that same old thing. I was caught in the middle. In the mostly all-white environment downtown, I was not fully accepted. Nor did it appear that I was fully accepted in the Black community, where I had been born and raised.

After that introduction I stayed away from ODBA meetings. It was not until a Black lawyer named Gerald Poindexter said to me, "John, you need to come on back" that I did. I went on to serve on the board and executive committee of the ODBA and to sponsor various events at the statewide meetings using funds provided by my law firm.

At Hunton, I stayed on the Vepco team for only a short while. The dispute over the construction of the North Anna nuclear power plant turned into full-blown litigation, and I ended up doing so much research for the litigation lawyers that I asked to be reassigned to their team. This request was a result of a change in my philosophy about the best type of legal work for a person like me at a mostly white law firm. When I first got to the firm, I figured that the best way to make myself indispensable was to master an arcane specialty and to be the go-to person in that field. But, after being at the firm a while and seeing supposedly hard-working people be told to leave, I decided that the thing to do was to learn a fungible skill that I could take with me wherever I went. In my mind that skill was litigation, and so I sought to become a "gator," a courtroom lawyer skilled in questioning witnesses and arguing to the court and to juries.

On the litigation team, I was assigned to work with Ken Wheeler and his associate Doug Davis. I was the junior guy. I got the grunt work. I was the one who had to stay on weekends and on my birthday to pore over huge legal research books looking for just the right case. I was at the office so much that my friends started calling it my home. They would call my office number, and when I answered the phone late at night they would say, "I see that you are at home." I didn't mind. It just did not bother me to be in the library at all hours, so long as I was making progress. And nothing was more exhilarating to me than finding that one case, the needle in the haystack.

When I moved from the Vepco team to the litigation team, all the important litigation was in federal court. Our lawyers were all over the country in federal court. But it seemed that I kept being assigned to cases in Virginia state courts. I was not happy that even brand-new associates were being hired and immediately flying off to litigate in federal courts across the country, while I was in Lunenburg, Mecklenburg, Fredericksburg, Alexandria, Botetourt, and Augusta counties in Virginia seeking access to property so surveyors could lay out the route for a power line, or I was litigating cases where people had been injured by coming into contact with power lines. When I started going to court, I had several early successes. I won a motion here and a motion there. I started to feel like I belonged in court. While I was handling these state court cases, I did not see where my life was headed. I thought that I was being unfairly relegated to working on small cases. In fact, though I did not realize it at the time, I was in a master class on the intricacies of Virginia law.

When Ken, Doug, and I went on the road to litigate cases, I was shocked to find out that each of us had our own room at the hotel or motel where we stayed. I had never before had my own room in a hotel. The first time we traveled together on a case, I said to Doug, "I guess you and I will room together and Ken will have his own room." Doug looked at me like I was crazy. "Are you kidding?" he said. "We don't do roommates. We have our own rooms." I could hardly believe it.

The big case for Vepco against Sun Shipbuilding concerning the construction of the North Anna nuclear power plant was still raging, and we were involved in discovery in Pennsylvania, where the support structures for the steam generators had been fabricated. Part of our claim was that the welding work had not been up to Nuclear Regulatory Agency standards. I had to tote, in my big, black litigator bags, heavy chunks of welded materials cut from parts of the reactor cubicles. We would use these exhibits to confront witnesses about the welding errors shown in the exhibit: things like lack of full penetration welding, like "bridging," like the use of untempered steel. To help litigate the case I had to learn the language and techniques of a master welder.

The Sun Shipbuilding litigation involved the largest amount of money ever disputed in a Virginia court at that time. Part of our claim was that because of mistakes in constructing the North Anna nuclear power plant, Vepco had been forced to continue to generate power with fossil fuels instead of being able to generate power more economically with nuclear fuel. We argued that Sun Shipbuilding was responsible for the difference in the cost of fossil fuel over and above the cost of generating the same amount of power with nuclear fuel. It was my job to find the law that explained how to recover the damages we were seeking.

That research memorandum became known at the firm as "the Damages Memo." It ended up being more than a hundred pages long, covering damages in contract, damages in tort, direct damages, consequential damages, delay damages, you name it. It was meant to be a one-stop resource for calculating and recovering damages in a construction dispute. This is the kind of assignment that can make or break a young lawyer. It was a big case, with big money on the line, for a big client, in the glare of the news, and with the most senior partners in the firm looking over my shoulder. It was pretty much do-or-die for me.

The case was so massive that we had to engage computer experts to help track all the errors in each of the thousands of welds. This was a daunting task because we were at the dawn of litigation support computing, and data had to be encoded on punch cards, a very laborious process. So much data was involved, and computers were so new, that the best we could do was to arrange for a truck with a generator to sit outside the courthouse with the card-reading equipment on board and a cable running through a window in the building to send us results. Though that arrangement sounds antiquated today, at that time it was cutting edge and remarkably high tech. But we never got to see how our plan would work at trial because the case settled. Even so, I had worked on one of the first efforts in Virginia to use computers in support of litigation. That alone was a lesson in being adaptable and creative in the practice of law.

While working with Ken and Doug, I had the chance to make my first arguments to a jury. We had a case involving a collision between a truck owned by one of our clients and a local workman in southwest Virginia. Doug and I first went to this rural part of Virginia to take the deposition of the plaintiff. We later returned to move to dismiss the case based on passive versus active negligence. The argument we were making was fairly esoteric, but what happened in court with me—a Black man in a nearly all-white environment—shows what life was like for me back then, traveling the state representing big businesses and often being the first Black attorney that anyone had ever seen representing large corporate entities.

The case was in Mecklenburg County off Route 58, just beyond the site of a large maker of mobile homes. When Doug and I got to court to argue our motion, we found to our surprise that the plaintiff's lawyer was the local commonwealth's attorney, who prosecuted crime in his community. This meant that people in that part of the state looked up to and trusted this man. As Doug and I sat in the court-room, we watched the man who would be opposing us on our motion make an argument to the jury in a criminal case and then go into the judge's chambers. When he and the judge returned to the courtroom, the judge sentenced the defendant, released the jury, and turned to his civil docket, which meant that Doug and I were up next.

I made the argument about indemnity based on active versus pas-sive negligence. Opposing counsel—who moments before had been on display as the local criminal prosecutor—got up and said that he had never heard of such an argument and urged the court to deny our motion. Because I had made the motion and thus had the burden of persuading the court, I had the right to speak last. As soon as I stood up to talk, the judge said, "Young man, I have never heard of the legal argument that you are making in this court. I am inclined to deny your motion." I felt the quicksand surrounding my ankles, and I thought to myself that I had better do something fast or I was going to lose. I replied, "Your honor, I promise you that I learned about active versus passive negligence at the University of Virginia School of Law, which I just finished last year. And, if your honor will give me a chance to brief this issue, I am certain that I can persuade the court that this is solid Virginia law and that we are entitled to relief." The judge replied, "You say they taught you this over at UVA's law school?" I replied, "Yes, sir. Just a year or so ago."

The judge then turned to our opposing lawyer and said, "Do you think we should let him brief this thing?" Courts rarely if ever ask one lawyer what the court should do about another lawyer's argument. Not surprisingly, my opponent said no. But, to my amazement the judge let us brief the issue. After the briefs were submitted, he denied our mo-tion. But that day in court I had been quick enough on my feet to think of briefing the matter, and thus I gave us a small additional chance of prevailing.

When that case went to trial, Ken decided that he would let me make the opening statement and that Doug would do the closing ar-gument, which wraps up the case and is the last thing the jury hears before it retires to deliberate. In the theory of trials, the opening state-ment is meant to be a dispassionate recitation of what you expect to prove in your case. It is like a table of contents. It is called an opening *statement* because it is not supposed to be an argument. Its purpose is to lay out a road map for the jury so that they will be able to recognize how the evidence they hear fits into the structure of the case. On the other hand, the closing argument is meant to convince the jury that you have proved the things that you set out to prove, to show them that you have met your burden of proof. In the closing argument, you can argue the facts and the inferences arising from the facts; you can invoke reason and common sense.

When Ken asked me to do the opening, he had no idea of what it meant to have been raised in the Black Baptist Church. He did not appreciate the tone and timbre of my voice. He had no idea of the passionate way that I would go about promoting the truth as I saw it in our case. My opening statement was far from a dry, methodical outline of what we hoped to prove. Instead of saying things like "We intend to prove this" or "We believe that the evidence will show that," I said: "We will prove to you that our client did no wrong in this case. We will show you that our client used his best efforts to avoid this accident, and yet it occurred anyway." When I sat down Ken whispered in my ear, "That sounded like a closing argument."

When Doug got up to do the closing argument, he sounded careful and methodical and precise and dispassionate. In other words, his closing argument sounded like an opening statement, while my opening statement had sounded like a closing argument. Ken told us later that he should have switched our roles. I recall that we lost that case.

On another case, I thought that Ken treated me unfairly, and my reaction to what he did probably changed the course of my career. Though I usually was on a steady diet of Virginia state cases, Ken was handed a case in federal court that involved travel to Mexico. We represented a rigging company that moved huge pieces of equipment from one place to another. I mean the kind of equipment that is so large, one might have to close an interstate highway, cover it with two feet of sand, move the equipment across the highway at 3:00 a.m. to avoid the heaviest traffic, and then remove the thousands of tons of sand.

The equipment in question had to be moved from California to Arizona, and the best way to do it was through Mexico. Ken assigned me to the case at the outset. I did all the research about how to do what we needed to be done. But soon a trip to Mexico was required to resolve a sticky issue. Ken said that he thought it was time to get Doug involved. I was not sure what he meant. I knew that on a big case all three of us would naturally be involved, and so I thought that Ken meant that going forward, Doug would be involved in research, writing, client advice, and all the things that we did in handling a case. But then I learned that he meant that Doug would travel with him to Mexico, not me. I thought that was odd. Usually, the associate assigned to a case stayed on the case. Ken's decision bothered me. But there was nothing I could do about it. After all, I was just a very junior associate at the firm.

Ken and Doug flew off to Mexico while I stayed back in Richmond. And then the phone calls started coming from Ken: "John, what does the contract say about who has the right to determine the route?" I pulled out the contract and answered the question. The calls kept coming. Several times a day Ken and Doug would call me because they did not know the case the way I did. I answered all their questions. It was clear that if I had been with them in Mexico, I could have answered these questions on the spot. But I was back in Richmond because the partner I was assigned to was either uncomfortable traveling with me or he thought he owed it to Doug to give him a chance to travel internationally on a case. Either way, I was the odd man out. And I did not like it.

14

The White Firm, All-Nighters, and Brilliance

I was sufficiently bothered by what had happened on the Mexico case that I asked the head of the litigation team to assign me to another partner. I was sent to work with Tim Ellis, a relatively new litigation partner. Tim had the reputation of being an extremely hard-working, very demanding young partner. Several associates who had been assigned to him had quit the firm. When Tim was working on a case, he could become a blur of activity: "Bring me that decision!" "What is your analysis?" "How can we distinguish this?" "Have you gone through the documents and marked the ones that relate to each issue?" "Have you tracked down that witness?" And so forth, all at once.

In our minds, Tim resembled the Tasmanian Devil, the Looney Toons cartoon character that was depicted as a whirring buzz saw. Because Tim seemed to be a blur of frenetic activity, everybody on the litigation team called him Taz. He knew what we called him, but he did not seem to care, and he might even have liked it. Working with the Taz could easily be a career-ending event if you did not meet his expectations. Most of my fellow litigation associates felt sorry for me when I was assigned to the Taz.

In my first meetings with Tim, he gave me a research assignment that had to be completed immediately. I met with him on a Thursday or Friday, and the assignment had to be done by Monday. My birthday was that weekend, but the assignment took priority.

This was long before computer research, in the days of legal encyclopedias, slip opinions, and regional digests of opinions, which were very thick books in small print with blurbs about cases and case citations. To thoroughly research a matter, a young lawyer could easily wind up sitting on the floor surrounded by stacks of books, turning pages and taking notes on legal pads. That was precisely how I spent my birthday that year. But, by Monday morning I felt that I had found all the cases and had decided on the approach we needed to take in the argument we had to make. I was ready to report my conclusions to Tim.

But I did not know that Tim had a reputation for doing something that I had never heard of any other partner doing. Sometimes when Tim gave a young lawyer a research assignment, he would research the matter himself. When he met with the young lawyer he would compare their research results, and woe to the lawyer who had not found all the cases and authorities that Tim had.

Tim and I started by talking about our client's situation. I brought up a case and said that it seemed to serve us well. Tim mentioned another case. I explained the difficulty with that case and pointed out that it had been decided before a change in the statute and thus was not very helpful. We went on like that for some time. I raised a case, he raised another case, and we hashed it out. In the end, Tim realized that I had read all the cases that he had brought up and that I had found the crucial authorities related to our issue. When he realized that, he accepted my approach to the case. I had gotten off to a good start with the Taz.

Tim and I started trying cases together, the intense cerebral former navy aviator educated at Princeton, Harvard, and Oxford and the young Black kid from the housing projects of Norfolk who was educated at UVA but raised in the oratorical traditions of the Black Baptist Church. As we won cases together, some of our litigation colleagues started calling us "Blackman and Robin."

One of our cases involved a very public dispute that was on a fast track to the Supreme Court of Virginia. An anonymous tipster had told the Richmond City Council that one of their members had been elected to the council even though he had been convicted of a felony and his civil rights had never been restored by the governor. The city council retained Tim and me to advise them how to proceed. We filed at the Supreme Court of Virginia the writ of quo warranto, which asks the question, "On what authority do you hold office?" The case was in the news because if this one person was removed from his seat, then either the city council or a circuit judge could fill the vacancy depending on which legal theory was applied.

Since we represented the moving party in the dispute, our side would get to make the opening argument to the Supreme Court. Then, after the other side responded, our side would get to make a rebuttal argument. In other words, we would argue first and last. Tim decided to let me make the opening argument and he would argue on rebuttal. The idea was that if I got into trouble in the opening, he could fix things on rebuttal.

As I argued the opening, the justices were highly engaged. They asked several questions. I explained the matters that they were concerned about. I sat down. The opposing lawyer got up to make his argument. Again, the justices were active. They asked opposing counsel about points that I had made in the opening. The opposing lawyer sat down. It was time for Tim's rebuttal.

Tim went to the podium: "May it please the court, I am Tim Ellis . . ." Almost as soon as he got his name out, one of the justices said, "Mr. Ellis, are you sure that you want to say anything?" For an experienced lawyer, that is a loaded question. Basically, it was a signal to Tim that the justices thought they had already heard enough from the opening argument. The underlying message is that if you say anything else you might risk messing up the case; you might snatch defeat from the jaws of victory. Tim quickly got the message. He immediately said, "No, your honor, I have nothing more to add. We ask that the court grant the relief we have requested on brief. Thank you." Then Tim sat down. We packed up and left the Supreme Court.

As Tim and I walked into the hallway outside of the courtroom, several well-dressed older Black men came up and hugged me. They told me that I had done a great job in court and that they were proud of me. One of the men turned to Ellis and said, "And you did okay too." I did not know any of these men, but I knew what they were trying to say. They could remember a time when a Black person could hardly be found in that building doing anything other than sweeping the floors. So, for them to see a young Black man standing before the Supreme Court of Virginia engaging in a give-and-take with the justices was the stuff of their hopes and dreams.

When we returned to our office, all Tim could talk about was how he did not have a chance to get a word in about the case. But he was not upset; if anything, he was quite pleased. Later that day, the court issued an order in the case granting the relief that we had requested. It was a good day.

That year the firm asked me to find a band for the annual Christmas party at the Country Club of Virginia. I called John "Chops" Turner, an older Black man who played the jazz organ and who was popular in and around Norfolk, my hometown. He had singers and musicians who could play anything from jazz to soul music. He agreed to drive to Richmond to play the party. We signed a contract for his band to play a certain number of hours. But my colleagues and their spouses liked the music so much that when his contracted time expired, some of the guys came to me to ask whether he would agree to play longer. I explained that he had already played for as long as the contract provided. Somebody said, "Ask him if he will play longer if we pay a little more." He agreed. The guys took up a collection and I handed it to him. I don't know how much it was, but we had a great time at that party. And sometime during the band's intermission, with the "Batman" theme playing over the sound system, Tim and I made an entrance dressed as, you guessed it, Blackman and Robin, to the shouts and cheers of our colleagues.

That same Christmas, I went to Norfolk to visit my mother and my family. When I got to her house, everybody looked in despair. My mother showed me an eviction notice: "We have to move out of the house." I had known nothing of what was going on; this was a total surprise to me. I tried to understand what was happening.

My mother had been talked into a business scheme where she would buy vending machines and put them in supposedly high-traffic locations, and thus she would make tons of money. The business was foolproof, she was told, and she need not tell her son the lawyer because as a grown woman she could take care of herself. All she needed to do to get these machines was to sign some papers and pledge her house as collateral. Well, the plan wasn't foolproof, the vending machines did not make money, and when she couldn't pay the note for buying the machines, the creditor foreclosed on her house.

I went scurrying around, trying to figure out how to stave off the foreclosure. First, I had to post a bond. Then I had to file suit on my mother's behalf against the vending machine people and everyone who had urged this plan on her. The case was set for trial in Norfolk. The firm let me handle it, and Tim came to Norfolk to try the case with me. We had sued to rescind the entire transaction for violation of consumer protection laws.

It was a bench trial. I put on some of the witnesses and made some arguments. Near the end of the proceeding, the judge made a comment that cut strongly against the theory of our case. He said, "I think she knew full well what she was doing. Her son is a lawyer at the biggest firm in the state; all she had to do was ask him. So, I don't think she was duped or misled." When I heard that, all the air went out of me, my legs felt weak, and I almost fell down. Tim saw my distress and leapt to his feet to argue the point that was being discussed. I cannot remember what Tim said, but I know he came to my rescue. Whatever he argued, he got the judge's attention and the judge ultimately ruled in our favor. We managed to save my mother's house from foreclosure. But that was not the last time that I was surprised by some drama at my mother's house.

Tim and I continued to try cases and handle disputes together. One of our cases involved the need to secure a preliminary injunction. Such cases come on in a hurry and move extremely fast in the court system. Everything is rushed because you are trying to get priority on the court's docket for an expedited hearing. You are working twenty-four to thirty-six hours at a time trying to get affidavits or line up live witnesses. There are briefs to be written and motions to be filed. It is a whirlwind of activity. While we were doing all this, I told Tim that I was working too hard, that I had not slept in a while, and that I was tired. Tim, who often had a wry sense of humor, said, "Let me see your hands." I did. He said, "I don't see the stigmata, which means that you are not being crucified, which means that you can work harder. So, don't be telling me that you're tired." At that moment I did not feel much like laughing, so I said, "Sure, Tim." And I kept going.

As I continued to work with Tim, I was getting closer to the time I would be considered for partnership. I had arrived at Hunton on

August 11, 1975, and I was up for partner on April 1, 1982. If I made partner at that time, I would have been at the firm six years and seven months.

In order to enhance my chances, Tim decided to have me work for all the partners who he knew were the most difficult to convince that someone was worthy of becoming a partner. I would see Tim and he would say, "Pusey needs some help on a research matter; I told him you would do it. Go see him." "Mr. Riley needs your help on the util-ity rate case he is working on. Go see him." And off I would go. I did research for just about every leading corporate partner in the firm. It was another do-or-die situation. Either I would work with these guys and dazzle them, or I would go down in flames. It was an intense time. I felt like I was in law school exams on a twenty-four-hour, day-after-day basis. I was researching and offering my judgment on a range of complex legal issues.

Amidst that vortex of activity, I received a serious set of mixed mes-sages within minutes. One of our corporate clients had a coal mine that was flooded in a downpour, which led to a cave-in. The corporate partner wanted my advice on an insurance claim that had been filed regarding the damage to the mine and to equipment that was buried in the collapse and was thus unusable. The policy contained an in-land marine sue-and-labor clause. I had never seen nor heard of such a thing. The policy also contained an exclusion saying that it would not cover the rebuilding of a collapsed mine. Sue-and-labor clauses were developed hundreds of years ago in the shipping industry. These clauses told a ship owner that if his ship was in danger, he could not just stand there and watch the ship and its cargo sink or be destroyed and then come to the insurer seeking payment for the loss. Instead, the ship-owner was required to fight—that is, to sue and labor—to save the ship and its cargo. Only then could the shipowner collect on the policy and the insurance company would pay the amounts expended in the effort to sue and labor for the ship.

Applying that theory to the problem of a collapsed mine, you can have a situation where very expensive equipment is down in the mine, and under the sue-and-labor clause the mine owner is required to fight to save that equipment. The owner cannot just sit by and watch the equipment get swallowed up. But in trying to save it, the owner might move debris out of the way, prop up a wall, or clear a passageway enough to get the equipment out of harm's way. Yet, there is an exclusion in the policy against coverage for rebuilding the mine.

How do you sort this out? I advised that we had a good claim under the sue-and-labor clause. The insurance company had said no. Based on my advice, the client stood its ground and recovered more than it had expected.

I went to my office on a Saturday, which was typical for young lawyers of that era. I opened a letter from the client. It contained glowing words of praise for the research I had done and the advice I had given regarding the insurance claim. The client said that had it not been for me telling it to stand tough, it might well have taken millions less on the claim. That kind of letter is a good thing when you are up for partner.

That same Saturday morning, I was called to the office of the head of the litigation team, E. Milton Farley, to go over my review for that year. Milton, who smoked cigars and generally had a brusque manner, sat me down and launched into his review: "Thomas, some of my partners say that you are brilliant. But other partners say that you do not pay attention to detail. I believe the partners who say the latter. So, let me just tell you this: you have one more year to be consistently brilliant or you are out of here! You understand me, Thomas?" Milton did not give me any details about the sources of the criticism. He did not tell me the way in which I was not consistently brilliant or in which I had failed to pay attention to detail, so I was left to wonder what I had actually done and who was complaining about me. There was no way for me to find out, so all I could do was keep plowing ahead.

I went back to my office thinking, "Now isn't this a blip? I just helped this client to a really good result, and minutes later the litigation team leader is handing me my head." I sat there stunned, wondering what it took to satisfy these people.

Another thing that was important in the quest to become a partner was doing pro bono work for the courts and the bar. One of the things that I did was to serve on the district committee of the bar in Richmond. This was part of the disciplinary structure when lawyers were charged with ethical violations. The district committees considered charges brought against lawyers, held hearings in those cases, and recommended various levels of discipline.

In my work on the district committee, I saw cases involving lawyers who I knew. One of the recurring claims against lawyers was the violation of escrow rules. If a lawyer holds money in escrow, it means that the money belongs to someone else and cannot be used for any purpose other than what it is designated for. It is an immediate violation to take money out of escrow, even if you put it back before it is needed for its designated purpose. We also had cases where lawyers missed deadlines for taking various steps in a case or in a legal matter like a closing. In other cases lawyers simply failed to communicate with their clients; either they didn't answer phone calls or they failed to respond to letters. In the cases we worked on, we could recommend a range of sanctions, from a private or public reprimand to temporary suspension of the lawyer's license or revocation of the license. We did not have final authority to impose these sanctions, but our recommendations were taken into consideration at the next level in the disciplinary process, which ultimately went all the way up to the Supreme Court of Virginia.

My work on the district committee was the closest thing to judging that I had engaged in prior to joining the Supreme Court of Virginia. As a committee member I had to evaluate legal arguments, assess facts, decide what I thought the truth was of a case, and recommend what the sanction should be. My committee work benefited me when I was on the Supreme Court.

15

Cocktail Parties, Making Partner, and Getting Married

From time to time in the 1970s and '80s, the firm would have cocktail parties at the home of John Riley, the chairman of the firm's executive committee. He lived in a beautiful home in Richmond's West End. The parties were usually catered by the Lamberts, a prominent Black family well known for their wonderful recipes and their classic style of catering. At my first cocktail party at Riley's house, I came directly from the office because I had been working late. I was solo that night, so aside from the Lamberts I was the only person of color there.

I was in the garden talking to some of my associates when I looked up and saw Justice Lewis Powell of the Supreme Court of the United States standing by himself holding a drink. I immediately thought that this might be my only chance to talk to one of the nine justices of the nation's highest court. I walked over and introduced myself. He knew who I was; he had long ago been told that the firm had hired its first Black lawyer. I decided to ask him a question for which I had wanted an answer for a long time. "Justice Powell," I said, "what difference does oral argument make after you have read all the briefs and read the cases and have been over the written arguments before you hear the oral argument?" He said, "Well, most of the time the oral argument does not change the view that you have of the case from reading the briefs and the cases. But, in maybe 5 to 10 percent of the cases, the argument of the lawyers can change your view of the case. This only happens when a lawyer finds the linchpin of the case and pulls it; this hardly ever happens if a lawyer simply stands there and rereads the brief, because then all the lawyer is doing is telling you what you already know." I said, "Thank you, Justice Powell, that makes a lot of sense."

A few years later when I was on the bench listening to oral argument, I saw the very thing that Justice Powell had described. I called it the Damascus Road effect, from the story in the Bible about how Saul had been converted to Paul. Every now and then a lawyer would make an argument that changed my mind about the proper disposition of the case. The first time it happened was during argument in a criminal appeal where the lawyer for the criminal defendant was trying to get the conviction reversed and the lawyer for the Virginia Attorney General's Office was arguing that the conviction should be affirmed. The lawyer arguing to uphold the conviction was a woman from the AG's office who seemed to get all the tough cases where a reversal might seem likely. I went on bench thinking that the commonwealth was probably wrong in the case, but the young assistant attorney general made such a strong argument that she changed my view of the case. When all the justices met to confer, I advanced the position that she had convinced me of. Ultimately we reversed the decision, but still this young lawyer had changed my mind by her advocacy.

At another cocktail party at Riley's house—for reasons that I don't now remember—I walked up to him and said, "Mr. Riley, how do you feel knowing that if you had won the argument in *Brown v. Board* cases, I would not have been able to come to this firm?" He was standing in a group of about five or six people. One of them was an associate of my seniority who jumped between me and Mr. Riley and said, "How dare you talk to Mr. Riley like that?" It was plain to me that this young lawyer was trying to curry favor with Mr. Riley, but it did not work. Riley turned on the young lawyer and said, "Sit down and shut up." Then he turned to me and started talking about the *Brown v. Board* case in which the firm had represented Prince Edward County in the suit that was brought on behalf of Barbara Johns of Farmville. As Riley and I talked, a crowd gathered round. There I stood in the center of a circle with Riley while my colleagues and their spouses sipped their gin and tonics and listened.

Riley said, "John, let me tell you about that case. We had a client come to us and ask us to take a lawful position in a court case. I did the research on that case myself, and I can guarantee you that the law of the United States at that time was separate but equal. So, in defending Prince Edward County we were doing what lawyers do all the time—we found the applicable law and presented it to the court on behalf of our client." What happened in *Brown,* he added, was that the Supreme Court changed the law. He went on: "I can tell you that I am happy you are at the firm, but the firm did not do anything wrong or out of the ordinary in taking that case. And one more thing," he said, "when Prince Edward County decided not to obey the ruling of the Supreme Court, we ended our representation of them."

I thought that Riley's answer made sense. I knew that separate but equal was once the law of the land, and I knew that in *Brown v. Board* the Supreme Court struck down that rule. I decided I could live with the idea that Hunton had played a lawyer-like role in the case and that when their side lost the firm moved on. I was part of the moving on.

A few months after that conversation with Mr. Riley, I went to him with a complaint about efforts to recruit lawyers of color to the firm. Because I was the first Black lawyer at the firm, when questions of recruiting more people of color came up, I was usually invited into the conversation: "John, we need you to help us find more Black lawyers." "Okay," I always said, and then I would go on the recruiting trips to the schools where the firm focused its hiring efforts. Over the years, a handful of lawyers of color came to the firm either as summer associates or first-year hires, but not many of them stayed.

Sometimes I would recommend a law student to be hired, but the recruiting committee would not make an offer. In one situation, the recruiting committee had gotten an application from a lawyer of color and had asked me to check on his references and credentials—in other words, to do due diligence. I made all the phone calls and read all I could about the candidate, and I received good reports. When I went to the recruiting committee to give my positive report, one of the partners said that he wanted more information and that I should continue my due diligence. I got upset and said, "I have had enough of this. I did what you wanted me to do and I came back with a good report, but that is not enough for you. It is as if you want to find a reason not to hire this man. I'm not playing this game anymore." Then I got up and slammed the door on the way out. My friend Alan Rudlin was in that meeting; he told me later that he had no idea what was going to happen after I stormed out of the room because no one had ever seen an associate slam a door on a partner. I did not know what would happen either. I suppose that I could have been fired that day, but at that moment I didn't care. I was tired of what appeared to me to be playacting about recruiting lawyers of color.

I went to see Mr. Riley to explain that on more than one occasion I had helped identify a candidate of color, but that it seemed to me the recruiting committee was looking for reasons not to hire minority students, and I was tired of it. Riley said, "John, let me tell you this. It is easy to hire someone, but the hard part is letting someone go when they don't work out. So here is what I'm willing to do: when you find a student who you think can do the work here, you come to me and tell me and we will make an offer. But you have to agree with me now that if that person does not work out, you will stand shoulder to shoulder with me when time comes to tell that person that they have to leave the firm." I thought his proposal was fair, so I said, "Okay, it's a deal. Let's start with the person who I was just discussing at the recruiting committee meeting." And not long thereafter, that person got an offer from the firm. He came to the firm for a few years then left to join another Richmond law firm. Later he became a judge.

Tim Ellis continued his efforts to make sure that I worked for every key partner in the firm. And I did. But even so, the effort to make partner at a big firm can be tough. Thus, a young lawyer needs all the help he or she can get to navigate that process. Some of the help I received came from unexpected sources.

A year or so before I was officially up for partner, I got a visit from a partner, Don Irwin, who was not on the litigation team and with whom I had never worked directly. The only way I knew him was because he had gone to Princeton and Tim had gone to Princeton, and the Princeton guys at the firm hung around together in and outside the office. Don came to my office to tell me that my billable hours were not as high as those of my contemporaries, and that I needed to get them up or it would count against me when it was time to consider new partners. I have always appreciated what Don did. He did not have to reach out to me. We did not work on the same subject matter team, and we had only spoken in passing at parties. Yet there he was standing in my office giving me advice to help me make partner. I thanked Don, and I asked Tim to find more work for me so that I could finish the year with higher billable hours.

I made partner on April 1, 1982. The story made the local news and was picked up by some of the publications focused on lawyers. When I made partner at Hunton, not only did I become the first Black partner at the firm, I became the first Black person in the history of the South to come to one of the old, white, southern law firms and to go up the line from associate to partner. The reason for that longwinded description is to distinguish me from the few Black lawyers who had become lateral partners at some white southern firms before I made partner at Hunton. A lateral is brought into a firm as a partner; they don't go through the years of scrutiny and toil that someone who starts as an associate has to endure.

One of the things that sticks in my mind about becoming a partner was signing the partnership agreement. The day after I made partner, I came to my office and found a thick packet of papers with my name on it in a sealed manila envelope marked "confidential." The envelope contained the partnership agreement along with a page for me to sign and date and thus add myself to the partnership. As I looked through that document, I saw the signatures of the partners who had come before me, signatures like Hunton's and Justice Powell's and other important leaders of the firm. I thought to myself, "This is historic." I took out my best fountain pen and signed the agreement. I put all the papers back in the envelope, resealed it, and sent it on its way. And then I exhaled.

I surprised myself when I exhaled because I had not realized that I had been holding my breath. It was as if I had been holding my breath all those years, from when I arrived until I made partner. I had been running hard, pushing myself, almost exhausted, determined not to fail, hoping that I could cross the finish line. I really do not think I knew how tense I had been until I felt the tension leave me as I signed that piece of paper. I had done something that no Black person in the American South had ever done. I felt all of that history. But, of course, that was not the end of my story.

A few months before the firm voted on whether I would make partner, I went to see Governor Charles Robb to talk to him about my hope to be appointed to the board of visitors of my alma mater, the University of Virginia. I spent only a few minutes with the governor telling him about my time at UVA and explaining why I thought I was a good candidate for the board. Nothing came of that conversation.

But the day I visited the governor, I noticed a very attractive woman working in one of the offices near the governor. The nameplate on her desk said "Miss Pearl Walden." That nameplate caught my attention. Women had started using Ms. instead of Miss, so it was a bit of a surprise to see that word. She had a pleasant voice and from what I could tell a good disposition, and I thought, "That's my wife." I asked about her and found out that she worked with my friend Judy Johnson, a lawyer I had known for years in the Old Dominion Bar Association. I called Miss Walden, but we kept having conflicts as I tried to set up a lunch date or a meeting after work.

Before I could arrange to see her, the firm elected me to the partnership. One of the rites of passage in those days was a roast of the new partners. I tried to get a date for the roast. I asked a woman who I had known for a short while, but she said she was busy. I thought about asking Miss Walden but heard from others in the governor's office that she would be busy at the Capitol at the time of the roast. I called Judy Johnson and asked her whether there was any way Miss Walden might be able to leave work at the Capitol in time to go with me to the partners roast.

Then I called Miss Walden and invited her to the party. She said she probably couldn't come because of demands at work, but after she checked she told me she could come after all. So, my first date with Miss Walden was the roast for the new partners. I am sure that for her that first date must have been something like a baptism of fire. Almost all the other people at the party had known each other for years. She was a completely new face in the room. People were introducing themselves and trying to find out who she was. We did not stay long at the roast, and shortly after Tim Ellis delivered his comedic lines about me (they were very funny and had the room laughing), we left. I took her to my condo overlooking Fountain Lake, where I had the makings of a late dinner that I prepared.

When I told my mother that I had met a young woman named Walden from Suffolk, she got very excited. "The Waldens from Suffolk? Really? Your granddaddy's best friend was Obadiah Walden, and if this is the same Waldens, our families have known each other for years." As it turned out, these were the same Waldens. Indeed, my mother had been the Women's Day speaker at the Waldens' family church back in 1956, and I remember being there because my mother had told me that the church was in Holland. When we arrived my mother said, "Here we are." And I said with all the understanding of a six-year-old, "Momma, this is not Holland. I don't see any windmills or any people wearing wooden shoes."

After our first date in April 1982, Pearl and I saw each other regularly. She invited me to Suffolk for Sunday dinner with her family. When we got to her family home, the first thing I noticed was that cars were parked all over the place. When we went inside, the house was filled with people. There were aunts, uncles, siblings, cousins—a big crowd. I said to one of her aunts, "Do y'all meet like this every Sunday?" Aunt Nita replied, "Yes, we do, and next week we are going to meet to talk about you." I thought, "Okay, this is fun. A big happy family with wisecracking aunts." I too came from a big family, so I was used to such gatherings.

Our relationship was on a good trajectory. Both of us had family members finishing Hampton University in June 1982, so we went to the graduation together. We both showed up that day wearing the blue and white of Hampton.

Later in the month we went to the state bar meeting at Virginia Beach. While we were there, I decided to propose to her. But I did not want to propose until I had an engagement ring. I had looked at rings back in Richmond at Schwarzschild's, and I had one in mind for her. I figured that I needed to go back to Richmond, get the ring, then propose to her at some nice restaurant on the way back to the beach. I told her that I had left some papers at my condo in Richmond that I needed at the bar meeting, so I had to make a quick trip to Richmond then back to Virginia Beach. Off we went.

When we got to Richmond, I got the ring, put it in my pocket, picked her up, and started back to Virginia Beach. As we drove, I tried to think of a good place to stop. But every place I thought of was closed. We kept driving. I got off the interstate and got on Shore Drive, figuring that some nice place had to be open near the water. I kept looking as we got closer to the bar meeting. Finally, I saw a place called the Duck-In that was open. It was not all that fancy, but it would have to do. We went in, ordered something to eat, and I proposed. She said yes! Great day.

When we left the bar meeting, we drove to Suffolk so that I could ask her father for permission to marry her. When we got to the house there were a few people present but not a big crowd.

I found her father and said, "Mr. Walden, can I see you for a minute? I have something to ask you." He said, "Young man, you have to have an appointment to see me." I said, "Mr. Walden, I would love to make an appointment, but this is urgent and I need to see you tonight." He relented and said, "Well, if it is so urgent come on back to my office." He and I left the living room, went to his office, and closed the door. I cannot imagine what the others thought was going on with me and Pearl's father behind closed doors.

When I had him alone, I said, "Mr. Walden, I love your daughter and have asked her to marry me. I want to ask your permission for us to get married." He said, "I want to hear what my daughter has to say about this." I went into the living room, got Pearl, returned to the office, and closed the door. Before too long, Mrs. Walden knocked on the door and came in to find out what was going on. Mr. Walden said to his wife, "Ruby, this young man says he wants to marry our daughter, and Pearl has said yes." Mrs. Walden broke into a big smile and Mr. Walden said, "Get out the wine glasses and tell everybody." That was June 17, 1982.

Later, Pearl and I talked about when we should get married. I said, "What's your birthdate?" She said October. Mine is in September. As it turned out, there are forty-two days between our birthdays, and each year they fall on the same day of the week. In 1982 our birthdays fell on a Saturday. The middle Saturday between our birthdays was October 9. That was the day we picked for our wedding. We had our first date in April. Got engaged in June. And got married in October. When we got married, we could not know that six months later I would be on the Supreme Court of Virginia. Events in our lives were moving with blinding speed.

We got married in Richmond. We moved into my condo at Fountain Lake, then we bought a house on Monument Avenue. In the mornings, she went to work in the governor's office and I went to work on Main Street. We were young, busy, happy, having a wonderful time together and with friends and families.

16

The Life of a Justice, a Brain Tumor, and Leaving the Court

Governor Robb announced my appointment to the Supreme Court of Virginia on April 11, 1983. By April 15 I had packed up, left the law firm, and was at the court. When I got there, I was out of sync with the court's calendar. The time for recruiting law clerks had come and gone. I dealt with that problem by hiring one of the staff clerks, Pat Davis, as my personal clerk. Pat knew her way around the court, knew the people in the clerk's office, and knew the personal clerks of the other justices. But still I felt like I had been thrown into a relay race long after the race had started. It was as if I had to put on my track shoes while running. And then I had to catch up, take the baton, and be sure not to drop it. I could not make a misstep because all of Virginia was watching.

The scrutiny I was under was palpable. How could a thirty-two-year-old lawyer be a Supreme Court justice? Isn't he too young? What does he know about life? How can the people of Virginia rely on someone so young to make critical decisions for the millions of citizens of Virginia? And then there was, Did they put him on the court simply because he's Black and they wanted to integrate the court, or does he really know what he's doing? I knew those questions were percolating because from time to time people would ask me directly. But by then I was on the court and had to get to work. And there was plenty of work to do.

One part of the work of a justice is to choose the cases that will be heard by the full court. In that process, the justices sit on panels—

typically in groups of three—and listen to arguments from the losing side at the lower court as they try to explain why their petition for appeal should be granted by the panel of justices and then heard by the whole court.

At the petition stage, the vote of one justice to grant the petition is enough to bring a matter on to be heard by the full court. Usually, more than one justice voted to grant a petition. And usually if a single justice granted an appeal, the others on the panel would give that one justice a little bit of grief. They would say things like "Since you are the only one who wanted to grant this case, it seems only fair that you should have to write the opinion in this case." But once a petition was granted the case was put on the argument docket for review by all seven justices.

To decide which of the granted cases would be assigned to which of the seven justices, we would draw numbers from a hat. The clerk of court kept an old fedora for this purpose. All the justices would gather in the chief's chambers and the clerk would put seven pieces of paper in the hat. Six were blank and the seventh had a "1" written on it. Whoever drew No. 1 would get the first case on the docket, then the next justice in seniority would get the next case, and so forth. If I, as the No. 7 justice, drew the first case on the docket, then the chief justice would get the next case. But because of the chief's administrative duties, he was only assigned two decisions per session, while the rest of us were assigned four decisions per session. Thus, in a normal session twenty-six cases would be decided—that is, six times four, plus two. In addition, there were some cases that, by statute, had priority on the docket. When these cases came to the court, they pushed the other cases back.

In general, there were seven weeks between court sessions. It went like this: at the end of a week of hearing cases, each justice would have a week apiece for each of the four decisions he had to write. Once the four weeks for drafting and editing the decisions were over, there were three weeks left for the justices to read the twenty-six sets of briefs and the key cases cited in the briefs to get ready for the next court session. This schedule was adhered to for the first few years I was on the court, but events made us change.

Court observers and lawyers often talk about whether an appellate court has a "hot" or a "cold" bench. A hot bench means that the judges are fully engaged with the lawyers, asking questions, making comments, and taking an active part in the proceedings. A cold bench is one where the judges might sit there for the whole argument and say nothing at all. In the '80s the Fourth Circuit was known as a hot bench; their questions might start even before the lawyer finished saying, "May it please the court." The Supreme Court of Virginia was known as a very cold bench. A lawyer could argue and get no questions at all. And even if there was a question, it might only be "Where can I find that statement in the record?"

Typically, lawyers like a hot bench because the questions from the judges let them know what the judges are concerned about. This helps the lawyers focus their attention on what the argument should try to clarify. In my own life as an advocate, I liked a hot bench. It was boring to me to argue to a bench where no one said anything. And when I was on the bench listening to arguments, I was usually curious enough about something in the case that I asked questions.

At the Supreme Court of Virginia, there was a rule of thumb among the lawyers that the justice who asked questions during oral argument was likely the justice who would write the opinion. Because each justice went on the bench with preassigned responsibility to write between two and four decisions, it was natural for a justice to find out as much as he could regarding those cases. Thus, the idea that a justice to whom a case was assigned would ask questions was not wrong. It's just that I was curious about all the cases, so I asked questions in almost all of them. This meant that it was hard to guess which decisions were assigned to me for writing.

Before I went on the bench, I read all the briefs. I might or might not read the appendices, depending on the nature of the case. But I would surely try to understand the legal arguments and the cited cases. Of course, I had more information on the cases assigned to me. I had the actual record of those cases in my chambers. I wrote questions and comments in the briefs. Sometimes I might clip a note to the front of the brief to remind me of what I wanted to ask about.

I don't know how the other justices prepared for oral argument, but I did notice that they almost never asked a question in a case assigned to another justice. During one court session, I found out why they acted that way. We were in the midst of oral argument, and I was almost in a dialogue with a lawyer who was arguing a case that was assigned to another justice. That case was the last on the day's schedule, so when we finished we left the bench, went to the robing room, then went upstairs to conference the cases and give our initial assessments of how we would vote on them.

As we left the bench, I was walking beside the justice to whom the case had been assigned. He was complaining: "It seems to me that if we don't give the lawyers more time to argue, somebody is going to take up all the time with questions and we are not going to get a thing from the lawyers." I was the "somebody" he was talking about as he walked beside me, but he kept on as if I wasn't there. "I don't know why somebody has to keep asking question after question." We took off our robes and went upstairs.

In the conference room we started with the chief's cases and went by seniority through the others. When we got to the cases for the justice who had walked beside me complaining about my questions, one of the other justices said, "I'm pretty sure that the lawyer in this case said something in response to one of John's questions that has conceded his whole case. Play back the argument tape." As the tape was playing, one of the justices said, "You hear that? That's a judicial admission, isn't it?" The other justices started chiming in: "That's right. What he just said means that we should never have granted this case. We ought to dismiss this as an improvident grant." And that is what happened. That meant that the justice who had complained about my questions had one less decision to write; he went from four to three. But he never thanked me for reducing his workload by 25 percent. But he at least stopped complaining about the questions I asked.

As we all talked about oral argument, I soon realized that the other justices had been taught something quite different than what I had been taught. I had finished law school in 1975; they had finished in the '50s or earlier. They had been taught that oral argument belonged to the lawyers, that it was the lawyer's time to explain the case and to make clear to the justices why the disposition the lawyer sought was appropriate.

My training had been completely different. My generation of lawyers was taught that oral argument was for the judges, that it was the time for the judges to let the lawyers know what questions or problems they had with the case. After the initial complaints about my questions, the whole court discussed the difference in the way the younger lawyers were being taught about oral advocacy. As a result, the bench at the Supreme Court of Virginia got a bit hotter than it had been.

At another oral argument, a lawyer gave me an answer that I thought was inappropriate. And I reacted immediately. A senior member of the bar was arguing the case. As usual for me, I had questions. While he was talking I said, "Excuse me, counselor, can you tell the court how the statute comes into play on the facts of this case?" Usually when a justice asks a question, the lawyer answers the question then moves on to the next point. That is not what this lawyer did. Instead, he looked at me and said tersely, "I'll get to that in a minute." My immediate internal reaction was that this is my courtroom, and a lawyer can't treat me that way in my own court. I thought that maybe he said that because I was the junior justice or because I was 32 or because I was Black—but I did not think any reason was acceptable. I replied, "No, you won't. You will get to this right now." The lawyer then answered my question.

As we were leaving the bench, one of the justices said that he was sure that lawyer had never been talked to like that by anyone, and that he had worried that the old lawyer might faint after being required to answer a question that he did not want to address. In my view, the lawyer had probably never been questioned by a person of color, and he was bothered that I had interrupted his argument with a question. Whatever was going on, I was determined that at least in court I would not accept being treated differently from the other justices.

I was treated differently on other occasions as well. For example, when Governor Gerald Baliles was inaugurated, several of the justices decided to attend to represent the judicial branch of government. Our robes were put in a room at the Capitol that was set aside for us. We entered the room in order of seniority, with the chief first, followed by Cochran, then Poff, then Compton, then Russell, then Stephenson, then me. A doorman held open the door to the room. As we walked in, the chief justice said, "Harry Carrico" and the doorman replied, "Mr. Chief Justice"; Cochran said, "George Cochran" and the doorman replied, "Mr. Justice Cochran"; and so on. When my time came I said, "John Thomas" and the doorman replied, "John." There it was again. That same old prejudice. No Negro is worthy of a title. It was the way that my grandmother and mother were called by their first name by any white person, even a white child. I decided that from then on I would introduce myself as Justice Thomas.

Returning to events in the courtroom, it's worth noting that sometimes things were not completely serious on the bench. One of the things that appellate lawyers are taught is not to distract the court during oral argument. For example, don't show up in an orange three-piece suit with pink elbow pads and wonder why the judges are fixated on looking at your clothes rather than listening to your argument.

During one session a lawyer came to argue who was obviously wearing a toupee; it was askew and was nowhere near the color of the rest of his hair. It was as if he had just laid a hairpiece on his head. It was impossible not to notice. It was one of those distractions that lawyers are warned about. The justices could not stop looking at this man's toupee, wondering whether it might fall off.

I was sitting in the far-left seat from the court's perspective. Justice Poff was sitting in the far-right seat. I wrote Poff a note and passed it down the bench. When it got to the chief justice, he gave me the eye but passed it along. When the note got to Poff, he did a spit take and pushed back his chair from the bench so he could not be easily seen over the rail. He was laughing. The note said this: "Richard, why don't you cut in abruptly from your end of the bench and make him snap his head in your direction, then I will cut in abruptly from my end of the bench and make him snap his head in this direction, and we will see whether his toupee stays in place." Well, poor Poff could hardly contain himself. And the chief was not happy. But I figured, what good was it being the youngest justice if you could not act like it every now and then?

Justice Poff was quick to laugh. He had an affable personality, and he and I got along well. I often told jokes when we were in conference. We did serious consequential work, and I thought we needed to be able to laugh together. In the '80s there was a book called *The Book of Royal Lists,* which contained all kinds of odds and ends about the British royal family. One list was about unusual things that had happened to Queen Elizabeth II while she was on royal tours. We were at the conference table, and I recounted the story that on a tour of an African country the queen was riding in a horse-drawn carriage with the local prince. As they rode along, one of the horses farted. The queen said, "Oh, I'm so sorry." The African prince replied, "That's all right; if you had not said anything I would have thought it was the horse." The moment I finished that story, Poff started laughing until he was nearly out of breath, then he got on his knees on the floor still laughing. Poff had heart problems, so I started to get worried and got on my knees beside him, saying, "Richard, Richard, what's the matter?" He replied, "John, I was raised on a horse farm. Have you ever heard a horse fart? It sounds like a trumpet. You could hardly mistake it for the queen of England." We had our share of laughter that day.

Before joining the court, Justice Poff had been a Republican congressman from Roanoke. But more than that, he had been nominated by President Nixon for a seat on the Supreme Court of the United States. According to historians, he would have gotten that seat had it not been for one thing: he had signed the Southern Manifesto, which said segregation today, segregation tomorrow, segregation forever. Because of that, Poff had to withdraw from consideration for the seat on the U.S. Supreme Court. Nixon subsequently nominated Lewis Powell.

While we were on the court, Poff talked to me about signing that manifesto. He said, "John, you will just not believe the power of the Speaker of the House in those days. I was a young congressman. The Speaker came to me and told me that I was going to sign the manifesto along with all the others. John, the Speaker could just ruin your life. He could control where your office was, your office budget, what assignments you got. He told me that I was going to sign it, and I did." What Poff was saying is that pressure from an authority figure is powerful. We all know that. But there are moments in our lives when we have to stand up for what is right even in the face of such pressure. I think that Richard took the wrong course all those years ago. But he paid for it in the most dramatic way, losing a coveted seat on the nation's highest court. I think that over the course of his life, he came to understand that what he did was wrong. At the end, Richard's family asked me to deliver his eulogy, which I did.

My father reentered my life momentarily while I was on the bench in the middle of an oral argument. I saw a state trooper enter the courtroom, approach the clerk, and hand him a note. The note was passed to me. It said: "A man claiming to be your father is drunk in the middle of the street cursing the police. What do you want us to do?" I wrote at the bottom: "Do what you would usually do in a situation like this. Don't think about me." I passed the note to the clerk, who gave it to the trooper. The other justices were curious about what had transpired. I told the chief what the note said and how I had responded. The chief then told me that he did not think the other justices needed to know. I wondered how long my father would continue to show up in my life. He had obviously told a policeman, "My son is on the Supreme Court." I was weary of it all.

Later, my father was a patient at the VCU hospital while being treated for alcoholism and hypertension. I was still on the court. When I learned he was at the hospital, I went to visit him. In a brief conversation with his doctor, the doctor said to me: "When I talk to your father when he is sober, I can see how he could be the father of the first Black and the youngest Supreme Court justice in Virginia history." I took that to mean that alcohol had altered the very course of his life, had diminished him, had made him less than he might have been. He might have lived a better life had it not been for alcoholism. It is a sad story that plays out in many people's lives. That hospital visit was the last time I saw him.

There was also a social side to the court. When all the justices gathered for a session of court, one of the justices, in rotation from senior to junior, was responsible for taking the other justices and their spouses to dinner. The justices would typically take everyone to a local restaurant and pick up the tab. I did not have the money to do it that way, so when my time came to host the dinner, my wife and I invited everyone to our home on Monument Avenue. We turned to the Lambert family to cater the dinner, and we hired one of their regular workers to tend the bar and serve dinner.

When our guests arrived, we started in the den with music, drinks, and chitchat. I had set up a bar with the things the bartender had told me he would need. While he was making drinks for the justices and their wives, I left the room. When I returned, I noticed that the bartender had taken a tonic water bottle from my cabinet and was pouring that into drinks instead of using the mixers that were on the table. What the bartender didn't know is that the tonic water bottle actually contained vodka that I had stored there because the bottle wouldn't break if I put it in my trunk for a trip. That means that instead of making a gin and tonic or a vodka and tonic, he was actually making a gin and vodka and a vodka and vodka. He had made drinks for several of our guests, but none of them noticed. When I asked each one about their drinks, they all said they were fine. Everybody seemed to be having great fun. I was playing Frank Sinatra, Robert Goulet, Barbara Streisand, Nancy Wilson; they were dancing and laughing. The chief justice said that he had never before been dancing with the court and he thought it was wonderful.

While we were still having fun in the den, one of my aunts brought in a platter of fried oysters that I had cooked myself using a family recipe from my Aunt Toppie. The fried oysters vanished quickly. A short time after all the oysters were gone, one of the wives came to me, got everybody's attention, then said, "John, we heard that you cooked these oysters yourself." I said, "Yes, I did." She said, "We don't believe you. We want to see you do it." What they wanted, of course, was more fried oysters. I had some left, so I invited everybody into the kitchen and fried more oysters.

Now this was a sight, the whole Supreme Court of Virginia and spouses standing in my kitchen watching the oysters fry, then grabbing for them as they were put on the serving platter. I have always remembered that scene with joy because they looked and acted just like my own family does when the oysters are being fried: they stand in the kitchen by the stove and intercept them before they hit the platter. I thought, "Isn't this something? People—despite race, rank, title, and position—are so much the same at a very basic level."

Early in my time on the court, my wife and I were at a Christmas party at one of the downtown hotels. As I was walking back from the restroom a man I did not recognize said, "Justice Thomas, hello." I responded, "Hello." The man then said, "By the way, I'm still pissed off at you, you asshole, for not ruling in my favor on my recent case." I did not know who this was or what he was talking about. I hurried back to the ballroom. Later, I told the other justices what had happened. They were shocked. They all said that nothing like that had ever happened to them. Then one of them said, "You know, that's contempt. There is a statute on that. A lawyer is not allowed to criticize a judge for a ruling the judge made in his official capacity. We should have the clerk issue a show cause order for him to demonstrate why he is not in contempt." The order was issued. An actual proceeding followed. At the end of the cases during court week, I left the bench, took off my robe, and sat at counsel table—before my own court—with a lawyer from the attorney general's office who was my counsel for the proceeding. I do not remember the outcome of the case; I do remember that it made me more guarded in my dealings with strangers.

But there were happier aspects of family life while I was on the court. All three of our children were born while I was serving, making them the first children born to a sitting justice of the Supreme Court of Virginia. The other justices' children had been born before they came on the bench.

Charles was born in October 1984. The question I had gotten all the time before he was born was whether I wanted a boy or a girl. Most people thought I would say a boy, but the truth was that since I had never had a father-son relationship, I was not sure that I would know what to do with a son. So, my answer was that I didn't know. But when our first child was a boy, we were as happy as we could be. Charles, like all babies, was prone to play with things at his eye level. We had him with us in the main courtroom at the Supreme Court one evening when we were showing family members around. He was crawling on the floor behind the bench and found a button that I had not paid attention to. He pressed the button. Alarms went off, and members of the Capitol police came running into the courtroom with me standing there holding my son and saying that I was sorry.

In July 1986 our daughter, Ginger, was born. She never set off any alarms at the courthouse. And she taught me right away that girls are different from boys in so many ways. In October 1987 our youngest son, Lewis, was born, which means that all three of our children were born within thirty-five months. The youngest justice had three babies all at once. We had three car seats. Three sizes of diapers. And we had all manner of traveling cradles and playpens to take on every trip. We soon graduated to a minivan to move around Virginia.

Because I was the first Black and the youngest justice in history, I got invitations to speak all over Virginia and the nation. And even when I had not been invited to speak, if someone noticed that I was present at a public event I always had to be ready to "say a few words."

Whether I was at a church or a school or a civic gathering, it was not unusual to hear the moderator say, "Ladies and gentlemen, we have here with us today the first Black and the youngest justice in Virginia history. Sir, would you say a few words?" It just did not work to say no.

I was invited to speak at Monticello on the Fourth of July in 1988 at the naturalization ceremony for new citizens. Since the 1940s, the United States District Court for the Western District of Virginia had convened on July 4 at Monticello to swear in newly naturalized citizens who lived in that part of Virginia. Leigh Cochran, the wife of my fellow justice George Moffett Cochran, was chair of the board of trustees at Monticello and invited me to make the speech. I agreed to do it. But I wanted to be sure that I was not an apologist for Jefferson and that I did not skip over the fact that Jefferson owned enslaved persons. I had long understood the contradictions that existed in Jefferson's life, but in the main I had come to think of him as a man who had conceived of and written down the great aspirational goals of our nation in the Declaration of Independence. As I thought about what I would say, I was determined not to let Jefferson off the hook. I did not want to give him a pass on the question of slavery, nor did I want to whitewash the issues of our fragmented, racially divided society as I welcomed these new citizens to our nation. I felt that I had to walk a fine line. One of my family members observed: "Obviously, you are being pushed out of your comfort zone by this speech. It is good for you to have to do this."

When I gave my speech that day, it was the first time I had ever been to Monticello. I had lived in Virginia all my life and had visited historic sites, but never Monticello. I had attended UVA for seven years, but had never been to Monticello. I had even been to eat at Michie Tavern, but I had no idea that Monticello was just around the next bend in the road. And while in law school I had been to Kite Day on Brown's Mountain, which overlooks Monticello, but still had not visited.

On that Independence Day in 1988, I talked about the benefits and burdens of freedom, about the importance of naturalizing new citizens as a means by which to strengthen our whole nation. I got a standing ovation. And then Dan Jordan, president of the Thomas Jefferson Foundation, told me that my speech had been carried live by the Voice of America in a nineteen-language simulcast to forty-one nations and 144 million people around the world—my largest audience.

At the end of the ceremony, a photographer asked whether she could use my speech with photos she had taken that day. I said no because the rules applying to Supreme Court justices frowned on our involvement in commercial ventures. But I have always wished to see such a book.

The other thing that struck me that day were the words of the Oath of Citizenship that naturalized citizens must take. Those of us who are born here never have to confront in one place what it means to be a citizen, to serve the nation, to take up arms in its defense, to repudiate all foreign princes and potentates, to accept our civic duties of voting. It is almost as if naturalized citizens know and care more about the rights and liberties we were born with.

While I was on the court, the American Bar Association did a study of the length of time it took from a final disposition in a state trial court to a final appellate decision in a state appellate court. The study showed that in Virginia it took almost three years, and the time was getting longer. The ABA recommended that it should take only one year from final judgment in trial court to a ruling by a state appeals court. Virginia did not have an intermediate court of appeals. Our sole appellate court was the Supreme Court of Virginia. But we traditionally reviewed only twenty-six to thirty cases each time the court was in session. With about seven sessions per year, we were hearing at most about 210 fully granted cases per year. We knew that the statewide bar associations were concerned about appellate delay in Virginia. The General Assembly was also aware of the problem and was looking at creating an intermediate appellate court as a means of cutting the time for appellate review.

In response to the growing concerns about the problem, the Supreme Court decided to take more cases each session. But we did this without doing anything to modify our longstanding court calendar. This increase in workload ultimately put me in the hospital.

Under the eliminate-the-backlog plan each justice would take one extra case. The chief would be assigned three and the other justices would be assigned five each. That comes to thirty-three sets of briefs and appendices. That meant that instead of having four weeks to write four decisions, we had four weeks to write five decisions. Instead of having twenty-six sets of briefs to read in twenty-one days, we had thirty-three sets to read in twenty-one days. These changes gave us less time per case, increased the size of the docket, and increased the time we were on the bench each court session.

I worked hard to operate under the new schedule. I felt like I was reading briefs, appendices, and cases all the time. For years I had suffered from obstructive sleep apnea, which caused me to snore heavily, stop breathing, then start breathing again, depriving me of deep, restful sleep. Early in my tenure on the court, I had been assessed at VCU's sleep laboratory and put on a CPAP machine. As I tried to do the additional reading and drafting, I was essentially burning the candle at both ends. I was staying up later, going to bed for a shorter amount of time, and waking up feeling exhausted. I was awakened one night with all the lights on in the bedroom and firemen in their turnout gear taking me out of bed and putting me on a stretcher. My wife said, "You had a seizure." I had had a grand mal seizure in my sleep. My convulsions had awakened my wife, and she called 911. They took me to VCU.

The next day I saw the chief of neurology. He told me I had a brain tumor, specifically a disembryoplastic neuroepithelial tumor affecting the amygdala and the tip of the hippocampus in the right temporal lobe, otherwise known as a DNET tumor. If you look at the word "disembryoplastic" you see "embryo." This was the injury that I had sustained on the day I was born when my head was squeezed and deformed on the right side. Though my mother had been able to push my skull into a more normal-looking shape, the injury to the brain tissue itself had already occurred.

A justice of the Supreme Court of Virginia with a brain tumor. It was obvious to me that those words did not go together. A justice decides life-or-death issues. How could the people of Virginia feel comfortable with someone deciding such cases while suffering from a brain tumor? I knew right away that I would have to leave the court. As I talked more with the neurologist, I learned that I had been having seizures for a long time but I had not realized what they were. As far back as law school I would get the sensation of smelling a scent of almonds, and if I was listening to music I would hear odd distortions in the sound. I learned that those sensations were petit mal seizures and that I had graduated from the little seizures to a big one.

My doctors explained that if a person has a weakness in their brain and is deprived of sleep, the weakness will manifest itself. Because I was sleep-deprived from trying to keep up with the increased workload at the court, the weakness that had been in my brain since I was born set off a tonic-clonic seizure. My doctors also told me that once the brain learns how to initiate a seizure, it is easier for it to do so the next time. The doctors at VCU wanted me to get a second opinion from the Mayo Clinic.

I told the chief justice and the justices about my brain tumor and about my decision to leave the court. There were expressions of sorrow and some tears. I told them that I would be returning to Hunton & Williams, which had agreed to take me back.

I left the Supreme Court on the last day of October 1989. I was thirty-nine years old. I had been at the court since April 15, 1983. I had been a justice for six years, six months, and sixteen days. In the time leading up to my last day, my cousin Bucky and I took pictures of my chambers to document how they looked and where things were. Then we packed up books and artwork and files and brought them home. It took several nights. On the last day I visited each of the justices who lived and worked in Richmond to say goodbye. I called the out-of-town justices. Then I went to see the chief. I gave him my state ID and my Supreme Court card. We shook hands. I left. I went to the clerk's office and said goodbye to the staff. Then I took the elevator to the garage, got in my car, and left the building. I was no longer a justice of the Supreme Court of Virginia, and I was not yet even forty years old. I had been a Supreme Court justice while I was in my thirties. Surely that is rare. So much had happened in those few years.

I returned to Hunton on November 1, 1989, and immediately made plans to travel to the Mayo Clinic. I got to the Mayo within a week, where they looked me over and agreed that I had a DNET tumor. It was not cancerous, but even a noncancerous tumor in the brain can wreak havoc, as I had already seen. The original plan was to put me on medications to suppress the seizures. But that approach did not work because the meds depressed my mental abilities, making it harder for me to do things that usually were routine. And, despite taking the meds, I had more seizures. In late 1989 the neurologists at the Mayo recommended that the damaged tissue in my brain be removed.

The tumor was removed at the Mayo Clinic in early 1996. My father died as I was recovering from surgery, when my head was still bald and a wrap was around my head. The family decided it was better if I did not attend the funeral. I have not had a seizure since the surgery. And years ago I stopped taking the medications associated with the tumor. As the doctors say, I had a good outcome.

When I returned to Hunton, I visited the senior lawyers and met new lawyers who had arrived while I was on the court. There were unkind news accounts of my return. One newspaper, apparently not believing that I faced a real medical problem, said that I had left the Supreme Court because I was suffering from "emptypocketitis." People can sometimes be very clever in their attacks. And there was some truth to the charge, because if I had stayed on the court I would not have been able to afford the brain surgery that I needed to get me back on my feet.

While I was dealing with the medical issues in the background, I was in immediate demand to discuss cases that were on appeal or were pending hearings and arguments at the Supreme Court. Everybody wanted to know what I thought about the way they had presented the case and the arguments they had relied on. But there was also an odd reaction to my return; some of the litigation partners did not want to tell their clients that I was available, because they thought the clients would want me to argue their appeals rather than having the litigation partner who had handled the case at trial make the argument. As it turned out, the way I had left the court made it so that I could go back and practice before the court. I had resigned; I had not retired. Indeed, when I left I was too young to retire. That makes a big difference. There are statutory rules that apply to whether a retired justice can practice in the courts of Virginia. But those rules don't apply to someone who resigns, like I did. Thus, I was able to work on a great many appeals to the Supreme Court of Virginia and to the Court of Appeals of Virginia, the intermediate appellate court that was created during my time on the bench.

Matters of race relations seemed never to be too far away from me, no matter where I was. I realized that again when I attended a cocktail party at the firm not long after my return. The wife of one of the partners came up and said, "John Charles, I have a story about prejudice and it involves you." I thought to myself, "What now?" She told me about her daughter, who attended one of the elite private schools in Richmond. She described how her daughter had always been an A student, particularly in English and history. In her daughter's history class the students had been told to pick a figure in history and write an essay about the person. Then she said, "My daughter chose you." She explained that her daughter had learned all about me and had written a wonderful paper. But her daughter got a D on that paper. When they asked why, they were told that it was because the subject of her paper was "unworthy."

The woman went on to tell me that everything worked out fine because her daughter got into the Ivy League school of her choice. With regard to the prep school teacher who had given the D, she said he had not been disciplined or let go, and that he was just "old school." I guess that meant that the view he expressed is what a white person in Richmond would expect from a teacher at one of the predominantly white prep schools in the 1980s. It made my stomach hurt then and still does now. "Unworthy." You can overcome all manner of obstacles, climb every mountain, learn from discarded textbooks, wrestle hatred to the ground, eat day-old bread, but to a privileged white man you are still unworthy. Sure. I keep waiting for our nation to grow and change to appreciate all its citizens, but it still seems a long way off. I was called unworthy years ago, but it is still happening. When the Senate majority said that they were going to block anything that President Barack Obama tried to do, they were essentially saying that they thought he was unworthy of leading our nation.

17

Wrestling with Jefferson and Confronting Racism

In 1990, I was invited to serve on the board of the Thomas Jefferson Foundation. I was the first Black person and the youngest in history to serve on that board. Part of the reason I said yes was my long history of involvement in things Jeffersonian. I already knew that there were many sides to Jefferson and that his thoughts were part of the intellectual DNA of America, and so I thought that it would be a good idea for me to have a front-row seat in the interpretation and presentation of the story of Jefferson and Monticello. But not all my friends looked at it that way. An older Black lawyer took me aside and said, "I thought you meant something to our people, so I want to know what the hell are you doing on the board of that slave-owning hypocrite Jefferson?" He did not give me the chance to respond; he concluded by saying that I should be ashamed of myself. My association with the Thomas Jefferson Foundation and Monticello has continued for more than three decades. I have seen real change in the discussion of Jefferson and slavery.

One of my roles on the board was to work with UVA's law school in selecting the Thomas Jefferson Medalist in Law. Because Jefferson did not believe in honorary degrees, UVA does not award them. Instead, UVA and the Thomas Jefferson Foundation jointly award medals in fields of endeavor that were important to Jefferson. There are medals in architecture, law, civic leadership, and so on. By long tradition, the medalists give a lecture at the related school, spend time with the students, go to dinner with faculty, administrators, and students, and are in residence for a few days. Another part of the tradition is a black-tie dinner at Monticello where each medalist is toasted by a member of the foundation board. I have made several such toasts over the years.

The dinner traditionally takes place inside the historic house. Works of art and sculptures are moved to the sides of the rooms, and tables are set up usually in the original dining room and the parlor. A doorway connects those two rooms, but no matter how you stand in that doorway your back is to a portion of the crowd, so the person speaking basically addresses the doorframe. It causes a few problems in being heard. But luckily, I have never had a problem being heard; I was born with a stentorian voice, which seems to bounce off the walls and resonate in both rooms. (The stentor was the herald of the Greek forces during the Trojan War; legend has it that he had a voice as powerful as that of fifty men.) When I made the toast, I always tried to relate it to something Jeffersonian. I would say things like "Mr. Jefferson himself would have appreciated the law medalists' multifaceted curiosity about the world."

In my time on the Monticello board, I got to meet and toast such luminaries as Marian Wright Edelman, William Rehnquist, Richard Posner, Lloyd Cutler, Rex Lee, Ruth Bader Ginsburg, Alan K. Simpson, Elaine R. Jones, Guido Calabresi, Mortimer Caplin, Anne-Marie Slaughter, Antonin Scalia, Peter J. Neufeld, Barry Scheck, Janet Napolitano, Cynthia Kinser, and George Mitchell. All these individuals loom large in the law, and it was exciting to meet them and get to know them leading up to the formal toast. I attended as many of the events at the law school as I could, and I would often ask the medal recipient or their family members what they would want me to say about them. I would ask about something in their lives that was not well known, such as their hobbies or their sense of humor. Usually, I would pick up little gems of information that would bring a smile to the face of the medalist as I stood in that doorway.

I was in awe when I met Marian Wright Edelman, who I remembered as a close advisor to John F. Kennedy and Bobby Kennedy on issues of poverty and the plight of children in the Deep South. She founded the Children's Defense Fund, which she championed all her life. It was a great honor for me to stand up for her at Monticello.

When I toasted Ruth Bader Ginsburg, I had the chance during dinner to hear her tell how she was treated as a high-achieving woman at two of the nation's eminent law schools and how, despite being at the very top of her class, she had trouble getting a job as a lawyer. I told her some of my own story of poverty and discrimination. At the end of the evening, she stood on her tiptoes, kissed me on the cheek, and said, "Now you take care of yourself, you hear?" "Yes, ma'am," I replied.

It was a real joy to toast my fellow Norfolkian Elaine Jones, who was the first Black woman to attend UVA law school. Though she is a few years older than me, I met her and got to know her when I arrived at UVA as an undergraduate in 1968. When I met Elaine, I was a first-year undergraduate, but I already knew who she was because I had heard about her from my family in Norfolk. They described her as an example of what working hard and persevering can do to change a person's life. It was widely known back in Huntersville how "that Jones girl, Elaine" had gone to college, then joined the Peace Corps and gone overseas to work. After Elaine finished UVA Law she went on to become director counsel of the NAACP Legal Defense Fund, a position once held by Thurgood Marshall himself. And so, I was filled with pride and joy as I stood in that doorway at Monticello praising Elaine's crusading spirit.

Mortimer Caplin had long been well known at UVA and the law school. He had been a generous benefactor, and his name graces several gathering places at the law school. One of his undergraduate sports was boxing, and he had quite a reputation for his tenacity in the ring. He had been in the treasury department when John F. Kennedy was president, and he had gone on to form one of the nation's renowned tax law firms, Caplin and Drysdale. But the thing that Mort Caplin did that made me so proud to toast him at Monticello was that on the night before the D-Day invasion he had been secretly placed on the invasion beach, where he and a few others had to conceal themselves so that early the next morning they could signal to the incoming boats the best places to come ashore. I always think about the peril he must have been in, with German patrols moving along the beach and with the German long guns in the cliffs above his head. It was frankly amazing to talk to someone who had been part of that great fight for freedom. I am sure that there was real emotion in my voice as I toasted Mort as the Jefferson Medalist in Law.

When I stood up for Janet Napolitano, she was still secretary of homeland security. I remember well that on that night she was wearing a green dress. The government had instituted color codes to denote the level of security and preparedness around the nation. As part of my toast I said, "You all can see that Secretary Napolitano is wearing green tonight, which surely signals that everything is all right up here on the mountain at Monticello." That remark got a laugh from the guests.

Aside from working with the committee on the law medals, I had occasion to meet with an array of guests who visited Monticello. Everybody seemed to show up on the mountain. There were presidents, prime ministers, governors, and world leaders. I met and talked with Mikhail Gorbachev on the West Front of Monticello. As we sat near each other in the bright sun that day, Gorbachev wore a baseball cap to keep the sun off his head. I asked him what he knew about Jefferson. He said that he had read the Declaration of Independence as a schoolchild and that he had also read about Jefferson.

When I left Monticello that day I did not expect to see Gorbachev again. But as luck would have it, as my family was checking out of the hotel the next morning so were Gorbachev and his wife, Raisa. He recognized me and we all took a photo together: the leader of the Soviet Union and me and my family.

By 1992, I had been off the bench and back at the law firm for almost two and a half years. I got a call from John Casteen, UVA's president at the time. He asked me to deliver the 1992 commencement address. That would be the twentieth anniversary of my own commencement; I said yes.

In the two decades since I had taken my baccalaureate degree from UVA, I had been on and off the Supreme Court of Virginia. I had married and become the father of three children. I had suffered a brain tumor and survived. I had become a trustee of Thomas Jefferson's Monticello. I had grown old beyond my years because of the problems that I had been called on to grapple with.

When Casteen called me that April, there was turmoil across the United States occasioned by the acquittal of the police officers who had been charged with beating Rodney King in Los Angeles. That month there were riots and protests across the nation complaining about police brutality. I did not have much time to get ready to make the speech because commencement was only about a month away.

As I thought about what I wanted to say to the graduates, I knew that I had to address questions of justice and injustice. I had to address questions of slavery and freedom that have existed since Jefferson's time. And I had to find something to say that would motivate these young people to make the world better than they found it. I was determined not to say the same old things that commencement speakers typically say: "May the wind be at your backs" and words of that kind. I thought about the reasons Jefferson had given for creating the University of Virginia. Roughly, he had wanted to escape the miasma of the Tidewater (the hot, humid part of Virginia where I was born), and he wanted UVA to be his last gift to the nation, a place to educate young people to "follow truth wherever it might lead" and to become leaders of the new nation. In the end, when our family headed to Charlottesville for commencement all I had was two sheets of notepaper but no fully prepared text. That was how I usually made a speech.

When we got to Charlottesville, my wife and our three children, who were eight, six, and five years old, were taken to Birdwood. This is an old mansion that sits on land that UVA had turned into a golf course. It is used for special events. To our surprise the other guests staying at Birdwood were Charles and Lynda Robb, along with their children and Lynda's mother, the former First Lady of the United States, Lady Bird Johnson, and her Secret Service detail. One of the governor's daughters was in the class of 1992.

I spent most of my time at Birdwood thinking about what I wanted to say the next day. The children were outside running around, throwing Frisbees, and generally having a great time. The night before graduation at UVA, as at most places, is filled with parties, gatherings, and celebrations. My friend Tony Pilaro, who had funded the Holland Scholarship program at UVA for students of color, wanted me to come to their gathering. I left Birdwood and drove to where the young Black graduates were gathered. I told them how proud I was of them and that I expected great things from them.

When I went back to Birdwood, it dawned on me that the Secret Service was guarding the house and that I needed to be careful as I approached the house so that they would know it was me. I certainly did not want to surprise them. I knocked first, then used my key to open the door. Though I had been ready to put my hands up as I came through the door, there was no problem and I went on up to my room.

The next morning, commencement day, the UVA police arrived to pick up my family and me. I was carrying my academic gown and hood and those few sheets of paper containing my notes for the speech. Pearl and the children were taken to the Colonnade Club. I was taken to the robing room in the Rotunda. The Rotunda is the iconic center of the university; it was the library of the original university back in 1819, and its dome with the oculus is known all over the world. It is a United Nations–designated World Heritage Site. Being in the Rotunda is a big deal at UVA.

Everybody robed up and the ceremonial marshal lined us up, with me walking beside President Casteen. We could see through the glass doors of the Rotunda straight up the middle of the Lawn to Old Cabell Hall at the far end. There was an immense crowd on either side of the passageway that had been roped off for the academic procession. As the music started we began walking, and I said to Casteen, "John, I have just about decided what I'm going to say today." Casteen did not think that was funny. I am sure that he did not know that I often stand up and speak based on a handful of notes hurriedly scratched on a piece of paper. Casteen responded, "Now, John, I hope that you are ready for this. Look at this crowd." I said, "Yeah, man, we got this."

The day was overcast, so we did not have to deal with a hot sun blazing down on us. It was almost cool and misty under gray skies. We came down the Lawn through cheers and yells and clicking cameras and people waving and calling out to me and to Casteen. It was a festive crowd, decked out in UVA's orange and blue, and the banners from the schools and departments were held high. We got to the far end of the Lawn and took our seats on the podium. In the front row I could see my wife and children, Chuck and Lynda Robb, and the former First Lady. It had been twenty years since I had been at UVA for graduation, and it was still exciting. In that time, so much had changed for me. It had been almost a magical transformation, from the young kid who had ventured from Norfolk to the mountains of Virginia to attend a school that was overwhelmingly white and all-male for two of my four undergraduate years, to the almost forty-two-year-old former justice of the Supreme Court of Virginia.

As I sat there waiting for when I would stand up to speak, I thought to myself, "Give them something that will make them think. Give them something to chew on. Don't waste this chance to influence these young people." I heard the start of my introduction; I gathered my meager notes; I stood up, went to the podium, and started talking. Soon I was fully absorbed in speaking. Even though I was creating much of the speech as I stood there, it flowed readily. Here is some of what I said that day:

> Whether you are medicine, law, business, or whatever your graduate degree, I tell you that just as Jefferson was part of the formation of America, all of you here must be part of the reformation of America. You must reform decaying cities. Reform the healthcare delivery system. Reform the teaching of science. Reform the importance of education in our country. Whatever your specialty is, you have a role to play in reforming America.
>
> This is a message of hope because as you sit here today— architects, builders, athletes, teachers, scientists, philosophers, doctors, lawyers, businessmen and women—you have within you the raw stuff of what it takes to grab this nation by the scruff of its neck and yank it back from the edge of self-destruction.
>
> Make no mistake about it, the forces that would rend this nation asunder are loose in the streets. And it will take all that is within you to reform it. But reform it you must.
>
> The needs of this nation are at this moment so great that we can no longer afford for those who are blessed with education simply to wring their hands and say, "Somehow we have to get out of this mess." We need you, in the best Jeffersonian tradition, to start telling people "how"—not "somehow" but "how."
>
> "Somehow" is all too often the watchword of those who criticize yet fail to offer solutions. "How" is usually the word used by those who think and analyze and resolve matters and help us set courses to move forward. You have it within you to calm the nation's turmoil, to restore its values, to reinstill its morality, to make it more perfect.

Some of you may be thinking that I ask too much of you, that the problems in America in the 1990s are intractable, that nobody can take them on and wrestle them to the ground. I don't recommend that you try to solve everything at once, nor do I think that Jefferson had that idea in mind when he established this university.

What I want you to do is to deal with wrong whenever and wherever you see it on an individual basis. Some of you may ask, "Why me? This is not my problem. These are the problems of our elected leaders." My short answer to you is, I do not believe that government can solve our problems; I think that government even is part of the problem.

But I am certain of this: that with each of you acting with fairness, honor, and determination in your own sphere, and I in mine and others in theirs, we can collectively reform America. You see, I was taught at my grandmother's knee that "little drops of water, and little grains of sand, make the mighty ocean and the pleasant land."

I tell you, *yes, you can*—right where you are, *yes, you can.*

The most profound changes in America will come from the goodwill and good works of people like you operating one-by-one on every street corner, in every alley, on every block, in every office building, in every way you can. No matter where you find yourself, if you see injustice or unfairness, whether in the laboratory, the office, the school, the courts, the country club, the Congress—speak out and say that it is wrong.

If you see hunger, bring food—not tomorrow, but right then. If you see hopelessness, bring hope—not tomorrow, but right then. If you see racism, or sexism, or any kind of -ism, stop where you are and say, "*I will not tolerate this.*"

There is a vast reservoir of good in America. Our citizens seek to do what is right. I believe that they yearn to be good. And sometimes the only thing that is needed is for one person out of thousands to say what is right, and others will respond.

Given what we now see across America, I don't think it would be too much to say that we are in the midst of a war for what is right, for what is just. But don't think that I am simply referring to the streets of any particular city in America. I am not. I am talking about a war for what is right on Wall Street, on Main Street, on Broad Street, in our souls.

Because you have taken a degree from this university, you were long ago enlisted as an officer in this war. We need your best thoughts, your deepest understanding, your most brilliant advice.

Our nation does thoughtless things. We spend billions of dollars developing labor-saving devices like computers and robots, but we take no steps to prepare for the people who will surely lose their jobs once their labor is no longer needed. Somebody here with careful thought and analysis could have fixed a problem like that, could have prepared for it.

Somebody here may see the wisdom in telling the nation that it may be time to change the standard workweek from forty hours to thirty or thirty-five hours, thus to share the blessings of labor-saving devices and put people back to work. Forty hours did not come from heaven. It was made by people right here on earth. It can change.

Somebody here may be the one to tell the nation that if some of our laborers are idle, we can put them to work repairing the cracks in the old tunnels under our great cities and fixing bridges and highways, picking up paper, doing something to make the nation better while they return to work.

Somebody here may have the wisdom to look at overcrowded jails and empty high-security military bases and wonder why we are spending more money for jails.

Somebody may wonder why is it that a match cannot be made between lonely senior citizens who are filled with knowledge and love and unwanted, warehoused infants lined up in hospital corridors starving for a human touch.

Somebody here may even start to understand that mountains can be moved.

I know mountains can be moved. I have seen evidence of it, and you have too. This very lawn was a mountain until it met Jefferson's will and it was leveled.

I know mountains can be moved because the power of Great Britain in India seemed like a mountain until it met the will of Gandhi and retreated.

I know mountains can be moved because a moon landing seemed like a mountain until it met the will of Kennedy and Johnson and was achieved.

I know mountains can be moved because institutionalized, legalized racism in America seemed like a mountain until it met the will of Rosa Parks and Dr. Martin Luther King and had to roll back some.

The will of the people brought down the Berlin Wall.

The will of the people crushed communism in the Soviet Union.

I say to you today that you have a mission. It was arranged long ago and set in motion for such a time as this. Jefferson intended for you to help America in times of need. You! He intended for you to help your country in times of need.

We know that you are able, because you would not be here today if you were not.

We know that you are ready, because if there is one thing our great university can do, it is to teach our students to be prepared for what will face them.

But the question is, are you willing? The answer is in your hands.

Do you have the will to help restore the family structure in America and take the latchkey out of the hands of babies?

Do you have the will to battle against drug use and save our nation from purchasing its own destruction?

Do you have the will?

Do you have the will to feed the hungry, comfort the suffering, make new jobs out of the ashes of the old?

Do you have the will?

Do you have the will to tell all who will listen that racial strife in America is nothing more than a time bomb that will rend the nation apart? Will you commit to helping heal racial wounds anywhere you find them?

I believe that you have the will. I believe that it is not coincidence that you have reached this moment of transition in your life just as America faces a moment of definition for itself. I believe that you are here for a reason. That you are part of a plan.

And so I tell you in closing as I told you at the start, *there will always be mountains.* But it is up to you whether the mountains you encounter will be obstacles or whether they will become mere stepping stones to new horizons. Use your will, have faith, keep your commitments.

God bless you! Thank you.

As I was speaking, I mentioned the names of some of the disciplines that were represented on the Lawn. I said something about builders; about architects, and the architects cheered; then about doctors, and the doctors cheered. And I thought to myself, too bad I had not made a list of all the disciplines because I could have caused the cheers from the several groups to reverberate around the Lawn. I realized that I had missed an opportunity. But no matter, at the end of the speech the graduates stood and roared.

After the recessional, when we were on our way to the robing room, one of the members of the board of visitors came up to me and said, "That was lovely. If your law career doesn't work out, you should consider joining the Royal Shakespeare Theatre." I guess there was some drama in my voice. I had had a great time at my alma mater.

18

World Travel and Lecturing at West Point

Bill Slate, a Virginia lawyer who had studied at the University of Richmond law school and who had been circuit executive of the United States Court of Appeals for the Fourth Circuit, became president of the American Arbitration Association in the 1990s. He invited me to serve on his board of directors. I said yes. The law firm thought it was a good business development idea and supported my involvement. The AAA board typically met in Manhattan, and so every few months off I went to New York City. On the board I met some of the most storied arbitrators in the world, people who had been instrumental in resolving major disputes and in allocating compensation following disasters like oil spills and mass injuries. After several years on the board, I was invited to serve on its executive committee, the small working group of board members who were called on to assure the proper functioning of the association when the board was not in session.

While I was on the AAA board, we created the International Centre for Dispute Resolution. We saw the need to do this because we learned that some participants in international disputes were concerned that the very name "American Arbitration Association" suggested that AAA was biased in favor of American entities. That surely was not true, but we thought that it was better to take that issue off the table by creating the ICDR. Also, during my tenure on the AAA board, I became national co-chair of the AAA's mediation committee, and thus I became deeply immersed in the world of dispute resolution.

One benefit of being on the AAA board was the dinner parties we had during our annual meetings. We went to iconic locations like the New York Yacht Club, which displayed replicas of the boats that had captured the America's Cup; the Rainbow Room at Rockefeller Center; a dinner cruise around Ellis Island. On the dinner cruise I ended up on deck reciting poetry, somewhat to the amazement of my fellow board members, who had no idea that I had so many poems tucked away in my head. My time on the AAA board set me on a decidedly international course.

The 9/11 attacks occurred while I was on the board. Our staff in Manhattan was traumatized, along with the entire city. One of the officers of the association had been scheduled to deliver a lecture in mid-September in Dubrovnik, Croatia, on interim relief measures in international arbitration under the 1954 New York Convention. In the aftermath of the attacks, the corporate officer decided to stay in New York and let someone else deliver the lecture. The AAA asked me to do it, and I said yes.

After we scheduled the trip, I saw that I had to leave the day after my friend Roger Gregory was to be sworn in as the first Black lawyer from Virginia to serve on the U.S. Court of Appeals for the Fourth Circuit. He had been nominated by President Bill Clinton, renominated by President George W. Bush, then confirmed by the Senate. Roger thus became the first federal judge in American history to have been nominated to his seat by presidents of opposing parties. There was no way I could miss this historic ceremony.

At Roger's swearing-in, the large formal courtroom at the Fourth Circuit's main courthouse in Richmond was overflowing with leaders from the legal community, from state government, from the national government, and from Black civic and social organizations. There were the usual speeches and resolutions, the reading of Roger's commission, and the handshakes and hugs and pats on the back. I could not help but think back to the day that I had come to the recruiting committee at my law firm with a good report on Roger, but someone wanted me to continue looking and I slammed the door and walked out. I thought of Shakespeare's All's Well That Ends Well. I was immensely proud to see Roger take his seat on the Fourth. And now, as I write these words, he is the chief judge of the Fourth Circuit, which covers West

Virginia, Maryland, Virginia, North Carolina, and South Carolina. Quite a job.

The day after Roger was sworn in, I got up early and headed to the Richmond airport on my way to Croatia. It had only been a few days since commercial flights had been restarted in the U.S. When I got to the airport I found that I was the only passenger who had shown up for my flight on US Air. The airline did not want to move their equipment with just one passenger, so they bought me a ticket on Delta. They had set up a folding table in front of the ticket counter and were asking all passengers to open their luggage so that it could be inspected for dangerous items. The infrastructure that we now have for screening luggage did not exist at that moment, but nobody was taking any chances.

I had been apprehensive about going to Croatia because I knew that it was not far from Bosnia and Herzegovina, where active fighting was going on and UN peacekeeping forces were on the ground. I did not know what to expect, traveling to a part of the world that had once been part of Soviet-dominated Yugoslavia. But I had agreed to make this speech, and so I went.

The flight was uneventful. After many hours in the air, I landed in Dubrovnik. I was taken to a hotel near the ancient walls of the city, where I met the other lecturers for the program that would be held at the Inter University Centre. I was the only American and the only person of color on the program. What else was new?

I was fully out of my element. Although most of the other lecturers spoke English, they also spoke French, German, Croatian, Russian, Italian, and Greek, and so I was easily left out of their ad hoc conversations. They would start a conversation in one language and change to two or three other languages. If someone noticed the questioning look on my face—which was almost perpetual—one of them would usually pause to explain to me what they had been talking about. I had that look of puzzlement on my face so frequently that one person basically volunteered to be my translator. I deeply appreciated the gesture because otherwise I would have been completely lost.

The conference itself was advertised as being in English, and so I was able to deliver my lecture in my own language. Basically, I had to follow the script that had been given to me by the AAA to discuss the technical issues of interim relief in international arbitration. I was talking about things like how to issue an injunction or sequester funds or mandate conduct when you do not have the power of the courts behind you to enforce your order.

I have never liked to be in an audience when someone onstage was reading a speech. I would much rather have someone talk to the audience, explain things, elucidate things, but not just stand and read. I can read for myself. And so, as I prepared to deliver my lecture in Croatia, I read the materials over and over so that I could just about memorize them and get to the point where to the audience I would appear to be delivering a lecture rather than just reading to them.

When I arrived at the lecture room there were about twenty people there. I went to the podium, identified myself, and started. When I finished, I got a standing ovation from an audience comprised of European-trained lawyers with English as a second, third, or fourth language. I was surprised by the reaction to the technical lecture I had just delivered. One of the attendees came up to me and said, "Are you a Black Baptist preacher?" I said, "No, why do you ask?" She said, "Because when you talk all I want to do is say 'Hallelujah!'" I did not know what to say. Yet, this was not the first time that someone had talked about the sound of my voice. I took her comment as a compliment.

When I got back to the hotel, the other lecturers had already heard about the standing ovation. One of them asked, "What did you say to them?" I told them that I had talked about interim relief measures under the 1954 New York Convention. They seemed not to believe what I had told them. But they left it alone.

While I was at the conference in Dubrovnik, I noticed something unusual when my European colleagues sympathized with me about the attacks on my country. It seemed that every time one of them told me they were sorry, there was an unspoken "but." It was a tone of voice at the end of their statement or a shrug of the shoulders. It was hard to describe, but I kept noticing it. Finally I asked, "Why the hesitation when you tell me that you are sorry for what happened? Why does it seem like there is something else that you want to say?"

The other lecturers were from England, Germany, and Italy. All of them had seen terrorism in their countries. One of them finally explained: "We are sorry for the attack on your country, but maybe now the United States will get off its high horse and stop preaching to the rest of us about what we ought to do to handle the terrorism in our countries. Maybe your country will finally come to understand what we have had to deal with all these years." I thought to myself, "Wow." They were saying that America had been self-righteous all these years but had now been placed on par with other parts of the world. Although this was my first international venture, I could understand where they were coming from. I thought it was a fair criticism.

Another important lesson I learned in Dubrovnik was just how young America is as a player on the world scene and why the nations of the Old World are not always happy to be told what to do by the U.S. When I was a schoolchild in Virginia, my teachers took every chance they got to talk about how Jamestown was the first permanent English settlement and how it dated from 1607. They instilled in us how old Virginia is. The "Old Dominion" is even its nickname. By contrast, Dubrovnik dates to the 600s. It is one thousand years older than Jamestown. There are stone buildings in Dubrovnik that are older than Jamestown. The whole situation taught me to think again about the United States' relations with the rest of the world, with cultures that have existed long before the U.S. came to be. And I realized for the first time that maybe Americans think too much of themselves.

It is funny how one thing leads to another, how the fabric of life is woven together. Many of the people I met in Dubrovnik had participated in the Willem C. Vis International Commercial Arbitration Moots in Vienna, sponsored by the United Nations Commission on International Trade Law. Following my lecture in Dubrovnik, I was invited to serve as one of the judges of the 2002 Vis Moots. I said yes.

The Vis Moots are something like the arbitral Olympics for international law students. Early in the year, a problem is posted on the internet. Law schools around the globe take the problem, prepare briefs on both sides of the issue, submit those briefs, register for the competition, and then travel to Vienna for several days of arguing the problem. It ends with the finalists arguing in front of all the participants to determine the winner.

When I arrived in Vienna as a judge and went to the University of Vienna's law school, I met teams from such places as the Honourable Society of the Inner Temple in London; the National Technical University of Singapore; the George Washington University Law School; Loyola University Chicago; and from Sweden, Switzerland, Iceland, France, and other places around the world. All had converged on Vienna to argue a complex commercial issue in English. And there I was participating as one of the judges. How on earth did I get from Huntersville to Vienna?

One of the things that was intriguing to me was to read the briefs written in English by sophisticated law students for whom English was not their principal language. These briefs were well written, but the sound of the language was attention-getting to a native speaker of English. The word choices were different; the analogies were different. I appreciated the difference. When we graded the briefs, we were told not to grade down because of incorrect use of English. I thought that was completely fair. I could not imagine how I would fare if I tried to write a complex brief in Icelandic or German. I would simply be lost.

Some of the arguments from those briefs have stayed with me through the years. In one brief, the writer was trying to say that his opponent's argument did not directly address the argument that the writer had advanced. He was basically trying to say that the two arguments were like apples and oranges, completely different. But what he wrote was that the two arguments were like "shoes and potatoes." I knew exactly the point he was making, but I have never forgotten "shoes and potatoes" and have always wondered whether there was something in his culture that would cause him to express himself that way.

One of the years that I judged at the Vis Moots, the United States ambassador to Austria was W. Lee Lyons Brown Jr. He was a UVA graduate like me. He had served on the board of the Thomas Jefferson Foundation like me, and he was present when I delivered the commencement address at UVA in 1992. I got word to Ambassador Brown that I was in town for the Vis Moots. He invited me to lunch at the embassy and allowed me to bring with me the leaders of the Vis Moots. I sat to his right at the long luncheon table that day. That poor colored kid from Norfolk at the right hand of the U.S. ambassador to Austria was having a good ol' time talking about the world. It was an exceptionally long way from where I started.

Later, I spoke in Delhi, this time at the International Federation of Commercial Arbitration Institutions. This was another speech for the AAA. I talked about electronic discovery in international arbitration. The conference attendees were all worried about the high cost of American-style discovery, and my remarks about the burgeoning costs of electronic discovery did nothing to calm their concerns. All the conferees knew that to resolve disputes in an American court was to almost go broke. Their main question to me was how to avoid American-style dispute resolution. I had no really good answer for that.

Though I was staying in a part of the city near the courts and government buildings, I quickly became aware of the great number of people in the city. I saw people sleeping in the medians of the highways. I saw groups of young children running up to cars stopped in traffic offering to clean the windows and then holding out their hands for money. One of my drivers told me that it was a crime to give money to beggars who came up to the car. When I was in the car, my windows were up.

I did not spend all my time overseas. One of the places closer to home that I enjoyed getting to know was the U.S. Military Academy at West Point in New York. One of my former law partners, John Lucas, had finished West Point in 1969. Unbeknownst to me, he had recommended to the chair of the Department of Law, Col. Patrick Finnegan, that I be invited to speak to the cadets. Because the cadets take an oath to support and defend the Constitution of the United States, all of them are required to take a constitutional law course while at West Point. And, some of the cadets choose law as their major; these cadets usually go on to law school and have as part of their military duties various law-related posts.

As part of the cadets' training in the law, West Point each year schedules a constitutional law lecture for the "Firsties," the seniors. The lecture has been delivered by justices of the Supreme Court of the United States, by attorneys general of the U.S., by solicitors general of the U.S., and other such leaders in the law. I was nominated to give the lecture in 2001. I was nominated before the 9/11 attacks, but the lecture itself was scheduled for November. When I got the invitation from West Point, I said yes. But after the terrorist attacks and the way in which the nation had been traumatized, I wondered whether West Point might want someone more prominent. I called Colonel Finnegan to ask whether under the circumstances they wanted someone else, like a military leader. Colonel Finnegan said, "No, sir. We want you."

Though I did not know it when I first spoke to Colonel Finnegan, he and I had been at UVA's law school at the same time. I was there from 1972 to 1975. He arrived in 1974 in the army's JAG (Judge Adjutant General) School, which was taught in part at the law school. So, we had passed each other in the halls, and he remembered me from his time in Charlottesville. He knew about my background and my career and had heard me speak. After I talked to Colonel Finnegan, I started getting ready for this lecture.

A lecture about the Constitution of the United States was different from the kind of speeches I typically delivered. A lecture is more narrowly focused, more concentrated and analytical than a commencement address. Indeed, to me this constitutional law lecture was more like the talk I had given in Dubrovnik. I would have to cover the material and talk about the structure and purpose of the Constitution. I would have to demonstrate the relevance of the Constitution to the cadets' role as officers in the U.S. military; and given the circumstances in the aftermath of the attacks, I thought that I had to give them words of encouragement about the importance of our nation to the world. In my college and law school days, the best lectures were engaging, inviting, thought-provoking, and inspiring. I had set a high bar for myself.

When I landed in Newark in November, I could see the plumes of smoke still rising from Ground Zero across the river. I was driven to West Point and checked in at the Thayer Hotel, which is near the front gates. I could look out the window of my room and see Buffalo Soldier Field, where I am told that in years past the cadets learned to ride horses as part of their training.

When I arrived at the lecture hall, I could see the cadets filling up the auditorium. They were dressed in their gray over white uniforms. It was quite a sight, all these strong young people who had signed up to protect and defend the United States against all enemies foreign and domestic.

I had told many of my friends and family members about the lecture, and several of them showed up. There was Al Carney, whose father had run the barbershop in my neighborhood. There was Tina Byrd, a law school classmate who practiced in California. There was the general counsel to the American Arbitration Association. And there was Uncle Charles, my mother's brother for whom I was named.

My uncle was wearing his Army Dress Blues, and he was proud that he could still fit into that old uniform. His oldest son, Walter Sears, had finished West Point twenty-two years earlier, in 1979. Uncle Charles got a special thrill that night because Colonel Finnegan basically looked at my uncle's chestful of medals and introduced him to the cadets by reading the medals. In the command voice that is known to all West Pointers, Colonel Finnegan said to the cadets: "We are honored to have with us tonight Lt. Col. Charles Sears, United States Army retired. He served in Vietnam. He was awarded the Bronze Star with four oak leaf clusters and the 'V' for valor, the Meritorious Service Medal, the Purple Heart, the Master Parachutist Badge, the Vietnam Parachutist Badge, and the Army Commendation Medal. His son, Walter, is West Point class of 1979."

My uncle was beaming from ear to ear. I was proud to see him greeted this way by West Point. He had served in the army during the years when it was not easy for a person of color to advance through the ranks. He had told me about times and places when he felt he was discriminated against because of his skin color. But he had persevered, and in his interactions with me throughout my life he had urged me to persevere too.

Then I was introduced and walked to the podium to deliver the lecture. It turned out to be the longest talk I had ever given, about forty-five minutes. I talked about each article of the Constitution and then about the Bill of Rights and the provisions that dealt specifically with the commander in chief and the United States military. At the end of the talk, I told the cadets that they were listening to a Black man born in 1950 in a broken, segregated America, but that nevertheless I wanted them to understand that I believed there is good in America and that our nation is worth preserving. I talked about the fact that our nation had endured as a representative democracy and that they had a crucial role to play in securing its future. As I spoke, I was fully aware that they would be called upon to go into harm's way to uphold our nation.

Here is what I said that night about the enduring nature of America and about the relationship between the civilians and members of our country's armed forces:

Let me turn for a moment to the relationship between the armed forces of our nation and the civilians of our nation. We have never been afraid of our army. This is so because our army was not imposed upon us from the outside; it was not a conquering force come here to oppress us. Our army arose from this soil, from these people. Our army has in the long history of America been, in many ways, ourselves.

Our army has not had a hereditary leadership caste born to rank and position. Our army has had leaders who earned their way to the front of the troops. Though our army was once, like our society, segregated by race, it was the first great institution to move towards the ideal of diversity with President Truman's 1948 order to desegregate the troops. This order came six years before the 1954 decision in *Brown v. Board* that struck down separate but equal as unconstitutional. And so it is today that this corps of cadets comes from all fifty states—men and women, Blacks and whites, Jews and gentiles, Protestants and Catholics. It is like America.

There has always been a closeness between the military and civilian authorities. Washington and Grant and Eisenhower left the army to become presidents. George Marshall and Colin Powell left the army to become secretaries of state. Douglas MacArthur, when ordered by the president to relinquish his command, followed that order. In another country a military leader of such prominence might have tried to raise an army and fight the president's order. But that is not the way of American soldiers, sworn as they are to uphold the Constitution. . . .

And so it is that we have a governmental structure that serves the ends of justice, we rely on principles of fair play, we cling to moral restraint in the exercise of our military might, and we have done so since the beginning of the union. But this leads me to a question for these times.

Can an eighteenth-century set of principles sustain us in the twenty-first century? Did the Founders achieve their hope of speaking in a way that would leave room for future changes for the good of our nation?

Indeed, we must ask the question that Lincoln asked: "Can any nation so conceived and so dedicated long endure?" Can this diverse land built on the principles of freedom endure in the face of those who would fly planes into buildings, send anthrax through the mail, do harm to the innocent, and then hide in caves?

Our history gives us evidence on this issue. Consider these facts: When George Washington was sworn in as president on April 30, 1789,

an emperor ruled China,
a czarina ruled Russia,
a kaiser ruled Germany,
a shah ruled Iran,
a shogun ruled Japan,
a sultan ruled Egypt,
and kings ruled France and Spain.

Today the presidency of the United States is the only one of those forms still remaining.

I think that there is good reason for the way our nation has endured. It begins with the fact that we are based on principles of individual freedom, principles that accommodate the sounds of many voices, principles that include the pursuit of happiness.

I think we have endured because we have a system that allows us to evolve and grow and move closer step-by-step to the ideals that lie at our foundation.

I think we have endured because our people know the taste of freedom and will not accept anything else.

And I think we have endured because of the special relationship our armed forces have with this nation. . . .

As we sit here tonight, our nation is under attack. The freedoms that have brought us thus far, the openness that is America, have been attacked in a horrific way.

We hear on the news about our troops being in harm's way. But for many Americans the very concept of being in harm's way is an item relegated to the news or a plot device in a novel.

Yet as I look into your faces, I know that "in harm's way" is a real part of your lives, that it is the course you have embarked upon for the good of our nation. I know that you will be in the fight.

And when you fight, you will do so having sworn an oath to uphold the Constitution that we have discussed here tonight. When you fight, you will be part of the tradition of freedom that has been passed down from the first soldiers who took up arms for the United States, from soldiers who may have occupied this very site, which is the oldest continuously used fortification in the nation.

Military historians and psychologists tell us the same thing about fighting wars. They tell us that the soldiers who believe in their cause fight more fiercely. And so it is my hope tonight to help you see that this is a rare nation. That though we are not perfect we strive to be more perfect; that though we have made mistakes along the way we have found the will to correct our mistakes; that until this nation came along no other nation on earth had put into place such a government.

And so in the end I want you to know deep inside that America is worth preserving, that it is worth keeping, that it is worth defending, that it is worth fighting for.

No matter what beachhead you find yourself on, no matter how dreary the foxhole, no matter how cold the cliff you might stand upon, I want you always to remember that you are there in the cause of freedom.

To drive this point home I want to say one more thing to you.

You have before you a Black man born in the segregated South of America in 1950 who has seen with his own eyes the whites-only signs and has known our nation in the days of injustice based on the color of our skin.

And yet still I stand before you to say with all that is within me that we must defend America.

We must not give up; we must not give in.

Because within us, within this great nation, there is the best hope for a better tomorrow, not just for us, but for the whole world. Go Army!

When I ended the speech, there was a moment of silence before the cadets—a vast sea of gray-and-white uniforms—came to their feet in a powerful roar of approval, the familiar army "Hooah." As I walked from the stage into the audience one of the officers said to me, "Sir, we have never seen the cadets come to their feet for a civilian lecturer."

After that speech, I was invited back to West Point on several occasions. I delivered the Martin Luther King Day speech. I spoke with the Black and Gold Society. I was invited to football games. I was invited to deliver the constitutional law lecture a second time. I helped organize a trip for some of the cadets to visit places in Virginia that were part of the fight for civil rights, like the Moton School in Farmville, where the young Barbara Johns led a strike of Black students protesting dilapidated conditions at the all-Black school, a fight that became part of the *Brown v. Board of Education* decision.

On one of my visits to West Point, it dawned on me that though Thomas Jefferson had signed the order to create West Point, and though he had helped select the first professors and the books that would be studied, there was nothing that honored Jefferson at West Point. There was the mighty Washington Hall. There were Thayer Hall and the Thayer Hotel. There was Michie Stadium. But nothing was named for Jefferson. I thought this was odd and asked about it. I was told that West Point was hoping to build a new library and that it might be named for Jefferson, given that he so loved books.

Months later I asked about the progress regarding the library. I learned that it appeared the library would be built, but that it would not be named for Jefferson because Jefferson had enslaved people. My first thought was that Washington had owned enslaved workers, too, so how could that be the differentiator, given that Jefferson had created West Point. I did not think that the explanation made sense, and I didn't think it was a fair result. I decided to call Senator John Warner of Virginia, the same John Warner who had been secretary of the navy when I was a young reporter at Channel 3 in Norfolk. I described the situation to him and asked him what he thought about it. He said he would look into it. Months later I learned that West Point was going to build a new library that would be named for Thomas Jefferson.

Let me talk about why I did that and what I think about Jefferson's legacy in America. Hardly anyone from the past can withstand the scrutiny of the present day. There is no perfection in the human condition, and as humanity matures and learns we can see the error of our ways. But I believe that imperfect mankind can, from time to time, have a perfect idea. And every now and then the perfect idea can move nations, institutions, populations, and people to a more perfect situation than where they started. Thus, when I grapple with those from the past, I always ask whether the totality of their lives moved mankind toward a better condition. I think that America is better today than it was when I was born in 1950. Then, the nation was segregated under the law. We were divided by skin color. No matter how brilliant or thoughtful or skilled a Black person might be, they were discarded as less worthy because of how they looked. But Jefferson wrote that "all men are created equal," that "they are endowed by their Creator with certain unalienable Rights," and that "among these are Life, Liberty, and the pursuit of Happiness." Because Jefferson expressed that powerful aspirational goal for America, he put in place an ideal that all of us could pursue. And so his idea was better than he was.

But suppose he had never expressed that idea. In that case, I think it would have been harder for the nation to achieve what it has achieved in all these years. This is so because even in the bitter days of slavery and Jim Crow and separate but equal, there was always looming in the background, ringing in the ears of our nation, the idea that "all men are created equal." And though Jefferson said "all men," I believe that people struggling for equality understand that his expression applies with equal force to both men and women. And so Lincoln invoked Jefferson's words, Dr. King invoked Jefferson's words, the women at the rights convention in Seneca Falls invoked his words. The way I look at it, the totality of Jefferson's life gets him over the line to a position where even a person of color can give him credit for helping our nation become more perfect. I did not say perfect; I said "more perfect," which is measured by where we started from—and by that measure we have moved in the right direction in part because of Jefferson.

While the new library was under construction, I went to the Monticello board and urged them make a gift to the library of a replica of Jefferson's desk and other artifacts that are at Monticello. The board agreed. Then I arranged with West Point for the board to travel to West Point to present the gift to the library when the new building was dedicated. The Monticello board was invited to the dedication ceremony. I was invited to speak at the dedication. We sailed from New York City up the Hudson River to West Point and tied up at their pier. The board stayed at the Thayer Hotel and invited the West Point command to dinner. The superintendent and the commandant and the dean of the academic board, Colonel Finnegan, now General Finnegan, accepted our invitation. We had a wonderful dinner with speeches and toasts.

On the day of the dedication, the other board members and my wife were given a tour of West Point. I went off by myself, thinking of what I would say at the ceremony. There were four speakers on the program: the four-star general, vice chief of staff of the army; the three-star general superintendent of West Point; the one-star general, dean of the academic board; and me. Immediately following the ceremony, the speakers and the guests went inside the building to look at a newly completed sculpture of Jefferson. As we stood there talking about the beautiful new building, an old soldier approached me and said, "While you were talking, I did not want you to stop. And when you stopped talking it was as if someone had suddenly turned off the music. I have never heard a speech like that." I said, "Thank you." I had heard people comment on my speaking voice, but what that old soldier said to me that day was the most vivid description I had ever heard of my voice.

Later in the day there was a parade of the cadets on the Plain. Dan Jordan, who was then president of Monticello and who had been a young army officer years ago, and Alice Handy, who was chair of the board of Monticello, were invited to stand on the Plain with the command of West Point to review the cadets. It was rare for civilians to be accorded such an honor. I was in the stands watching all this, and I was pleased about what I was seeing.

On another occasion I was invited to address the members of the West Point class of 1969 at their memorial service for the members of their class who had died in Vietnam. They gather every five years to remember their fallen. I accepted the invitation, but I was deeply worried about what I could say to these soldiers. They had fought in Vietnam while I had not; I had gotten a high number in the draft lottery back in the '60s when I was at UVA. I thought that I needed to understand who these fallen soldiers were, where they came from, what they had hoped for and dreamed about. My former law partner John Lucas had arranged for me to make the speech, so I asked him to send me information about all of his fallen classmates. My idea was to create a composite of these soldiers while having enough specifics to remind their living classmates of exactly to whom I was referring.

On the day of the ceremony, we met on a grassy area with the wall of the Vietnam Veterans Memorial in our field of vision. The members of the class and their spouses were there, along with the spouses and families of some of the fallen. In that setting, with tourists walking by and people in the foreground stopping as they found their loved ones' names on the wall, I delivered these remarks about the fallen members of the class of 1969:

> When one reflects upon those members of your class who died in Vietnam, were missing in action in Vietnam, and were severely injured, one sees a picture of the very best that America has to offer. In their lives leading up to their time at West Point they were "readers and writers" of poetry. They were track stars, Eagle Scouts, Golden Gloves champions, state champion football players. They lettered in football, and in basketball, and in track. They were in the honor society and on the debate team. They were in the German club and the French club. They were president of the student body, vice president of the student body, senior class president, members of the Key Club. They were in the senior play, on the yearbook committee, on the prom committee. They were the pride and joy of their families, their communities, their churches, their schools—from one end of America to the other. They were the promise of this nation, and they all wanted so much to come to West Point.
>
> They came to West Point because they were born in the army, lived in the army, loved the army. They came to West Point because as seven-year-old boys they told their fathers that they wanted to be airborne. They came because they were born warriors who had to live the life of a soldier. They came because they had faith in the goodness of mankind and of America. They came because they thought their country needed them.
>
> At West Point they were fiercely competitive. They were the boxing champion of the regiment, they were champion marksmen, their pistol team went 29 and 0. They were cross country champions, they were gymnasts, they played lacrosse. They were

in the skydiving club, the ski club, the military affairs club, the rocket club, the scuba club, the amateur radio club, the behavioral sciences club. They were on the honor committee and in the Century Club.

They did not let curfew stand in the way of a proper goodbye to their dates. Wrapped in their brown boys, they could sleep through any natural or man-made event. They were as happy-go-lucky as a summer breeze; they were in the midst of every prank. They were mature and determined; they were cheerful and the best of friends; they had a radiant sense of humor; they had wry wit. They were completely selfless; they were the ultimate friend; they were loud, happy, and unrestrained; they had caustic sarcasm. They wore jungle hats, smoked pipes, put army insignia on their Brobes. They helped their classmates in the sciences, in math, in engineering.

They got their airborne wings during the summer and wore them proudly on their cadet uniforms. They were editors of the yearbook. They were quiet and unassuming; they were the strong, silent type.

They were called "Snake" and "Greaser" and "Schroeds" and "Dellwoo" and "North" and "Chip" and "George" and "Jon" and "Smiling Jim" and "Old Man," and they built with all their classmates a firm foundation of friendship that rivals the very granite that West Point is built from and stands on.

And when the time came, they chose the infantry, they chose artillery, they chose armor. They went to jungle school together; they won their Ranger tabs together. They became pilots and flew gunships; they became Pathfinders; they won their wings at jump school. And they volunteered for Vietnam, they moved their names up on the rotation, and they served.

While in Vietnam, they heard the poet say to them, "In the world's broad field of battle, in the bivouac of life, be not like dumb, driven cattle, be a hero in the strife." And heroes they were, every one. They volunteered to stay with their South Vietnamese unit even when American soldiers were ordered to leave. They extended their tours of duty. They died in hand-to-hand combat. They led their armored cavalry platoon to save an infantry platoon, and they died. They flew escort for a medical evacuation mission, and they died. They were the victims of multiple mine explosions, but they continued to direct the evacuation of their troops, and they suffered grievous injuries. They climbed to the top of a water tower to call in an air strike, and they vanished. They volunteered to lead an extraction team to bring out a wounded ranger, and they died. They drew sniper fire away from their men to allow them to withdraw to safety, and they died. Surely they filled the unforgiving minute with sixty seconds' worth of distance run. They earned the Combat Infantryman Badge, the Silver Star, the Bronze Star, the Army Commendation Medal, and the Purple Heart. They died for the country they love; they died for principles that they believed in. They died at the call of duty; they died with honor. And when they died their mothers and fathers exclaimed through tear-filled eyes, "These are our sons, in whom we are well pleased."

And so it is for us the living to do all that we can to remember them with the honor that they so fully deserve. Memory is a powerful force; the strongest memories are forged in the most difficult circumstances. You and your fallen classmates have faced the most difficult circumstances that any American citizen can face. And as we stand here today within weeks of Memorial Day and within a day of the anniversary of D-Day, we must all remember the dire price of freedom. We too must hear the voice of the poet telling us, "Let us then be up and doing, with a heart for any fate," and saying to us, "Act, act in the living present. Heart within, and God o'erhead."

We must all ensure that every veteran of war is provided for by this nation. We must ensure that every citizen is aware that the call to defend our nation is not answered by everyone, that they served so that America will be free. We must ensure that those who stand up and fight must never be let down by this country.

God bless the members of the class of 1969 living and dead; God bless the United States Military Academy at West Point; God bless America.

That speech affected me more than any of the hundreds of other speeches I've given in my life. It is a sobering proposition to think of all the sacrifice that has been made to preserve our nation and our freedoms. None of this is easy, and none of this is free. I so hope that all our citizens can be inspired to help their neighbors and each other, to lift us up, to bind our nation together.

19

The Poetic Justice and Carnegie Hall

Governor Tim Kaine appointed me to the board of visitors of the College of William & Mary in April 2006. I went on the board just prior to the inauguration of Gene Nichol as the college's new president and the investiture of Sandra Day O'Connor as the newest chancellor. When I came on the board, my friend Taylor Reveley III—who had been managing partner at Hunton and who had been on my robing committee when I went on the Supreme Court of Virginia—was dean of the law school at William & Mary.

Since about 1990 I had been delivering the First Day, First Year law lecture at the University of Virginia's law school. One year I delivered that lecture at both UVA and William & Mary, but that was when the two schools did not start on the same day and at the same time. When I went on the W&M board, Taylor asked me to again deliver the First Day, First Year lecture at W&M. I delivered that lecture each year from 2006 until I left the board in 2016.

During my time on the William & Mary board, I attended a dinner for the academic affairs committee that led to me performing poetry at Carnegie Hall. It is one of those unlikely stories of chance meetings and leaps of faith. Kathy Hornsby was also on the academic affairs committee, and the dinner was at her house. As we arrived and started introducing ourselves, there were several faculty members present— which was typical for an academic affairs dinner. One of the professors taught music at the college. When she said, "Hello, I'm Sophia Serghi, a professor of music," I replied, "I am Judge Thomas, a poet." I don't know why I said that. I don't think I had ever introduced myself as a poet. But in that setting, with professors in various fields like English, philosophy, and music, for some reason I didn't want to be thought of as a lawyer or a judge.

When I said I was a poet, Professor Serghi asked, "What kind of poet are you?" I said, "A lyric poet." She wanted to know what my poetry sounded like, so I started reciting from memory. Some of the poems were mine, and others were from Longfellow and Kipling. I went from one poem to another. We sat next to each other at the dinner, and I continued to recite poems.

After dinner, Professor Serghi asked permission to play one of Bruce Hornsby's pianos, so we went to another room and the professor played a piece she had written called "Allure." A few days later I got an email from her in which she asked whether she could see the written versions of my poems. She thought that based on what I had recited at the dinner, she could write music inspired by my poems.

I was caught off guard by the professor's request. I had never thought about a poem inspiring music. And I had no desire for her or anyone to read my poetry. I had not let anyone except family members see or hear my poems since that episode in high school.

I told her that I was not interested in sending her my poems. She asked again, and I thought, "Why not?" I sent her copies of my poems.

She chose a poem called "Crystal Trees," which I wrote in 1998 following an ice storm in Virginia that had covered the trees in what looked to me like crystal. She wrote a musical piece with the same title. I was unfamiliar with such a process. What she had done was completely different from what I did in the law. She was using one art form to inspire another. It was intriguing.

Not long after she composed "Crystal Trees," she had another idea. This time she said, "If I can write music inspired by your poetry, I wonder if you can write poetry inspired by my music." I told her that I would try. She sent me the musical piece "Allure" that she had played at the dinner meeting in Williamsburg. In short order I wrote the poem "The Allure of the Muse," which I finished on April 19, 2011. We went back and forth like this for a while, with Professor Serghi writing music and me writing poetry.

On one of my trips to Williamsburg for a board meeting, she took me to a recording studio at the Swem Library. She wanted to record me reciting my poems so that she could hear my words in my voice as she composed music. Later she asked if she could use my poems in her music class to see what they would inspire in her students. I visited her class to listen to and comment on the student compositions. One student created a choral piece, another created electronic music, and another created a piano piece. I heard multiple types of compositions inspired by what I had written.

Then Professor Serghi came up with her big idea: why don't we put together a program and perform at Carnegie Hall? I could not see how we could get from a music classroom in Williamsburg to the great Carnegie Hall. But she had another idea. She proposed to the director of the Muscarelle Museum of Art at William & Mary that the museum sponsor the program and use it as a fundraiser for the college. From there things took off.

On February 23, 2013, the Muscarelle Museum of Art sponsored at the Weill Recital Hall in Carnegie Hall a program titled "The Allure of the Muse" with John Charles Thomas, poet; Sophia Serghi, pianist; the Harris Simon Trio; and Anna Kijanowska, solo pianist. I was the emcee for the program. I introduced the poems, talked about the music, and provided continuity. That night I recited sixteen of my poems. I recited the first poem I had ever written, "The Morning," at the start of the program and at the end. Four of the poems were accompanied by music written by Professor Serghi. Five were accompanied by jazz and the rest by classical music. I was a long way from the side porch at my grandparents' house and from that classroom at the white high school in Norfolk.

At the end of the concert, I walked from behind the podium that held my notes and the copies of the poems. I walked to the edge of the stage with nothing in front of me but the audience. All the music had stopped. I talked about how damaging it is to crush the spirit of a young person based on prejudices that a person might have within them. As I talked, I started crying. And as I cried, I thought to myself, "Please don't forget the words to 'The Morning.' That poem has been with you all these years, and this would be a terrible time to forget its words." I kept talking about not crushing hope, about caring for one another, and I cried more. Finally, I started the poem, and the words came to me as they have all these many years. And the room fell silent, then it erupted in applause. And all I could think was, "Thank God, we did it."

Afterword

By the time I stood onstage at Carnegie Hall, I had been around the world. I had spoken to hundreds of audiences. Throughout my life the poetic voice that I first learned in my childhood had stayed within me. My grandfather's idea to teach a four-year-old classical poetry may well have been the secret sauce of my whole life. It taught me the power of words, not to fear an audience, not to doubt my own ability to persuade. It taught me how to stand in front of a group and how to ask for support and for help and for unity.

In my time at West Point I came to understand that the teaching method there is called adversity training. The cadets are put under stress in many different settings and taught to cope with it, to grapple with it, to wrestle it to the ground. Their adversity training lasts the four years that they are at West Point. But as I look back at my life, I think that I was in adversity training full-time day and night, year after year. I had to cope with violence at home and in the streets, with material poverty and racism, with sorrow and some joy. When you live with adversity all the time, I guess it will either crush you or you will find a way to survive. And if you can survive constant adversity, maybe you can live and thrive in most environments.

My life was not easy, and I would not want to try to live it again. But having lived it and having survived thus far, I can see that I learned positive lessons along the way. Looking back, I know that I am blessed to still be here, to have a loving wife and happy family, with bright-eyed grandchildren and wonderful friends. It is a poetic story.

The message that I have learned from life and want to pass on to everybody is embedded in the words of a poem that I wrote in 1996:

LIGHT THE SOUL

Light lay quietly at the Beginning
'Til it was called into action by God
Then it split the darkness, warmed the cold
Brought motion to the stillness, touched our souls

And they say there is light at the end
As we brace ourselves for the final journey
The Word is there is light even then
Light that Blinds you, Binds you, then sets you free

From Alpha to Omega, the Light shines through
From dawn to dusk it orders what we do
By particle and wave it prompts the birds to sing
By pulse and reflection, it points out the way

Light can lift depression, dispel despair
Bring Hope to the weary, lead us from fear
Light can raise up emotions, quiet the storm
Beckon us from rolling seas into the calm

We learn by light, we grow by light
We sit in the dark transfixed by its sight
As the light flickers our hearts respond
We can see the connections we can feel the bonds

It has been given to some to handle the light
To mold it, to craft it, to bend it to right
It has fallen to some to sculpt what we see
To sharpen, to brighten, to make it run free

To those who would hold light in their hands
There is much to remember, to understand
In the Right Light, Love can shine
In the Right Light, We can leave Wrong behind
In the Light Justice can grow
By the Light there is good we can know: Light the Soul

My message is that each one of us is the light. It is within us, and we must let it shine. I have been curious all my life. I have always wanted to learn from and about other people and where they come from, how they live, what they care about, what words they use and love. There is so much that our children and grandchildren can do if we ask them and encourage them and smile at them and cheer them on.

ACKNOWLEDGMENTS

From the time I made partner at Hunton & Williams on April 1, 1982, historians started telling me that I needed to write my story. I listened to their advice, but I was only thirty-one years old, and I was busy. Basically, I thought that I could wait. When I was appointed to the Supreme Court of Virginia at the age of thirty-two, becoming the first Black and the youngest justice in the history of Virginia, the chorus of voices telling me that I had to write my story reached a crescendo. But again, I was still young, I was a newlywed, and I was very busy. So I thought that writing my story could wait. Part of that reluctance had to do with my notion that the writing of memoirs is the business of older, gray-haired people. Anyway, as time went by, from one person or another I often heard, "When are you going to sit down and write?" It took me until I had retired from my law firm and had more time to sit and read and think and remember. Finally, I called the University of Virginia Press and asked the then director whether they might be interested in my story. The answer was yes. And then I started the process: writing a proposal, providing an outline, discussing the possible relevance of my life's story—all that and more.

While the process was underway, I sat down at my computer and started writing. As I wrote, we started contract talks. As I wrote, I started remembering vividly the many ups and downs of my life. In the midst of the process, Suzanne Moomaw became the new director of the University of Virginia Press. She made a cold call to me and said, "I just want you to know that I want to publish your book." Now that was a jolt. I thought to myself, "Well it looks like this might actually be happening; it's time to get busy." In short order, we signed a contract, an editor was assigned to me, and the process shifted into high gear. Now the book is done, and I want to thank the many wonderful people who helped me get from a blank sheet of paper to this book.

I want to thank Suzanne Moomaw for her direct get-the-job-done approach. I want to thank my acquisitions editor, Dr. Nadine Zimmerli, for first guiding me through the early stages of the process then suggesting early edits for my manuscript and then advocating for the book with her colleagues at the press. I must also thank my copy editor, Lynne Bonenberger, who has the patience and the memory to read and remember every word to the point that she would ask questions like, "Why is it that on page 23 you referred to your cousin one way but on page 97 you referred to him a different way?" I was amazed by the level of detail of her comments, and I deeply appreciate her work. Thanks also to Amber Williams, who was the proofreader for my book. It was her job to make sure, at the end, that no typos had crept into the manuscript. That is a seriously demanding job. I know this well from my own days of proofreading my decisions for the Supreme Court of Virginia, and then after they were published, being told that a typo was found in the published decision.

When it comes to the images in the book, I have to start by thanking my aunt Lula Sears Rogers—the youngest of the fifteen Sears children; my mother's baby sister, and my youngest aunt—who sorted through the old family albums to find pictures that went back to my earliest days. I thank too my cousin Eunice Taylor-Joseph, who also sent me old family photos. I also must thank my friends at the Thomas Jefferson Foundation who gave permission for me to use photos taken there and John McKee of the foundation staff, who helped us locate the best of the images of me with world leaders at Monticello. And on the technical side I want to thank the Librarian of Virginia, Sandra Gioia Treadway, for agreeing to assist in the digitization of the photos used in the book, and I also want to thank Ben Steck, the digital collections specialist at the Library of Virginia, who spent a goodly portion of a day carefully removing old photos from their frames, digitizing them, then putting them back where they came from. It was an interesting process to observe, and I deeply appreciate his skill.

Thanks are also due to members of the University of Virginia Press who worked in-house on my book. I want to thank Anne Hegeman,

Cecilia Sorochin, Rachel Laney, and Ellen Satrom, who oversaw the editing, design, and production of my book. Thanks to Jason Coleman, who is responsible for marketing my book. I did not know how many people were involved in publishing a book; I am so pleased that the wonderful people I have named here worked on my book, because they have taught me about this process and made it understandable for me. All's well that ends well.—jct